D0857789

Bilingual Children: Guidance for the Family

Multilingual Matters

This new series of books covers some of the many aspects of multilingualism and multiculturalism throughout the world. The series title is meant to be inclusive rather than exclusive, for we hope to publish works on languages in contact — and sometimes in conflict — in varying types of community. Our aim is to establish the advantages of bilingualism and multilingualism in their wider cultural settings, while at the same time identifying problems and working towards solutions. At times the series will cover fundamental theory, at others policy implementation in an educational system, and at others again, the factors involved in bringing up children bilingually in the home.

1. "Bilingualism: Basic Principles"
   HUGO BAETENS BEARDSMORE

2. "Evaluating Bilingual Education: A Canadian Case Study"
   MERRILL SWAIN AND SHARON LAPKIN

3. "Bilingual Children: Guidance for the Family"
   GEORGE SAUNDERS

4. "Language Attitudes Among Arabic-French Bilinguals in Morocco"
   ABDELÂLI BENTAHILA

5. "Conflict and Language Planning in Quebec"
   RICHARD Y. BOURHIS

6. "Bilingualism and Special Education"
   JIM CUMMINS

Please contact us for the latest information on recent and forthcoming books in the series.

Derrick Sharp, General Editor,
Multilingual Matters,
Bank House,
8a Hill Road,
Clevedon, Avon BS21 7HH,
England.

MULTILINGUAL MATTERS 3

Bilingual Children:
Guidance for the Family

George Saunders

MULTILINGUAL
MATTERS LTD

British Library Cataloguing in Publication Data

Saunders, George
    Bilingual children –
    — (Multilingual matters; 3)
    1. Bilingualism   2. Children — Language
    I. Title   II. Series
    404'.2   P115

    ISBN 0-905028-12-0
    ISBN 0-905028-11-2 Pbk

Multilingual Matters Ltd,
Bank House, 8a Hill Road,
Clevedon, Avon BS21 7HH,
England.

Typeset by Wayside Graphics, Clevedon, Avon.
Printed and bound in Great Britain at the
Pitman Press, Bath.

091658

Contents

PREFACE   ix

GLOSSARY   xi
1 BILINGUALISM   1
    Introduction   1
    What is bilingualism?   7
    Is bilingualism an advantage or disadvantage?   14

2 ESTABLISHING BILINGUALISM IN THE FAMILY   23
    The family   23
    Motives for creating bilingualism   26
    Infant bilingualism   29
    Method employed   34

3 COMMUNICATION IN THE FAMILY: HOW IT WORKS   42
    General remarks   42
    The children's communications strategies   48
    The children addressing both parents simultaneously   50
    The children addressing father plus monolingual(s)   52
    Brother to brother communication   54
    Brothers to sister communication   63
    Private speech   65
    Communication with animals   71
    Communication with toys   73

4 DEPARTURES FROM NORMAL LANGUAGE CHOICE IN THE FAMILY .   75
    Introduction   75
    Role play   84
    The mother's knowledge of German   87
    Storytelling by the parents   89

Code switching and triggering 92
Quotational switching 98
Quotational switching in storytelling 106

5 INFLUENCES FROM OUTSIDE THE IMMEDIATE FAMILY 113
Attitudes of monolingual English-speakers 113
Relatives and friends 118
Playmates 121
Peer group pressure 127
Use of the "wrong" language 128
The children and German-English bilinguals 129
Kindergarten and school 134

6 FURTHER POSSIBLE PROBLEMS IN ESTABLISHING BILINGUALISM . . 138
Children's reluctance to speak the home language 138
Effect of the father's not being a native speaker of German 146

7 MEASURING PROFICIENCY IN BOTH LANGUAGES 159
Introduction 159
Receptive vocabulary 159
Estimating fluency and accuracy 165
Storytelling 165
Free speech 171
A look at the children's accuracy over time 172
Types of errors and reasons for their occurrence 174
Syntactic transference 175
Semantic transference 180
Lexical transference 194
Phonological transference 201
Communicative competence 204
Conclusions about the children's accuracy 206
Measuring degree of bilingualism 207

8 BILITERACY 210

9 HOW THE CHILDREN VIEW BILINGUALISM 219
The children's attitudes to their two languages 219
The children and language and languages 227

10 OTHER AIDS TO THE DEVELOPMENT OF BILINGUALISM 232
Books 232
Records and cassettes 233
Radio and television 234
Games 238
Outings 238

Shops, restaurants, etc. 239
Ethnic schools and playgroups 239
Visits to and from the linguistic homeland 241
Correspondence 242
Language maintenance for parents 242

11 CONCLUSIONS 244

NOTES 247

REFERENCES 255

INDEX 263

Preface

This book arose from a suggestion by the publishers, Mike and Marjukka Grover, and I would like to thank them and Derrick Sharp, the General Editor of Multilingual Matters, for their enthusiastic encouragement and patience during the book's longer than expected gestation period.

I would also like to express my gratitude to various friends and colleagues, in particular Jim Hunt of the University of Tasmania and Michael Clyne, Monty Wilkinson, Walter Veit, Leslie Bodi, Howard Nicholas and Anne Pauwels of Monash University for their continued interest in the project, for their encouragement, and for many stimulating and fruitful discussions.

My debt to various scholars in the field of bilingualism, especially Michael Clyne, will be evident from the numerous references to their work throughout this book.

Many other people, too numerous to mention by name, deserve thanks for assisting in various ways, for example relatives, friends and acquaintances for their ungrudging acceptance and in some cases active support of the experiment in bilingualism described in this book; without this, the going would undoubtedly have been difficult. In this respect I am particularly grateful to my parents, Kate and Tas Saunders, for their unfailing interest and good-humoured encouragement over the years.

Special appreciation is due to my wife, Wendy, who has helped in many ways, to mention but a few, by risking eye-strain to read the manuscript in its initial rough draft forms and offering valuable suggestions on content and clarity, and by showing an unflagging conviction that raising children bilingually was not only possible but also a beneficial and enriching experience for the whole family.

Last, but definitely not least, to the subjects of this study, Thomas and Frank, for many pleasurable hours of conversation and play, for the many insights into bilingualism which they have given me, as well as for their cheerful willingness to be recorded and written about, I would like to say simply, but very sincerely: "Danke schön".

George Saunders

Glossary

Ambilingual: Equilingual (see).

Balanced bilingual: Someone who is approximately equally skilled in two languages (but not necessarily passing for a native speaker in both, or even in one of them).

Bilingual: Able to use two languages (for some or all of the skills of speaking, listening, reading and writing).

Biliteracy: The ability to read and write in two languages.

Code switching: Switching from one language (or variety of a language) to another for part of a sentence or conversation (because of triggering [see], situation, stylistic reasons, etc.).

Cognate: A word in one language which is historically related to a word in another language and which in the present form of the language may still have basically the same meaning, e.g. German *Mutter* (=mother) and English *mother*, or a somewhat different meaning, e.g. German *Baum* (=tree) and English *beam*.

Dominance: The degree to which a bilingual is more proficient in one language than the other; the language in which there is greater proficiency is said to be his or her "dominant language".

Equilingual: Having an exactly equal command of two languages, usually with the added implication that native speakers of both languages would assume that one was a fellow native speaker.

Homophonous diamorph: A word having the same meaning and sounding the same or similar in another language, e.g. German *Bier* and English *beer*.

Intelligence quotient (IQ): A ratio of mental age to chronological age. A child with a mental age of 6 years and an actual age of 5 years has an IQ of 1.2, usually expressed as 120.

Interference: Transference (see).

Interlocutor: A person taking part in a conversation.

Language maintenance: Continuing to use a language in the face of competition from another language.

Language shift: Giving up using one language in favour of another (the opposite of language maintenance).

Lexical transference: The use of words from one language in another but which are not normally considered part of the other, e.g. "I'll meet you at the *Bahnhof*." (German for "station".)

Linguistic: Of or relating to language or linguistics (see).

Linguistics: The scientific study of language. A person engaged in such study is a linguist.

Loanword: A word which originally belonged to one language but which is now also considered part of another, e.g. English has *kindergarten* from German, *spaghetti* from Italian, *kangaroo* from Guugu Yimidhirr, and so on. (In many cases loanwords started out as lexical transfers [see] but have now gained acceptance in the language.)

Mental age: The degree of mental development or intelligence of an individual in comparison with the average intelligence of normal children at different ages.

Monoglot: Monolingual (see).

Monolingual: Having only one language.

Multilingual: As for bilingual, but involving more than two languages.

Phonological transference: A sound in one language is identified with and pronounced like the closest available sound in another language, e.g. a German, lacking the /ð/ sound of "*th*at" in his native language, may, when speaking English, substitute /d/ for it, thus "*d*at"; the result of phonological transference is perceivable as a foreign accent.

Polyglot: Multilingual (see).

Quotational switching: Leaving quotations in their original language while speaking another language, e.g. "And Dad said, '*Paß auf!*' " (German for "Watch out!").

Receiving bilingual: A person who understands two languages but who can speak only one.

Receptive vocabulary: One's hearing or "passive" vocabulary, i.e. the amount of words one understands (but does not necessarily actively use, e.g. one might *understand* the work "gargantuan" but never *use* it oneself).

Semantic transference: The transference of the sense of a word in one language to a word in another language which is sometimes an equivalent (e.g. a German-English bilingual using "card" in English instead of "ticket", because German *Karte* means not only "card", but "map" and "ticket" as well), or which sounds similar but never has the same meaning (e.g. a German-English bilingual using *Rente* in German in the sense of "rent", whereas the German word means only "pension"). Included here are also literal translations of words and idioms in another language (e.g. a German-English bilingual using "washbear", a literal translation of German *Waschbär*, instead of the normal English "racoon").

Syntactic transference: The use in one language of sentence patterns and/or system of inflections belonging to another, e.g. a German-English bilingual's "I had my school jumper all day *on*" (which has the word order of the corresponding German sentence).

Switching: Code switching (see).

Transference: The use by bilinguals of any elements of one language in another (also referred to in the literature as "interference").

Transfer: Any example of transference (see).

Triggering: A switch from one language to another in a sentence or a conversation, brought about by a trigger word (see), a quotation said or heard in the other language, or the context of the situation.

Trigger word: A word which, because of its similarity in both languages, causes a bilingual to forget which language he is speaking and to switch from one language to the other, e.g.:

"This is called *edelweiss* — das ist eine kleine Blume . . ."
        (trigger word)   (German: *that's a little flower . . .*)

Trilingual: As for bilingual, but involving *three* languages.

Unilingual: Monolingual (see).

1 Bilingualism

Introduction

This book has been written primarily with the non-specialist reader in mind who is interested in bilingualism, particularly in the bilingual upbringing of children in the home. Care has been taken to explain terminology and procedures in terms which, it is hoped, will make them easily understood by the general reader. Explanations of the more technical terms are also listed in a glossary for easy reference. An English translation is provided for any material quoted in other languages.

For readers wishing to refer to any of the publications mentioned in this book, a small raised number in the text refers to a note at the back of the book, where the author, date of publication and specific page numbers are given; the publication in question can then be easily located in the bibliography.

Bilingual families are by no means a rarity in today's world. Indeed, bilingualism is a far more common phenomenon than the predominantly monolingual native speakers of a world language such as English might realize. In fact, bilinguals outnumber monolinguals. According to Fishman,[1] a prolific writer on bilingual matters, more than half of the world's population today uses more than one language while engaging in the activities basic to human needs. In many societies (e.g. in Papua and New Guinea, Africa, South America, India and South-East Asia, etc.) bilingualism has long been considered the norm rather than the exception. In Aboriginal Australian communities, for instance, as Dixon[2] points out in his recent book *The Languages of Australia*, there has always been a great deal of bilingualism "due to intermarriage, meetings at intertribal gatherings, and simply interest in acquiring new languages. Most people will speak at

1

least two languages (and probably understand one or two others), while some may speak six or seven . . . A child will often have parents speaking different languages." With the arrival of European settlers in 1788, "Aboriginal Australians – naturally multilingual in their traditional society – found no difficulty in learning to understand and speak good English" – a marked contrast to the predominantly monolingual English-speaking settlers, few of whom ever learned to communicate with the original inhabitants in their own languages.

In this century many people have, for various reasons, left their home-lands to settle or work in other countries where they have, of necessity, had to acquire some knowledge of the local language, thus becoming to varying degrees bilingual. In Australia, for instance, the 1976 Census[3] revealed that 12.3% of the Australian population over the age of five regularly used a language other than English, compared with 1.4% who did not use English and 86.3% who used only English. (The actual percentage of bilinguals would undoubtedly be somewhat greater if account were taken of [i] people who know, but do not *regularly* use a language other than English; [ii] people who know more than one language but do not know or regularly use English.)

Parents who speak a language other than the officially recognized language of a country and who wish their own language to be retained in the home both by themselves and by their children, often do not succeed in achieving this. For example, the 1976 Australian Census[3] shows that 44% of Dutch immigrants, 31% of Maltese immigrants, 28% of German immigrants, 20% of Polish immigrants, 10% of Yugoslav immigrants, 6% of Italian immigrants and 3% of Greek immigrants had shifted to using English only. In most cases this means that these immigrants will not pass, or will not have passed, the language on to their children. Indeed, in the second generation, the Australian-born children of immigrants, the shift to the use of English only is even more striking. If we take Maltese immigrants as an example, we find that about 31% of them have shifted to the use of English only; yet about 57% of second generation Australians of Maltese parents have shifted to using English only, this rising dramatically to about 97% where only one parent is Maltese.

Various reasons can be put forward to explain why such language shift takes place and why some individuals and groups are more successful than others at maintaining their language in another country. A factor favouring language maintenance is an immigrant's settling in an area of his new country where there is already a considerable number of people who speak his language — he then may have greater opportunities to use the language frequently in a number of domains, e.g. in shops, clubs, church, cinemas, perhaps even in employment; this in turn increases the likelihood that the language will continue to be used in the home and be passed on to the children. A family settling in a neighbourhood where their language is spoken by very few people has a much more difficult task in retaining their language. Yet such a situation may be looked on as a challenge and definite language maintenance efforts be undertaken. Other factors may also (as pointed out by Kloss[4]) either aid or work against the retention of a minority language, for example, the attitude of the majority group in the society towards the minority language. A hostile attitude towards, or even attempts at suppression of, the minority language may cause its speakers to shift quickly to using only the majority language. On the other hand, such hostility may cause the minority language speakers to fight determinedly to retain their language.

The same applies if the majority group is tolerant of the minority language. Such tolerance can give minority language speakers, especially children, confidence in using their language. In some cases, however, lack of opposition to a minority language may lead to complacency among its speakers and result in no particular effort or interest being shown in retaining it or passing it on to the children.

Even when parents themselves retain their own language in a new country, why is it that so many fail to pass it on to their children? In some cases they simply do not try to do so; they see little point in their children speaking any language other than the language of the new country, since that is where they will be living and growing up. They are often reinforced in their attitude by the popular view, called by the Australian linguist Clyne[5] a "prize fallacy", that the children of immigrants will learn the majority language better if they forget their home language and if only the majority language is spoken in the home. (This is discussed further on pages 30 and 31.)

In other cases parents do wish to pass their language on to their children, but are discouraged by the seeming impossibility of doing so. The views of Margret Hofmann,[6] a German immigrant in the U.S.A., are typical in this respect. She answers the question asked in the title of her article, "Can the mother tongue be retained for children of German immigrants?", in the negative:

> "I believe that Americans will not have much success in their efforts to raise their children in the German language or bilingually . . . The quickly established rule, 'At home we will talk only German' can be followed for a very short time at best."

Referring to her own experiences with her own child, she writes:

". . . we were enthusiastic, and with the little one, as well as in his presence, we talked German. But, perforce (*sic*), our enthusiasm waned soon. After all, we were not the only ones who talked to him. All our guests, of course, spoke English. Whenever he visited he heard English . . For each item he had to learn two words: one German and one English, and that took him too long. As a result he began to stutter . . ."

She pessimistically concludes that the best that can be hoped to be done under such circumstances as far as the language is concerned is to get children "to practise typically German sounds frequently", so that they can learn the language more easily later on on a visit to Germany.

This book looks at the possibilities of bilingualism in the home much more optimistically, yet realistically. It aims to show that whilst difficulties will arise, as they do in most aspects of life, they are by no means insurmountable, and that parents *can* achieve a reasonable standard of bilingualism for their children. This is a view shared by, among others, readers who responded to the article by Margret Hofmann, e.g. Thomas Brandt:[7]

"I believe that the answer to the question raised depends a great deal upon the manner and method of approach, upon genuine interest, and circumstances of the project discussed. If German immigrants preserve their native tongue as a living thing without allowing it to disintegrate . . . , if they are careful not to have it compete with the American language, and if they provide for a natural setting within their family, children will offer no resistance to speaking, reading or even writing it."

To which can be added the words of Henriette Vent:[8]

"Even if children do not learn all the German words and even if their speech may sometimes be halting, it is, in my opinion, far better to teach them to know and speak some German than to drop it altogether for fear of achieving mediocre results. I do not think that in bringing up normally intelligent children bilingually, there is any danger that their English will suffer and turn into a hodgepodge. Their schooling, as well as the fact that most of their day is spent speaking English outside the home should prevent that."

A country's stock of languages can be seen as an important and valuable national resource, and the loss of any of them is to be regretted. After all, the ability to speak a language other than the majority language is seen as a desirable educational attainment in most societies, with one or more foreign languages usually forming part of the school curriculum. Yet, paradoxically, often little is done in many societies to encourage the preservation of languages already spoken by many children at home. As Smolicz[9] succinctly puts it:

> "It is a curious fact that bilingualism in 'migrant' children is often discouraged, while the same phenomenon is favoured for the élite of the dominant group through the painful process of the acquisition of a second language at school."

Moreover, the number of children, at least in English-speaking countries, who persist long enough with a school language programme to acquire a good level of competency in a foreign language is not great.

However, even when educational authorities show a more enlightened attitude and make provision for children from certain minority language groups to have some of their schooling in those languages as well as in the majority language, for many children this is already too late for them to benefit from it, since their competency in the minority language is by school age already minimal or non-existent. There is a need for information and encouragement to be given to families in which one or more parents speak a language other than the dominant language, but are unsure how to go about it, and perhaps apprehensive about the possible consequences.

This book looks closely at how one Australian family has gone about raising its children bilingually over a period of eight years. It is hoped that by documenting in some detail what has happened, and is still happening, in one family, as well as drawing on other relevant research, other parents who are contemplating raising their children bilingually can be shown that whilst such an endeavour is not all plain sailing and does require some effort, it *is* possible and can be a rewarding experience for both parents and children. Much of the book is anecdotal; the anecdotes have been chosen not only to illustrate various aspects of bilingualism but also in the hope that they will reveal an actual normal family living its everyday life, a family in which two languages co-exist more or less harmoniously. The family is, however, not a model to be followed unswervingly. Obviously each family is unique, with its own particular set of circumstances. Readers will quickly realize whether certain things will work in quite the same way in their family and make appropriate modifications. It is hoped that this family's experiences will also show that it is possible for fluent non-native speakers of a minority language to create a bilingual home environment from which their children can derive considerable benefit.

Whilst much of this is anecdotal, it is by no means just impressionistic. The anecdotes are based on careful observation and are in most cases illustrated with actual dialogue taken verbatim from over 400 hours of tape recordings. Moreover, the children's performance and progress in their two languages are analysed not only interpretatively but also using objective measurements.

During the course of the book an attempt is made to give or suggest answers to many of the questions people raise concerning bilingualism in young children. Among the typical questions asked are:

— Should a child be exposed to two languages simultaneously or should one be established before the other is introduced? (See pp. 29–48.)

— Won't acquiring two languages simultaneously place too great a mental burden on a young child? (See particularly p. 21 and pp. 29–41.)

— Will a child spoken to in two languages from birth begin to speak later than a child spoken to in only one language? (See p. 43.)

— Is the developmental sequence followed by a child acquiring two languages simultaneously the same as that followed by children acquiring only one? (See pp. 42–48.)

— What influence will one language have on the other? Will a child be able to keep his two languages separate? (See pp. 29–48 and chapter 7.)

— Will bilingualism retard a child's progress in the majority language of the community? (See pp. 29–48 and chapter 7.)

— Won't the effort of becoming bilingual retard a child's intellectual development? (See pp. 14–22 and chapter 7.)

— Will children simply acquire the home language if the parent(s) use(s) it to communicate with them, or do they have to be formally taught the language? (See especially pp. 29–48.)

— Will family harmony be jeopardized if each parent speaks a different language with the children? (See particularly chapters 2–5.)

— What happens if a child wishes to address both parents at the same time? (See pp. 50–52.)

— Will bilingualism be effective with young children in a two language household if the parent who is to pass on the minority language has reduced contact with the children because of employment? (See particularly pp. 42–48 and chapter 6.)

— Won't the use of a minority language cause friction with acquaintances, friends and relatives who do not understand the language? (See chapter 5.)

— Won't being required to speak two languages cause young children to have difficulty expressing themselves or to stutter? (See especially pp. 114–117.)

— Won't children's desire to conform to their peers cause them to reject the home language when they start kindergarten or school? What can be done if children refuse to speak the language? (See particularly pp. 121–128 and pp. 134–146.)

— Won't attempting to teach children to read and write the minority language interfere with and impede their progress in reading and writing in the majority language at school? (See chapter 8.)

The suggested answers to these and other questions are based both on careful observation and evaluation of one family and on evidence from other studies of bilingual children.

What is bilingualism?

The word "bilingual" has different connotations for different people. To some people, bilingualism means "a native-like control of two languages", a definition put forward in 1933 by the American linguist Leonard Bloomfield.[10] However, such a definition leaves many speakers of more than one language unaccounted for, people who do not have "native-like control" of one (or even, in some cases, both) of their languages. Some writers refer to the type of bilingualism as defined by Bloomfield above as "true" bilingualism, and some are even more demanding in their definition than his "native-*like* control". Thiéry,[11] for example, calls a "true" bilingual someone who would at all times be taken for a native by native speakers of both the languages concerned. He justifiably refers to this definition as restrictive and as representing the highest degree of bilingualism. Such bilingualism represents an ideal which is very rarely attained and which is perhaps best referred to by the less emotive term *equilingual* (also known as *ambilingual*), although a more precise description would probably be "dually monolingual", since a person at this level of bilingualism would in effect be able to function as if he or she were two monolinguals.

Some writers, unfortunately, use the term bilingualism without defining precisely what they mean. Andrews,[12] in an article on bilingualism published in 1980, for example, dismisses out of hand Leopold's[13] classic study of his daughter Hildegard's acquisition of bilingualism, THE SPEECH DEVELOPMENT OF A BILINGUAL CHILD: A LINGUIST'S RECORD (which is referred to often in this book), with the words:

> "Looking for literature on bilingualism . . . , I discovered that this field of inquiry had had a very slow start in the 1930s, and that the early studies yield but little insight. Leopold's frequently quoted study of his daughter Hildegard turned out to be especially disappointing because *it does not deal with bilingualism, its title notwithstanding*." (This writer's emphasis.)

However, she offers no explanation as to why Hildegard should not be considered as a bilingual. Presumably she does so because Hildegard's ability in German was considerably less than in English. Contrast this with Leopold's[14] own assessment of Hildegard at age 6 years, two months:

> "Hildegard is now, for all practical purposes, bilingual. She understands in both languages everything within her range of comprehension and is capable of expressing her thoughts, feelings and wishes in both. The expression is, however, much more restricted and halting in German."

Andrews' judgement of Leopold's work is surprising, since none of the bilinguals mentioned in her article are equally proficient in both their languages. Moreover, to show that motivated adults can become bilingual, she quotes and lends credence to the far-fetched claims of a nineteenth century German, Heinrich Schliemann,[15] who wrote:

> ". . . I succeeded in acquiring in half a year a thorough knowledge of the English language. I then applied the same method to the study of French, the difficulties of which I overcame likewise in another six months . . . This unremitting study had in the course of a single year strengthened my memory to such a degree that the study of Dutch, Spanish, Italian and Portuguese appeared very easy, and it did not take me more than six weeks (*sic*) to write and speak each of these languages fluently."

It is extremely doubtful if Schliemann's knowledge of English and French after six months of study, let alone his knowledge of the other languages he learned in six weeks, would match Hildegard Leopold's knowledge of German acquired over a period of many years.

How proficient does a person have to be, then, to be classed as a bilingual? Haugen,[16] an American linguist who has worked extensively in the field of bilingualism, suggests that bilingualism begins "at the point where a speaker of one language can produce complete, meaningful utterances in the other language". Diebold[17] considers that a type of bilingualism has even commenced when a person begins to *understand* utterances in a second language without being able to utter anything him- or herself.

Bilingualism, therefore, simply means having two languages (and bilingualism is often used in the literature to mean the same as multilingualism, that is, having more than two languages). Bilinguals can be ranged along a continuum from the rare equilingual who is indistinguishable from a native speaker in both languages at one end to the person who has just begun to acquire a second language at the other end. They are all bilinguals, but possessing different *degrees* of bilingualism. A monolingual (also called a unilingual or monoglot) is thus someone who knows only one language. (In this book monolingual is used, for the sake of convenience, to refer also to persons near the extremity of the bilingualism continuum, namely to persons who are minimally bilingual, that is, who have very little proficiency in more than one language.)

A bilingual's degree of bilingualism can be assessed in the four skills of listening comprehension, speaking, reading comprehension and writing. There are many possible combinations of abilities in these skills. Many children of immigrants, for instance, possess all four skills solely in the official language of their country of residence (e.g. English in Australia), whilst they may be able to understand only the spoken form of their parents' language (e.g. Italian) and barely be able to speak it. Haas[18] would class such children as "receiving oral bilinguals", since they are bilingual only in receiving the spoken form of two languages, in listening comprehension. Someone who is bilingual in all four skills would, using this system, be classified as a "receiving sending oral visual bilingual". Again, within each skill there could be differing abilities in each language, e.g. an English-Chinese bilingual educated through English could be much more proficient at writing English than Chinese, whereas his spoken Chinese could be better than his spoken English, and so on.

The term "balanced bilingual" is frequently encountered in the literature on bilingualism. Whilst some writers (e.g. Haugen)[19] use it as a synonym of equilingual, most researchers use "balanced bilingualism" in a different sense which does not imply perfect mastery of both languages (e.g. Peal & Lambert[20]). Balanced bilinguals in this sense are bilinguals who are roughly equally skilled in their two languages, i.e. a balance exists between the two.

This means that someone who could pass for a native in both languages would be considered a balanced bilingual, but so too would someone whose performance in one (or both) of his languages was less than perfect, as long as his ability in both was roughly equal. Much of the recent research comparing bilingual and monolingual children has been done with balanced bilinguals. Various tests are used to determine which bilinguals are balanced. For example, in 1978 Doyle et al[21] used the Peabody Picture Vocabulary Test (see pp. 159ff. for further details of this test), and called those children balanced bilinguals who had a discrepancy of 20 IQ points or less between the French and English forms of the test. One of the tests used by Peal & Lambert was a word association test in which children had to write down in 60 seconds as many words as they could think of in the same language as particular stimulus words. A child who overall scored 20 words in French and 20 in English was obviously classed as balanced on this test, but so too was someone scoring 20 words in French and over 11 in English (or vice versa). A similar leniency of assessment is shown by other researchers (e.g. Balkan[22]).

Even a balanced bilingual is therefore usually "dominant", that is, more proficient, in one of his two languages, although he or she may not be dominant in the same language in all areas. There may be domains or situations in which a bilingual usually uses only one of his or her two languages, e.g. an Australian child may use only English at school but speak only Greek with his or her mother at home; consequently he or she may have a greater English school vocabulary and be better able to talk about events at school in English, yet be better able to talk about, say, cooking in Greek. A number of tests can be administered to determine language dominance in various domains or contexts (see pp. 207ff. for discussion and examples).

The term "dominant" is also used (e.g. by Macnamara[23]) to describe two other aspects of bilingualism. Firstly, for one language to be used when, from the point of view of speaker, topic, situation and so on, the two languages are equally suitable, e.g. a German-English bilingual might keep a diary in English, when he could equally well use German; such a preference when there is a choice could be taken as an indication that his dominant language is English. Secondly, "dominant" is used with reference to the tendency for a bilingual's two languages to have some influence on each other, that is, for what Weinreich calls "interference" to take place between the two languages. In his book LANGUAGES IN CONTACT, Weinreich[24] defines interference as:

> "Those instances of deviation from the norms of either language which occur in the speech of bilinguals as a result of their famil-iarity with more than one language."

Clyne,[25] in his work TRANSFERENCE AND TRIGGERING, a perceptive study of the language of German-speaking immigrants in Australia, prefers the term "transference" to refer to this transferring of elements of one language into another, and this is also the term which will be used in this book. Transference may be of various types, as shown in the following examples from the speech of English-German bilinguals (more detailed explanations of the terminology with illustrative examples are given in the section beginning on p. 92): *lexical*, e.g. Frank (4;5,11) (= age four years, five months, eleven days; all ages will be given in this form): I'll *lösch* this match in this little bit of water (from German *löschen*="extinguish"); *semantic*, e.g. Thomas (6;7,8): *Before* two weeks Craig's dog had pups (from German *vor*="before", "in front of", "*ago*"); *syntactic*, e.g. Frank (5;0,29): And then we'll walk the hill *up* (from the German sentence pattern where "up" [*rauf*] would occur at the end: Und dann gehen wir den Hügel *rauf*); *phonological* (using sounds from the other language, resulting in a foreign accent); etc. Transference can occur in both directions, that is, from language A to language B as well as from language B to language A. The language in which transfers (instances of transference) occur least is thought to be a bilingual's dominant language.

But, as has been seen above, there are also various other factors which may be taken into consideration when determining a bilingual's dominant language, and for some bilinguals it may be difficult to decide with any precision which language could, overall, be considered dominant. Although very few bilinguals manage to avoid interference or transference altogether, they usually have one language in which it is reduced to a minimum (as in the English of the children in this study; see, for example, chapter 7).

As will be seen, the type of bilingualism attained by the children in this book falls within the definition of balanced bilingualism given above. An effort is made to achieve some sort of balance between the two languages in all domains. A realistic achievement to be aimed at would seem to be what Anastasi & Cordova[26] call "bilingual parallelism", that is, a type of bilingualism where the individual learns to express himself in *all* types of situations *in at least one language*. The other language "provides a parallel means of expression in some *or* all situations, depending on the thoroughness of its mastery."

An important aspect of bilingualism is *code switching*. Code switching, or switching from one language to the other, in the course of a conversation, even in mid-sentence, is usually carried out by bilinguals without any significant pause in the flow of speech. (Speakers of only one language also switch in a similar fashion between varieties of that language, e.g. between an English dialect and Standard English.)

Switching may be due to a number of factors, both linguistic and extralinguistic. Among the extralinguistic factors the following are the most common. Firstly, the person being spoken to is obviously an important consideration. A monolingual speaker of either of a bilingual's languages will clearly be addressed in the language which he or she can understand, e.g. the children in this study, if speaking German to their father, will switch to English to address people who understand only English. But what if both speakers know both languages? Often one of the two languages becomes established as the one mostly used. This is the case in families where communication between certain members of the family may take place in one language, between other members in another, e.g in this study communication between children and father is in German, between children and mother in English, so that in a family conversation the children switch frequently from one language to the other depending on which parent they are addressing, e.g.:

> **Frank** (5;6,0) (to father): Das war Klasse (*That was terrific*), wasn't it, Mum?

Young children quickly become very skilled at this type of switching, switching automatically and seemingly effortlessly whenever required to do so.

Some bilinguals may switch languages according to domain, e.g. in some Australian families children speak a non-English language in the home to certain members of the family, but the moment they leave the home domain and go out into the community they switch to English to speak to the very same people.

Amongst themselves bilinguals may also switch languages for stylistic reasons, e.g. according to topic; they could be discussing school or work in one language, yet switch to another to talk about sport (perhaps because each topic is strongly associated with a particular language). Similarly, while speaking one language to each other, bilinguals may switch to their other language to quote something written or something said in that language (see p. 98), in much the same way a speaker of Australian English might attempt a British English accent when quoting an Englishman. In discussions and arguments between bilinguals a speaker may switch to a language in which he feels he can make his point more forcefully or eloquently.

Much depends on the attitude of bilinguals towards language switching as to how much switching actually takes place in any interaction. Some bilinguals like it to be kept to a minimum, preferring one language or the other to be used, whilst other bilinguals are quite happy to switch languages constantly according to topic, etc. In the home children are, with regard to switching, guided to a large extent by their parents' preferences and example.

Another kind of switching is what Clyne[27] calls "internally conditioned switching", that is, switching caused by linguistic factors. The occurrence of a word which belongs to, or at least appears to belong to both languages (e.g. a proper noun such as Canberra) causes a speaker to forget momentarily which language he or she is speaking, and he or she continues in the other language, until it is realized what has happened. Clyne[25] calls such words "trigger words", since they trigger a more or less unconscious switch from one language to another. The switch may be made just before trigger words ("anticipational switching") or, more commonly, immediately following them ("consequential switching"), e.g.:

Frank (5;5,3): Mum, what can I have to drink?
Mother: Do you want some Prima?
Frank: Ja, bitte. (*Yes, please.*) (PRIMA, which is an Australian brand of orange juice but also a German word meaning "terrific", has triggered a switch from English to German.)

Although some involuntary switching and transference do occur between a bilingual's two languages, albeit to different degrees in different individuals, bilinguals are usually remarkably adept at keeping the two functionally separate when speaking. (For remarks on very young bilingual children see pp. 42–48.)

Haugen[28] points out that a crucial factor in the kind and extent of a person's bilingualism is the age at which the two language are acquired, because the aptitudes, opportunities and motivations for learning are so different at various ages. He thus refers to *infant, child, adolescent* and *adult* bilingualism.

Infant bilingualism is the type under close scrutiny in this study, although the other types, particularly child bilingualism, are also referred to. Infant bilingualism is the *simultaneous* acquisition of two languages from birth (see p. 29 for further details). Child bilingualism implies *successive* acquisition of two languages, that is, a child acquires first one language within the family and then acquires a second language through kindergarten and/or the early school years. The distinction between infant and child bilingualism is in some cases difficult to draw. For example, a child may be exposed to only one language in the home but have some informal contact with speakers of the other language right from the beginning. Infant and child bilinguals usually acquire both their languages with a native or native-like pronunciation, whereas adolescent bilinguals (who become bilingual after puberty) and adult bilinguals (who acquire their second language when adults) usually speak their second language with a non-native accent (see pp. 201ff. for further discussion of this phenomenon).

Balkan's[22] major study of Swiss 11–16-year-old bilinguals, published in 1970, suggests that infant and early child bilingualism could have certain advantages over later child bilingualism. Balkan first compared all his bilinguals with monolinguals, with whom they were matched for non-verbal intelligence and socio-economic status. The bilinguals scored at a significantly higher level on tests of numerical aptitude, verbal flexibility, perceptual flexibility and general reasoning. Balkan then divided the bilingual group into two: those who had become bilingual *before* the age of 4 and those who had become bilingual *after* the age of 4. He found that the early bilinguals were not only markedly superior to the monolinguals but also significantly superior to the later bilinguals.

Is bilingualism an advantage or a disadvantage?

For many of the world's bilinguals this question is purely academic: they have no choice but to be bilingual. But for parents who are in a position to decide whether they are to raise their children bilingually or not, the arguments for and against bilingualism are an important consideration in making that decision.

Much controversy has surrounded the question of whether a person's, particularly a child's, bilingualism can be considered an advantage or a disadvantage. Much of the writing on the subject during the first half of this century concentrated on what were seen as the detrimental effects of bilingualism. In 1922, for instance, Jespersen[29] wrote in his book LANGUAGE. ITS NATURE, DEVELOPMENT AND ORIGIN:

> "It is, of course, an advantage for a child to be familiar with two languages, but without doubt the advantage may be, and generally is, purchased too dear. First of all the child in question hardly learns either of the two languages as perfectly as he would have done if he had limited himself to one . . . Secondly, the brain effort required to master two languages instead of one certainly diminishes the child's power of learning other things which might and ought to be learnt. Schuchardt rightly remarks that if a bilingual man has two strings to his bow, both are rather slack . . ."

Bilingualism has been seen as something unnatural. In 1933, Weisgerber,[30] a German linguist, believed that bilingualism could impair the intelligence of a whole ethnic group. Thirty-three years later, Weisgerber[31] still believed that any possible advantages of bilingualism were outweighed by what he saw as "the certain detrimental effects", that by nature man was basically monolingual, and that being bilingual was like trying to belong to two different religions at the same time.

In an article published in Switzerland in 1928, de Reynold[32] expressed the opinion that bilingualism leads to language mixing and language confusion which in turn results in a reduction in the ability to think and act precisely, a decrease in intelligence, an increase in mental lethargy and reduced self-discipline.

Besides such evidence against bilingualism based on personal intuition, many studies also seemed to indicate that bilingualism had a negative effect on intellectual development. In 1923, Saer,[33] for instance, studied 1,400 7–14-year-old Welsh-English bilingual children in five rural and two urban districts of Wales, and concluded that bilingualism results in lower intelligence. However, Saer failed to consider social differences between the bilinguals and monolinguals. Even so, it was only in the rural districts that the bilinguals were found to score lower on intelligence tests; in the urban districts the bilinguals' average IQ was slightly higher than that of the monolinguals:

	AVERAGE IQ	
	Urban districts	*Rural districts*
Monolingual children	99	96
Bilingual children	100	86

It seems that the urban bilingual children had much more contact with their second language before beginning school and then outside school hours than did their rural counterparts. There would thus be much more balance between the urban bilinguals' two languages than would be the case with the rural bilinguals, and this would allow them to compete on a more equal footing with monolinguals in verbal intelligence tests. Subsequent research in Wales (e.g. by Morrison[34] in 1958) shows also that if the occupational status of parents is taken into consideration when comparing rural and urban children no differences are found.

Caution must be exercised when comparing monolinguals and bilinguals on tests of intelligence, particularly on tests of verbal intelligence, and particularly if, as often happens, the bilinguals are tested in only *one* of their languages, perhaps their "weaker" language (see pp. 159–165 for further discussion).

In 1956, Haugen,[35] in a review of studies conducted in America to that time, concluded that knowing two languages did not appear to affect non-verbal intelligence. He noted further that the verbal intelligence of bilinguals was retarded at most by two years at any point, and that this difference disappeared by the time bilinguals reached college age.

However, even these conclusions have been convincingly challenged by research carried out since the early 1960s which shows bilingualism in a very favourable light. In 1962 Peal & Lambert, for example, studied the effects of bilingualism on the intellectual functioning of ten-year-old children from six Montreal French schools. The bilingual children, who were selected for being balanced bilinguals, were compared with a group of monolingual children, with whom they were matched for socio-economic class, sex and age. At the start of their study, Peal & Lambert predicted that their findings would be similar to those of previous investigations, i.e. that whilst non-verbal IQ tests would reveal little difference between the bilinguals and monolinguals, the monolinguals would perform significantly better than the bilinguals on verbal tests of intelligence. However, both of these predictions proved to be wrong. Not only did the bilinguals perform *significantly better* than the monolinguals on the *nonverbal* IQ tests, but also scored significantly higher on all the tests of *verbal* IQ. Moreover, the bilingual children were found to be in a higher grade at school than the monolingual children of the same age, and also to achieve better results in their schoolwork than the monolingual children in the same grade. Peal & Lambert[36] thus concluded: ". . . it appears that our bilinguals, instead of suffering from 'mental confusion' or a 'language handicap' are profiting from a 'language asset'." These findings seriously question the not uncommon belief, such as expressed by Wilkinson[37] in his book THE FOUNDATIONS OF LANGUAGE, that "learning a second language imposes a burden on development in both languages and on educational attainment."

Peal & Lambert[38] sum up their research as follows:

"Intellectually [the bilingual's] experience with two language systems seems to have left him with a mental flexibility, a super-iority in concept formation, and a more diversified set of mental abilities, in the sense that the patterns of abilities developed by bilinguals were more heterogeneous. It is not possible to state from the present study whether the more intelligent child became bilingual or whether bilingualism aided his intellectual develop-ment, but there is no question about the fact that he is superior intellectually. In contrast, the monolingual appears to have a more unitary structure of intelligence which he must use for all types of intellectual tasks."

These results were criticized (e.g. by Macnamara[39]) on the grounds that the bilingual students were chosen for the study if their English vocabulary was comparable to their vocabulary in their mother tongue, French; since there is generally a relationship between vocabulary and intelligence — the greater the vocabulary the higher the intelligence — it seemed probable that only the intellectually brighter children were chosen for the bilingual group. Lambert & Anisfield (née Peal)[40] convincingly refuted this objection: the important criterion for selecting the bilingual children was that they had to approach a balance of skills in their two languages, i.e. they had to be approximately equally good *or poor* in both languages.

A large-scale follow-up study by Anisfield[41] in 1964 confirmed the conclusions reached in the 1962 investigation: groups of immigrant children who, because of their circumstances, had no choice but to be bilingual, were found to score better on intelligence tests than monolingual control groups.

Other studies also indicate that bilingualism can have a positive effect on intelligence and can give a child certain cognitive advantages over his or her monolingual peers. Segalowitz,[42] for example, states in an article published in 1977 that "the bilingual's verbal and cultural background is inherently richer because of its bilinguality, and thus produces an earlier occurrence of certain experiences critical to intellectual development". Some of these cognitive advantages can be summarized as follows:

(a) Earlier and greater awareness of the arbitrariness of language

Ianco-Worrall's[43] 1972 study of Afrikaans-English 4–9-year-old bilingual children in South Africa showed that bilingual children analyse language more intensively than do monolinguals and are better able to analyse language as an abstract system. The bilingual children become conscious at a much earlier age of the fact that names are arbitrarily assigned to objects and are subject to change. That is, that there is no intrinsic connection, for example, between the word *dog* and the animal it symbolizes. A word is just what people use it to mean; it is not an attribute of the thing it names.

The bilingual and monolingual children in Ianco-Worrall's study were asked questions such as: "If you were making up names for things, could you call a dog 'cow' and a cow 'dog'?" The great majority of the monolingual children replied that the names of objects could *not* be changed, whilst the majority of the bilingual children agreed that in principle this could be done.

Feldman & Shen's[44] 1971 study of 4–6-year-old Spanish-English bilingual American Headstart children and Cummins's[45] 1978 study of grade 3 and grade 6 Irish-English bilingual children confirmed Ianco-Worral's findings: 68.8% of the Spanish-English bilinguals and 70% of the Irish-English bilinguals, compared with only 31.1% and 27.5% respectively of the children in the monolingual control groups, asserted that the names of things could be interchanged.

It would seem that the experience which bilingual children have in acquiring their languages, part of which is an early realization that most things are referred to in at least two ways, not just one (e.g. dog/*Hund*), promotes this sort of awareness.

(b) Earlier separation of meaning from sound

The ability to separate the *meaning* of a word from its *sound* is, as Cummins[46] points out, "necessary if a child is to use language effectively as a tool for thinking". The available evidence suggests that bilingualism can give children a head start here. Ianco-Worrall,[43] for example, found that the bilingual children in her study were capable of separating the meaning of a word from its sound at a much earlier age, in fact some two to three years earlier, than their monolingual peers. The children were given 8 sets of 3 words, such as *cap, can* and *hat*, and asked, "Which is more like *cap — can* or *hat*?" 54% of the 4–6-year-old bilinguals consistently interpreted similarity between words in terms of *meaning* rather than their sound, whereas almost none of the monolingual children did this. Thus, monolinguals chose *can* as being more like *cap*, because of the similarity in sound, whilst the majority of bilinguals chose *hat* because of its similarity in meaning to *cap*.

These findings are confirmed by Ben-Zeev's[47] 1972 study of Hebrew-English bilingual children and offer support for Leopold's[48] claim that:

> "A bilingual, who constantly hears two words for one thing, is compelled to pay more attention to the meaning expressed than the word used to express it, whereas the monolingual is often satisfied with a hazy definition of a word and will use it without understanding it fully."

(c) Greater adeptness at evaluating non-empirical contradictory statements

Cummins[45] found in his 1978 study that grade 3 and grade 6 bilingual children (whose home language was English but who at school were being taught through Irish) were better able to evaluate non-empirical contradictory statements than monolingual children with whom they were matched on IQ, socio-economic status and age. This type of statement takes the form: "The counter in my hand is blue and it is not blue." The children had to answer true, false, or whether it was not possible to know, and then had to justify their responses.

(d) Greater adeptness at divergent thinking

In 1973, Scott[49] published the results of a seven-year study of a group of English-Canadian children who were given the opportunity to become bilingual by doing most of their schooling in French. He found that these bilingual children performed better than monolingual peers on divergent thinking tasks. Divergent thinking is a special type of cognitive flexibility which some researchers see as an index of creativity while others look on it more cautiously, for example Lambert,[50] who calls it "a distinctive cognitive style reflecting a rich imagination and an ability to scan rapidly a host of possible solutions". Measures of divergent thinking provide a person with a starting point for thought and ask him or her to produce a whole series of permissible solutions, such as "Think of a paper clip and tell me all the things you could do with it".

(e) Greater adeptness at creative thinking

In 1974, Carringer[51] measured the creative thinking ability of 15-year-old "balanced" Spanish-English bilingual children and compared it with that of monolinguals. The bilinguals scored higher than the monolingual control group in all respects (verbal and figural fluency, flexibility and originality). In his discussion of these results, Carringer says:

> "Although only exploratory, this study suggests that bilingualism does promote creative thinking abilities and at least in part serves to free the mind from the tyranny of words. Since the bilingual has two terms for one referent, his attention is focused on ideas and not words, on content rather than form, on meaning rather than symbol, and this is very important in the intellectual process as it permits greater cognitive flexibility."

(f) Greater social sensitivity

There is some evidence indicating that having two languages can give children a greater social sensitivity than monolingual children. For example, Genesee, Tucker & Lambert[52] found in 1975 that English-speaking children in French school immersion programmes (i.e. receiving most of their instruction through French) proved to be more sensitive to the communication needs of blindfolded listeners than other children.

In 1977, Ben-Zeev[53] found that bilingual children tended to be more sensitive to cues, being more open to correction and guidance than monolinguals.

(g) Greater facility at concept formation

The experiments of Liedtke & Nelson[54] in 1968, using a Concepts of Linear Measurement Test with 6-year-old monolinguals and children exposed to two languages in the home, confirmed Peal & Lambert's[55] conclusion in 1962 that bilinguals were significantly better at concept formation, which is a major part of intellectual development. They surmise that this is because the bilingual child, by virtue of his or her two languages, is exposed to a more complex environment and to a greater amount of social interaction compared to a child acquiring only one language.

These studies certainly give a brighter picture of the effects of bilingualism on children's intellectual development. However, it should be noted that the bilingual children in these studies were chosen because they showed no great difference in ability between their two languages, that is, they were all types of "balanced" bilinguals (although they were by no means equally proficient in their two languages). Also, in some cases other tests were conducted in which there was no significant difference in results between the bilinguals and the monolinguals, e.g. the bilinguals' performance on empirical questions (e.g. "The counter in my hand is yellow and it is not green. True or false?") in Cummins's[45] 1978 study was not significantly better than that of the monolinguals.

Cummins[56] hypothesizes that "those aspects of bilingualism which might accelerate cognitive growth seem unlikely to come into effect until the child has attained a certain minimum or *threshold level of competence* in his second language". However, it would seem that this threshold is well within reach: the children in the studies just mentioned who were, according to fairly lenient assessment criteria, considered balanced bilinguals, had clearly reached this hypothesized threshold level of competence.

Various researchers, such as Doyle *et al*[57] in 1978 and Ben-Zeev[58] in 1977, have found that there is one type of test in which bilinguals frequently perform worse than monolinguals, namely in tests of vocabulary. The reason for this would seem to be that bilingual children have to learn two different labels for everything, one for each language. This reduces the frequency with which they will hear a particular word in either language. In other cases particular words may be associated with certain situations in which only one language is regularly used and the corresponding names in the other language may not (yet) be known (see pp. 161–165 for further discussion). And since bilingual children are usually tested on their knowledge of vocabulary in only one language, or if in both, in each language separately, it is possible that they will perform less well than similarly aged monolingual speakers of either of their languages. However, this does not mean that they know fewer *concepts* than the monolingual children. If the bilingual children's *two* languages are taken into account, their overall performance will usually improve significantly and they may then equal (as found, for example, by Bergan & Parra[59] in 1979), or even outperform monolingual children (see pp. 162–163 for elaboration of this point).

From the evidence, therefore, it appears that if bilingual children have a reasonable degree of balance between their two languages, their overall intellectual development is not hindered and is, in fact, in many ways enhanced.

As far as the bilingual's brain is concerned, Segalowitz,[60] in a review of research on neurological aspects of bilingualism, concludes that:

". . . there does not seem to be strong neurological evidence indicating a basic difference in the way language is represented in the monolingual and bilingual brain . . . the evidence presently available does not indicate that a bilingual brain suffers some neurological burden that a monolingual brain escapes. From the strictly neurological point of view, a brain can handle two languages just as easily as one."

With regard to memory, there is no evidence to indicate that it is impaired in any way by bilingualism. One theory regarding the structure of memory in bilinguals is that they have two separate memory stores, one for each language, with information presented in one language not being readily available in the other (a view put forward, for example, by Macnamara[61] in 1967 and also in 1971). However, evidence from many studies (reviewed, for instance, by Segalowitz[42] in 1977, and McLaughlin[62] in 1978) suggests that concepts are not segregated in the brain according to the language with which they are associated; bilinguals store words in memory in terms of meaning, i.e. there is one semantic system underlying the two languages. Items are then in some way "tagged" with the right language at the time of speaking. An implication of this is that a bilingual who hears information first in one language and then repeated in his or her other language will retain the information just as well as if he had been given the same information twice in the same language. Kolers[63] gives a concrete example of this in an article published in the SCIENTIFIC AMERICAN:

". . . suppose one wanted to give a student two lessons in geography. If the student knew two languages, he would retain as much geography from one lesson in each language as from two lessons in one of them. Moreover, he would be able to talk about geography readily in both languages."

Most of the problems associated with bilingualism are really social or cultural problems, that is, problems brought about by a hostile attitude of the majority group in a society, or sections of it, towards the presence of other languages and cultures, as well as the conflict faced by children expected to live in one culture at home and in another in the world outside. These factors can, of course, adversely affect a person's bilingualism: a child who wishes to conform to the majority group in society may reject the culture and language of the home. Much depends on an understanding and supportive home environment if this is to be avoided. If children's bilingualism (and biculturalism) were viewed favourably both by their families and by the population in general, few problems would exist.

Within the family itself, particularly where each parent speaks a different language to the children, it is probably necessary, to avoid problems, that each parent understand the other's language, and that the parents co-operate and be supportive of each other's efforts to transmit his or her language to the children. Such co-operation may mean, for example, giving preferential treatment to the language which is in the weakest position. These questions are discussed further throughout this book.

2 Establishing bilingualism in the family

The family

This study looks closely at two Australian-born boys's acquisition of bilingualism in English and German. The two boys, Thomas and Frank, were born on 9 November 1973 and 1 October 1975 respectively and have never been outside Australia. They have a sister, Katrina, born on 13 February 1981, but she features only peripherally, since, at the time of writing, she has not begun to speak. From birth, the children have been addressed by their mother and most other people in English, whilst their father has always spoken to them in German. This situation differs from most of those reported in the literature on bilingual families in that not only is English the dominant and official language of the community in which the family lives and the native language of the mother, but it is also the native language of the *father*. Such a situation makes possible the observation of many factors affecting the fostering and maintenance of a minority language, and, since the father is not a native speaker of German, it also affords some insight into difficulties experienced by parents who, by choice or necessity, communicate with their children in a second language.

Both parents were born in the Australian island state of Tasmania. They both come from monolingual English-speaking families and speak General Australian English as their native language. As far as can be ascertained, both sides of the family have consisted of only English-speakers for at least six generations. The father's great-great-grandfather, for example, was born in England in 1814 and, like the forefathers of most Australians, arrived in Australia as an immigrant, albeit not a voluntary one. He ran foul of the harsh penal system of the time, being sentenced in Nottingham at the ripe old age of thirteen to transportation for life to Van Diemen's Land (present-day Tasmania) for the obviously serious offence of misappropriating a brace-and-bit.

Both parents' first contact with foreign languages came in high school, an experience which had not been available to their own parents. The mother learnt French for four years and did moderately well at it, but she did not like the subject particularly, finding the pronunciation of the language strange and difficult.

The father studied both French and German for five years at high school, where, encouraged by enthusiastic and skilful language teachers, the two languages quickly became his favourite and best subjects. This interest continued on to university, French being studied for a further three years and German for another four years as major subjects in a Bachelor of Arts honours degree at the University of Tasmania. He attained the degree with First Class Honours in German. This was followed by four years working on a doctoral dissertation in German linguistics. Fourteen months of this time were spent studying German linguistics and Dutch and carrying out linguistic field-work at a university in Germany. Since completing his doctorate the father has taught languages at a high school, colleges of advanced education and a university. Because of his occupation, and also because of his interest in shortwave broadcasts, particularly those in German, he has been able to maintain a high degree of competence in the language. His German could not be called perfect in the English sense of the word, i.e. not entirely flawless, although errors in grammar and pronunciation are rare. Native speakers of German have referred to his German as *perfekt* which, in its German sense, means "excellent". Some native speakers of German, particularly those not from North Germany or those who have lived in Australia for a number of years, have mistaken him for a native speaker of the language. He feels confident about using German in most situations, although he is aware that his command of the language is not equal to that of his native language, English. (See p. 209 for details of the father's language dominance, and pp. 146ff. for references to his accuracy.)

The mother's motivation to learn German came shortly after her marriage at the age of twenty-one. There was a distinct possibility, which later eventuated, that her husband would receive a travelling scholarship from the German Academic Exchange Service which, together with an Australian Government Postgraduate Scholarship he already held, would enable him to conduct research for his doctorate in Germany the following year. Since she wished to continue practising her profession of nursing sister while in Germany, and since her return fare to Australia would have to be earned in this way, motivation to learn some German was, understandably, strong. After eleven months of tuition from her husband she had acquired a rudimentary knowledge of German grammar, a vocabulary of about 1,500 words, and a reasonably accurate pronunciation, which enabled her to participate somewhat hesitantly in simple conversations. She took care to learn carefully the medical terminology she thought she would need in a German hospital.

Even so, her minimal competence was not to be enough to shield her from a number of rather traumatic linguistic experiences, experiences most likely encountered by many an immigrant, guest-worker or simply traveller abroad. On arrival in Germany, the mother took up employment firstly as a nursing aide, then, when her qualifications were finally recognized, as a sister on a private ward of a large hospital where the medical personnel and cleaning staff were predominantly monolingual speakers of German. Recourse to English when faced with a linguistic predicament was therefore not possible. Aided only by a small pocket dictionary, she had to cope with being in sole charge of the ward three hours a day, answering the telephone, dealing with emergencies, and so on. Whilst this experience was initially rather nerve-racking and stressful, it did bring about a dramatic improvement in her comprehension of and fluency in German. Within a short time, patients unaware of her origin thought she was Dutch, in itself a kind of compliment and an indication of her progress in German.

On her return to Australia, she decided to consolidate the knowledge of German she had acquired by studying it more formally as a subject for the Tasmanian Higher School Certificate (H.S.C.), the prerequisite for studying the subject at university. This year of study proved very beneficial in increasing her proficiency in German grammar and giving her much practice in writing the language. During the year she won first prize in a German essay competition run by the German Australian Club in Tasmania, and in the end-of-year H.S.C. exam gained 166/200, the second highest mark. Since then she has maintained her German mainly through reading and, of course, through being consistently exposed to the language in the home. She still speaks it fluently and her level of comprehension is very high. Moreover, her experience with German had aroused her interest in other languages and cultures. As a hobby, she and her husband studied Indonesian together at H.S.C. level, both reaching a good level of competence.

The father also sat, for interest's sake, the H.S.C. Dutch exam and obtained a good mark. In addition he has acquired a good reading knowledge of the closely related Afrikaans.

It needs to be pointed out that in this study the children usually address their father as Bert, pronounced [bɛɐt] as in German, and that in German Thomas is usually addressed and referred to as Ernie, pronounced [ɛɐni]. These are nicknames which date from when Thomas was aged 4;9 and was fascinated by the television show SESAME STREET and by German comic books (*Sesamstraße*) which the father had about the same show. Thomas subsequently assigned each family member the name of a character from SESAME STREET, and these two have remained and become the usual forms of address in German. Before this time the father was referred to as either Dad [dad] or Schorsch, and these forms of address will also occur in some of the quotations given.

As would no doubt sooner or later become obvious to the reader, the present author and the father referred to in this study are one and the same person; such constant, close observation of the children would be very difficult, if not impossible, for an outsider to carry out effectively. The account has been written in the third person in an attempt to look at the children's linguistic development more detachedly. Of course, as any parent knows, it is difficult for someone so closely involved with the children to remain completely objective; nevertheless, every effort has been made to give an honest picture of their bilingual development, with the problems and failures being recorded along with the benefits and successes. Fortunately, as will be seen, the successes have outweighed the failures by a considerable margin.

Motives for creating bilingualism in the family

In this case there were several motives for the parents' decision to raise their children bilingually. Firstly, both parents believed in the intrinsic value of a knowledge of more than one language, providing as it does an awareness and appreciation of another culture and its way of thinking. They themselves had gained much pleasure and insight from their acquaintance with other languages and wished to share this with their children, just as music-loving parents might encourage their children to appreciate music and perhaps even to play a musical instrument.

Secondly, on a more practical level, due to the father's profession and interests, it was probable that the family would at some time in the future be visiting or living temporarily in a German-speaking country. In view of the difficulties encountered by the mother during her stay in Germany, both parents were convinced that, if the children were fluent in German, the time needed to adjust to the new environment would be significantly reduced and such a stay would consequently be much more enjoyable for both children and parents, particularly if the children had to attend school while there. Observations of difficulties encountered by the children of guest-workers in Germany and by recently arrived immigrant children in Australia reinforced this conviction.

Thirdly, both parents were curious about the difficulties seemingly associated with attempts to maintain a language other than English in the Australian setting. They knew of many parents who had as their native language a language other than English and who had not succeeded in passing it on to their children. This seemed to be particularly so when one marriage partner was Australian-born. Clyne's[3] analysis of the 1976 Australian Census shows, to take one example, that 27.8% of Australian residents born in Germany no longer regularly used German. The shift to exclusive use of English among Australian-born children of two German-born parents is about double this figure: in Melbourne, for example, 58.3% of such children use English only. The chances of languages other than English being passed on diminish even more in mixed marriages, that is, marriages where one spouse is born overseas, the other in Australia. For example, if we look at marriages in Melbourne in which one parent is German-born, the other born in Australia, the U.K. or Eire, we find that only 6% of children with a German mother and 4% with a German father speak German. Moreover, such mixed marriages are by no means unusual in Australia: for the period 1969–1973, for instance, Price[64] shows that 38% of males and 24% of females from twelve different groups of immigrants born in non-English-speaking countries married Australian-born persons.

Fourthly, the father was also interested in the problems faced by parents who, by choice or necessity, use a language which is not their native language to communicate with their children, a situation also by no means unusual in immigrant families in Australia where English has in many cases become the language of the family.

Fifthly, the father felt a need for a regular conversation partner willing to talk only German with him at all times and on all topics. He had, it is true, in his work and in various organizations he belonged to, some opportunities for speaking German on a reasonably regular basis. However, by their nature, such conversations tended to be rather formal and technical. Informal conversations about ordinary, everyday, even mundane matters rarely took place. The father could have used German in the home with his wife for such conversations, which they indeed did do occasionally for practice, but these interchanges, whilst enjoyable and helpful, did have an air of artificiality about them. In addition, the father had discovered that many German-speaking immigrants who had lived for some time in Australia were unfortunately often more interested in demonstrating their knowledge of English, even if it was poor, than conversing in German, even among themselves.

It was felt (and hoped) that a child would have no inhibitions about speaking German to his father, and would regard it as natural to use it at all times with him. As will be seen, this feeling proved in large part to be justified.

The experiment was begun not without a certain amount of apprehension as to its possible outcome. The literature on the subject had, at that stage, not been consulted extensively, and the parents relied heavily on accounts from immigrant families; most were pessimistic, forecasting failure at various stages in the children's development: before kindergarten age, on beginning kindergarten, at the start of school, etc. Other people expressed fears that the children would become confused. However, the parents had fortunately also encountered some children, and read of others, who seemed to be coping happily with two, or even more languages. In particular, a visit one year before the birth of their first child to friends in Sarawak (East Malaysia) had impressed them with the feasibility and advantages, not to mention the pleasures of family bilingualism. Danny, the friends' three-year-old son, chattered happily with his visitors in English, with the maid in Teochew (a Chinese language), with his parents in Teochew and English, with his paternal grandparents in Teochew, and with his maternal grandparents in Malay. Of course, the conditions prevailing in the city of Kuching were very favourable to some form of bi- or trilingualism: Teochew (together with the closely related Hokkien and Hakka) was the language of the large Chinese population, English was the main language of a largely overseas-educated administration, and Malay, as the national language of Malaysia and long a lingua franca in the region, was steadily gaining in importance. Hobart, Tasmania, on the other hand, was a predominantly monolingual city where support outside the home for the speaking of a language other than English would be minimal. An indication of the position is given by the 1976 Census[3] which reveals that only 4% of Tasmania's population over five years of age regularly uses a language other than English. Of these languages other than English, German is, admittedly, the one most widely used in Tasmania, but by only about 1% of a total population of just over 400,000.

Of course, not all parents will have the same motives for wishing to raise their children as bilinguals. The native language of the parents (or one of them) may, for example, be different from that of the society in which they live and their native language may represent their most effective means of communication. This language may also be the only language of relatives and friends in the country of origin. To *not* pass the language on to the children could be seen by the parents, and later perhaps also by the children (as found by Pauwels[65] in her questioning of children of Dutch-Dutch marriages in Australia), as reducing the effectiveness of communication in the family, perhaps drastically, and as depriving both children and monolingual relatives of the means of unhindered communication, and cutting them off from part of their cultural heritage. Rūķe-Draviņa,[66] a Latvian-born linguist, considers that it may at times have a lifelong effect on children if they do not acquire the language of their parents, as they are then cut off from the family's circle of relatives and friends.

Infant bilingualism

As already mentioned in chapter one, infant bilingualism is the term often used by linguists (e.g. by Haugen[28]) to describe the type of bilingualism resulting from a child's being exposed simultaneously to more than one language from birth. Other terms are also used to refer to this type of bilingualism; for example, Swain[67] calls it "bilingualism as a first language", Wode[68] "first language bilingualism", and Huerta[69] "native acquisition of two languages".

The child has, therefore, as these terms suggest, from the beginning two (or more) first or native languages, although this does not imply that he or she will have equal command of both. Circumstances rarely ensure that a child will have even approximately equal contact with both languages in all situations. Consequently, it is highly likely that one language will predominate and be spoken more fluently, more accurately, or with a greater range of vocabulary. If circumstances change, for example when the child begins school, a shift in language dominance may occur. This is perfectly natural and should not cause parents undue concern or discourage them. Perfect balance between the two languages is an ideal, an ideal which is hardly ever realized by children, or for that matter by adults. In fact, this writer has never met an adult whose ability in two languages was equal in *every* respect. This does not mean that a very high standard cannot be attained in both languages. Unfortunately, some parents who are attempting to pass on their native language to their children in an environment in which the dominant language of the community is another language, become upset and despair because their children's ability in the language is not on a par with that of monolingual children in the parents' homeland. Because of this, some parents have even come to regard the attempt as a failure and to consider it a waste of time to continue. This is a tragic loss both to the family and to the country as a whole. For, as Leopold[70] points out, children *can* acquire a serviceable knowledge of their parents' language, being able to communicate with relative ease at a level appropriate to their age and experience, even if perhaps not with grammatical exactitude, while at the same time acquiring a perfect knowledge of the dominant language of the community. This would seem to be a perfectly reasonable and worthwhile accomplishment. In any case, the children's ability in a language acquired naturally through inter-action with their parents in the home will usually be far superior to any ability they may acquire later through studying it as a foreign language at school, particularly as far as a native-sounding pronunciation is concerned. And if a child does wish to study his or her parents' language formally at a later stage, he or she can already have a solid foundation on which to build. Instead of laboriously acquiring a second language, he or she will then be consolidating and developing one of his or her first languages.

Of course, not all children who are bilingual have been exposed to their two languages from the beginning. Studies of bilingual children generally distinguish between infant bilingualism, as outlined above, and the success-ive acquisition of two languages in childhood (called by Haugen[28] "child bilingualism" and by Baetens Beardsmore[71] "consecutive bilingualism"), in which the child has reached an age (an arbitrary cut-off point of 3 years being suggested by McLaughlin[72]), where one language has become relatively well established before exposure to the second language occurs (e.g. as with the children mentioned in Rūķe-Draviņa's[73] study). This is a situation many immigrant children find themselves in, the second language being acquired in many cases in a natural environment, that is, through contact with playmates etc., but without any systematic formal instruction. In many respects the problems facing such children and their parents as they strive to acquire the language of the community and continue to use their own language in the home, will be similar to those encountered by families attempting to establish infant bilingualism.

Many immigrant parents believe, or are led to believe by their children's teachers, that they will best serve their children's interests if they attempt to speak only the dominant language of the community in the home. The assumption is that the more of this language the children hear, the sooner they will become competent in it; speaking another language in the home would only reduce exposure to and hinder acquisition of the dominant language. Such an assumption seems to imply that by subtracting one of a bilingual's languages his or her other must necessarily improve. Indeed, that is the belief of quite a number of (monolingual) Australian teachers, includ-ing teachers of English as a second language, with whom this writer has spoken and who are working in schools with a high percentage of children from a non-English-speaking background. However, this assumption fails to consider some important factors. Firstly, the parents' command of the dominant language of the community may be defective or even very meagre. For them to attempt to speak this language exclusively to their children may mean that communication between parents and children is far from spontan-eous or efficient. Moreover, the children are being presented with an imperfect model of the dominant language of the community, perhaps with faulty pronunciation and deviant grammar, which is scarcely going to improve their proficiency in the language. The children may even come to look down on their parents' deviant variety of the language. Rūķe-Draviņa,[74] writing on her observations of Latvian children in Sweden, supports this view:

> "Those Latvian children who spoke their mother tongue at home had, as a rule, greater success in Swedish, the language of the school, than those bilinguals who spoke mainly Swedish with their parents . . . An explanation for this apparent contradiction is that the children who had spoken Swedish at home with their non-Swedish parents had learnt it with a poor pronunciation and faulty expression, which meant a much worse start for Swedish instruction at school than the other alternative, namely to speak the mother tongue at home and to learn the second language outside the home from a good 'pure' source, that is, from its native speakers."
> (Translated from the German)

Oksaar[75] noted much the same for Estonian children in Stockholm. Similarly, Clyne,[76] in his investigation of two hundred German-English bilinguals in Australia, concluded that maintaining a good standard of German did *not* go hand in hand with inferior English.

Using the parents' native language within the family, a language in which the parents most probably feel more at ease and are more proficient, would also have the advantage of improving the children's esteem for them.

Another aspect worthy of consideration is that discarding the parents' language can mean problems for the children of those immigrant families which decide to return to live in their original homeland. Stephanie Thompson,[77] in her study of 138 settlers who returned from Australia to Italy, describes how many children (who were either Australian-born or had arrived in Australia when very young) had to repeat years of study in Italian schools because of difficulties with language:

> "Often (the children) were more proficient in English than in Italian, particularly in the written language; and even in their homes in Australia some of them had insisted on speaking only English. As a result, most of the school-age children had language difficulties to overcome following their return to Italy."

Even in cases where there is no permanent return to the original homeland, loss of the language by the children cuts them off from close contact with grandparents, etc., still living there. Even if the grandparents migrate with the family and manage to acquire a reasonable knowledge of the language of the new country, it would still seem advisable for the grandchildren to acquire or retain competence in the home language, since there is evidence (e.g. from research by Clyne[241]) that migrants over 60 revert more and more to their first language, this reversion being accompanied by a clear decline in ability in their second language; communication between the elderly and their family is hindered if the children and grandchildren have lost the ability to speak the home language — this is a common complaint emerging from Hearst's[245] 1981 study of immigrant elderly from eighteen different ethnic communities in Australia.

Whilst the number of possible kinds of infant bilingualism is, in theory, and no doubt also in practice, quite large, published research reports mainly on the following types:

1. The two parents have different native languages, one of which is the dominant language of the community. Each parent uses his/her language to the child from birth. Each parent has some degree of competency in the other's native language, e.g. Ronjat[78] (mother German, father French); Leopold[13] (mother English, father German); von Raffler-Engel[79] (mother Italian, father English); Volterra and Taeschner[80] (mother German, father Italian).

2. The child is exposed from the beginning to two languages, but has minimal contact with the second language until kindergarten. In such cases, the two parents may have different native languages, one of which is the dominant language of the community, but it is the language which is not the dominant language of the community that is used by both parents to the child, e.g. Fantini[81] (mother's native language Spanish, father's English, residing in the U.S.A., Spanish used to children), Zierer[82] (mother's native language Spanish, father's German, residing in Peru, German used to child).

3. The parents may share a common native language which is different from the dominant community language and which they use to the child, e.g. Haugen[83] (Norwegian in the U.S.A.), Bubenik[84] (Czech in Canada), Oksaar[85] (Estonian in Sweden and Germany), Ruķe-Draviņa[73] (Latvian in Sweden). Haugen was born in America of Norwegian parents, with whom he always spoke Norwegian, whilst he spoke English with most people outside the home:

> "Thanks to my parents' adamant insistence on my speaking their native language at home, the threshold of the home became the cue to my code switch."

4. The parents may have different native languages, both of which differ from the dominant language of the community, and use one of them to the child, e.g. Elwert,[86] whose parents, a German and an English-woman residing in Italy, spoke to him only in English. From most other people he heard Standard Italian or the local Italian dialect.

However, reports on cases of infant bilingualism where one of the languages acquired by the child is not the native language of either parent, nor the dominant language of the community, are rare; apart from his own research,[87] only three are known to this writer: Past,[88] Dimitrijević[89] and Stephens.[90]

Past reports on his daughter Mariana's acquisition of English and Spanish in Texas. Both he and his wife are native speakers of English, and both also speak Spanish, although far from perfectly. On a Foreign Service Institute type language proficiency test, where a score of 0 represents a complete lack of communicative ability and a score of 5 indicates the ability of an educated native speaker, Past and his wife scored 2^+ and 3^+ respectively.

The Past family's situation differs in several ways from the present study, the principal difference being that the parents attempted to spend 60–90 minutes a day talking only Spanish to each other and to their daughter. That is, in the home there was no clear division of language according to interlocutor. Instead, Mariana was encouraged to speak Spanish, and not English, to both parents at certain times of the day. To increase her exposure to spoken Spanish, her parents encouraged her to watch bilingual television programmes, gave her opportunities to play with Spanish-speaking children, and at age 5;0 enrolled her in a bilingual kindergarten. As another means of exposing Mariana to native quality Spanish, her parents began to teach her to read the language, along with English, when she was only 1 year 11 months old and just learning to speak.

And what were the results of this experiment? Although Mariana preferred to speak English whenever she had a choice, and although her speech was not as rapid in Spanish as in English and she occasionally had to grope for a Spanish expression, she could communicate well in Spanish if she wanted to. The Oral Language Dominance Measure administered at the start of school showed her English to be only slightly superior to her Spanish and she was rated as a balanced bilingual capable of receiving instruction in either language. Her reading ability was assessed as second grade level in both languages (see chapter 8 for further comments on biliteracy). Her experience with speaking and reading the two languages resulted in practically no confusion and she enjoyed normal relations with her peers.

Dimitrijević[89] gives an unfortunately very brief report on a case which seems very similar to that described in the present study. Although not stated specifically in the article, Dimitrijević and his wife are apparently both native speakers of Serbian living in Yugoslavia, yet Rayko, their son, is spoken to in English by his father and Serbian by all others. Rayko's two languages seemed to develop equally well until he started to have Serbian playmates, at which point he began to show a preference for Serbian and his English lagged behind. Nevertheless, although his father did not insist on it, Rayko still continued to use some English with him when there was no urgency involved and they were alone together.

Stephens,[90] in an even briefer and more unusual report, writes that he spoke to his four-year-old son exclusively in Esperanto, while his wife always used English, making the child undoubtedly one of the very few native speakers of Esperanto! Stephens states that his son spoke both languages equally well and that his English was at least of the same standard as that of a monolingual child of the same age.

What such children experience could be called a "home language immersion programme", since in many ways it parallels the experience of children in so-called immersion programmes which in recent years have proved to be popular and particularly effective in schools in Canada and the United States. Of course, children in a bilingual home obviously begin their "immersion" at a much earlier age than the children in these school programmes. In these, children from English-speaking homes are, from the start of schooling, "immersed" in French or Spanish, that is, receive all or a significant part of their instruction in these languages. The children receive some instruction in English language as a subject and outside school hours use mainly English, the dominant language of the society in which they live. Careful evaluation of such language immersion programmes (e.g. by Swain et al[91] in 1981) has revealed how very effective they are. At first the children show some retardation in English compared with their peers being instructed in English, but this rapidly disappears. At the same time, however, they acquire a knowledge of their second language which in many ways approximates that of native speakers. Moreover, their performance in subjects such as mathematics and science is on a par with that of children being instructed in English.

Method employed

In the literature, a number of methods are advocated for fostering and maintaining bilingualism in the family. The method employed in this study is similar to that followed by the French linguist Jules Ronjat who in 1913 wrote one of the first detailed case studies of infant bilingualism. Ronjat's native language was French, his wife's German. They lived predominantly in France, but had frequent contacts with German speakers. When their son, Louis, was born in 1908, Ronjat[78] received a letter from the linguist Grammont, in which he offered the following advice for raising the child bilingually:

> "There is nothing to teach him. It is sufficient that when something is said to him it be said in one of the languages you want him to know. But the important thing is that each language be represented by a different person; that you, for example, always speak French to him, his mother German. Never reverse these roles. In this way, when he begins to speak, he will speak two languages without being conscious of doing so and without having made any special effort to learn them."
> (Translated from the French)

Ronjat and his wife followed this advice closely. They consciously created a one language-one parent home environment. To their son they always spoke their respective native languages, whilst to each other they spoke German, unless a monolingual French-speaker was present. Whilst not discounting the possibility that infant bilingualism could be achieved by other methods, Ronjat[92] was convinced, as a result of observing his own son and other children, that this one person-one language method not only offered the surest guarantee of success but also required the least mental exertion on the part of the child.

Until the age of 5, at least (where Ronjat's account unfortunately finishes), Louis's progress under this method was impressive. He acquired both French and German with a native pronunciation and there was little evidence of the vocabulary or syntax of one language influencing the other. Louis was able to express himself fluently and appropriately in either language.

The German-born American linguist, Leopold,[13] whose four-volume study, published between 1939 and 1949, gives perhaps the most detailed account of the acquisition of infant bilingualism, followed this method with his daughter Hildegard. Hildegard was usually addressed in English by her mother, a native speaker of that language. The family lived in America, except for a summer holiday in Germany when she was five. Leopold's wife, a third-generation German-American, could understand German and express herself in it faultily, but fluently. During courting they had spoken English to one another, but after marriage, Leopold[93] reports, ". . . I was obstinate enough to speak German to her regularly . . . She usually answered me in English." When Hildegard was born, this well-established practice was simply continued, the mother speaking to her in English, the father in German, but with the expectation that, unlike in interactions with the mother, he would receive German in return from his daughter.

Leopold did not apply the formula of "one person, one language" as rigidly as did Ronjat. Leopold, for instance, addressed Hildegard in English when monolingual English speaking playmates or visitors were present. There was also some indecision in the family regarding the mother's choice of language when speaking to Hildegard. During their six month stay in Germany in 1935 the mother began speaking only German to Hildegard.[94]

Since she was practically her daughter's only contact with English there, Hildegard's use of that language declined rapidly. Wishing his daughter to retain her English, Leopold persuaded his wife to revert to speaking it to her. This she did, but a month later Leopold had second thoughts: "I am now in favour of [her mother using] German in order to reinforce the position of German to induce Hildegard to speak only German at home after her return to America."[95] However this resolve was forgotten until the family returned to America at the beginning of 1936, but even then it was not put into effective practice: "Her mother is by no means consistent in carrying out the principle of 'German at home'. She accepts Hildegard's English."[96] The situation was, therefore, as Leopold himself[93] readily admits, far from ideal, since he represented Hildegard's only real contact with German in America. When Hildegard was aged 6;2,2, Leopold summarized her linguistic progress to that point in time as follows:

> "At the moment . . . I can state that she speaks both English and German fluently. Both languages are fully formed. There are no significant gaps in the grammar. The vocabulary is large in both languages, but it is more complete and ready at hand in English . . . she often hesitates [i.e. when speaking German], which shows that English expressions come to her mind first."[97]

Two years later, just after Hildegard's 8th birthday, he wrote:

> "Hildegard keeps on speaking German to me. In longer narrations she has considerable difficulty in expressing herself, but eventually, haltingly, she can say everything."[98]

Hildegard's use of German had no adverse effect on her English. At an early age (4;2,13) she was judged to be far ahead of her age with regard to purity of pronunciation and vocabulary.[99] Her ability in English and generally at school was considered above average.[100] At high school and college Hildegard studied German and achieved her best results in it. In 1950, then aged 20, she went to Germany for the summer to help with postwar reconstruction. She spent 10 days in France en route, where "she struggled with her meagre college French. She breathed a sigh of relief when she entered Germany and people really understood her".[101]

This result might not be ideal, but it is surely a very satisfactory achievement in the circumstances.

Leopold's experience with his second child, Karla, born six years after Hildegard, is perhaps even more interesting in that it shows that even when an attempt at raising a child bilingually seems to have achieved little success, the child may be unconsciously absorbing the language and establishing a foundation on which he or she can later build. Leopold and his wife followed the same procedures with Karla as they did with Hildegard. Hildegard herself announced her intention of speaking German to her little sister so that she would learn it, but this did not eventuate, mainly because their mother was nearly always present speaking English.[102] Leopold always addressed Karla in German but, whilst she understood almost everything he said, she rarely answered him in German. In other words, she was basically a receiving bilingual. Commenting on her speech to him at age 5;0,1, Leopold writes:

> "Her German is extremely limited. She . . . scatters some German words over her English sentences when she speaks to me, as a sort of concession to my way of speaking. Her German is restricted to such fragments, words and brief sentences."[103]

However, she accepted that her father spoke only German, and at age 5;9,10 even objected when he addressed her in English because the maid was present and involved in the topic: "Don't talk to me in English."[104]

Karla's exposure to German did not impair her knowledge of English. Leopold writes,[105] for instance, that when she was in fourth grade her teacher drew attention to the fact that she had "a remarkable flair for English writing". Like her sister, she took German at high school and it was also her best subject. At the age of nineteen she visited Germany where, as Leopold reports, she was able to activate her dormant German:

> "For the first few days there she did not try to speak German because her parents were along and did the talking. Then she opened up and spoke German fluently and with surprising correctness. In view of the lack of practice in speaking, I had not expected her to be able to converse so well; but the long, deeply embedded preparation, although passive in her case, asserted itself amazingly."[101]

Since the studies by Ronjat and Leopold are perhaps the best known in the field of infant bilingualism, they will be referred to frequently in the following pages and comparisons will be drawn between their observations and those made by other researchers, including the present writer.

Not all researchers agree that this type of one person-one language approach to achieving infant bilingualism is advisable. The most forceful objections are perhaps those presented by Zierer.[82] Zierer, a native speaker of German residing in Peru, and his wife, a native speaker of Spanish (each having a good knowledge of the other's native language), decided to raise their son bilingually. However, they decided to make German the language of the home and not to expose him to Spanish until he had first become reasonably proficient in German, because they believed that:

1. Simultaneous acquisition of Spanish and German would "produce perturbations in the child's cognitive and affective control" and "would undoubtedly constitute very considerable mental exertion for the child".

2. "Considering the powerful unifying force that a language exercises on its speakers, the integration of the family would have been affected if the child had spoken to his mother in one language and to his father in another."

These assumptions are not supported by the evidence presented by Ronjat, Leopold, or, as will be seen, the present study, and would seem to underestimate the young child's ability and adaptability. There is at times undoubtedly some mental exertion involved for the child who is simultaneously acquiring two languages, but whether delaying exposure to one of the languages would lessen any such exertion would be difficult to refute or confirm. The assumption of a danger to the integration of the family would probably only be valid if one marriage partner did not have a good understanding of the other's language. This could have a detrimental effect on relationships within the family, since the parent not understanding one of the languages might resent not being able to understand conversations between spouse and child. However, even in such a situation, friction could possibly be avoided if the child and parent used the language only when the monolingual parent was absent or, more practicably, by providing him or her with a running summary in translation, which is, in any case, often done by young bilingual children before they realize that both parents understand both languages; Harrison & Piette[106] mention an apparently successful example of the first type of arrangement in a family in which the mother and the two children speak Welsh to each other except when the monolingual

English-speaking father is present, in which case they all use English in order to accommodate him.

Elliott[107] gives a deliberately exaggerated, yet amusing account of the difficulties which can be encountered in a family if one parent is not very proficient in one of the languages being acquired by the child. Elliott's family lived in America, and his French wife Gisèle spoke only French to their son, Nicholas, while he himself addressed him in English, as well as occasionally in broken French. He reports that he had considerable difficulty in following his son's French utterances and "In self-defence, I kept a French dictionary by my side . . ." However, even this did not work all the time. On one occasion Nicholas told his father: "Papa, le potage est en train de bouillir." (= Dad, the soup's boiling). By the time Elliott had puzzled this out with the aid of his trusty dictionary, the stove, walls and floor were covered with soup!

In Zierer's family, however, both parents were proficient in both languages, and it is unlikely that any conflict due to lack of comprehension would have eventuated. It appears that restricting the child to German until he was 2 years 10 months old may not have been entirely conducive to "the integration of the family", since his monolingual Spanish-speaking maternal grandmother, who visited the home daily, was requested not to speak to him in Spanish until that time.

There is probably no single method which can guarantee success in achieving bilingualism in the family, since there are simply so many variables involved. A method which works well in one family may encounter difficulties in another. The studies mentioned above have endeavoured to separate the child's two languages according to interlocutor or according to certain fixed times. All the parents, including those in the present study, have avoided indiscriminate code-switching, believing this would confuse the child.

Ronjat[108] mentions, for example, a Swiss friend whose mother tongue was French and whose wife was a native speaker of (Swiss) German. In the home, situated in the German-speaking part of Switzerland, the parents used Swiss German and French to each other and to the children, but without any system. Once the children started school, they no longer wanted to speak French. Ronjat believed that this would not have happened if the one person-one language method had been applied:

> "The children, who are affectionate and intelligent, would un-
> doubtedly have remained attached to a language which they

would have, above all, felt to be the language of their father."
(Translated from the French)

But again we may well be underestimating the child. Huerta[109] reports on a Mexican-American boy's simultaneous acquisition of Spanish and English in a home environment where frequent switching between the two languages is the dominant style of speaking, e.g. his mother speaks to him in both Spanish and English. Although she describes only the period from age 2;1–2;10, Huerta concludes that this method has no detrimental effect on the child's developing bilingualism and believes it may even enhance it. A special feature of this situation, though, is that this system of communication in the home receives support from the linguistic behaviour of the community. According to Huerta, such code-switching is common among Spanish-English bilinguals in the American South-West where the family lives.

Another study in which most of the persons in the community with whom the child comes in contact use two languages alternately is that by Padilla & Liebmann.[110] They studied the speech development of three young Californian Spanish-English bilingual children whose language input was not dichotomized by person, and found no evidence that the bilinguals had a reduced rate of linguistic development in comparison with that of monolingual children.

In a two-year investigation of 13 Canadian French-English infant bilinguals with a commencing average age of 34 months, Doyle *et al*[57] in 1978 also came to the conclusion that there is no evidence that the bilingual child's languages must be separate by person or location, at least as far as optimal vocabulary growth is concerned.

Experiments by Bain[111] in 1974 did, however, indicate some advantage ·for dichotomizing the child's two languages. Bain tested and compared three groups of children on their ability to relay messages from one parent to the other. Two of the groups were two types of Alsatian-French bilinguals, one in which the children were being raised according to the one person-one language principle, and one in which both parents used both languages indiscriminately with their children. The third group consisted of monolingual children who spoke either only Alsatian or only French. The bilinguals from the one person-one language group scored 69.7% correct responses, whilst the other bilinguals and the monolinguals scored almost the same, namely 55.0% and 55.7% respectively. These results suggest that separating a child's two languages by person results in accelerated cognitive development compared to using them indiscriminately or even compared to using only one language. The results also suggest that bilinguals exposed indiscriminately to two languages fare just as well as monolinguals.

A possible danger of *not* separating a child's two languages by person can be seen in an account by Burling.[112] Burling, an American anthropologist, and his wife worked for two years in the Garo Hills of Assam, India, among the Garo people. Their son, Stephen, aged 1;4, was spoken to in English by his mother and in English and Garo (a Tibeto-Burman language) by his father, and he also had constant contact with monolingual Garo-speakers. When the family left the Garo Hills when Stephen was aged 3;4, Burling writes that: ". . . there was . . . no doubt that Garo was his first language . . . , but English had become a flexible means of expression as well." Back in America, his father, who then became his only source of Garo, tried to speak the language with him "*from time to time*". However, this was not sufficient to maintain Stephen's Garo:

> "For a couple of months he would respond to Garo when I spoke
> to him, but he refused to use more than an occasional word.
> After this, he began failing even to understand my speech . . .
> and within six months of our departure, he was even having
> trouble with the simplest Garo words . . ."

This severely reduced contact with Garo and the fact that even in India the father had not established himself as a Garo-only interlocutor for Stephen (". . . when he was two and one half years old . . . he developed a taste for speaking English with native English speakers and to my chagrin he came to prefer to speak English with me."), meant the loss of Stephen's Garo. Had the father consistently spoken Garo to his son, it seems probable that Stephen would have (eventually) recognized him as someone to whom he was to speak Garo and would have considered using it to him (cf. the temporary reluctance of the two children in this study to use German to their father, described in chapter 6).

3 Communication in the family: how it works

General remarks

Each individual bilingual family will, of course, have its own particular circumstances which will determine who speaks which language to whom, and when. What may evolve as a satisfactory linguistic arrangement in one family may, therefore, need to be modified in some way in another family. And not only do circumstances vary between families, but even within the one family. Children will have differing personalities, and their position in the family may also exert considerable influence. What works with one child may not necessarily succeed with another.

The description of communication in the family in the present study is therefore offered merely as a guide to what can be achieved, and indeed in a situation which is in some ways less than ideal for creating bilingualism. The father is virtually the children's sole contact with German, and consequently their exposure to English is at least four times greater. Such a situation would not appear conducive to achieving a good standard of bilingualism. If it were the mother passing on German, for example, the hours of contact the children would have with the language, particularly in the years before commencement of school, would be significantly increased. Nevertheless, such drawbacks can be countered to a certain extent and it is hoped that the results obtained in the case in question and detailed in the following pages will prove encouraging to any family which is contemplating, or is in the process of raising its children bilingually.

This study gives a more accessible insight into the effect of fathers' speech to children than would be the case in a monolingual family, since *all* of the children's German comes from him. Rondal[113] calls fathers "the forgotten contributors to child language development". Friedlander[114] offers some encouragement to fathers who are solely responsible for passing on a language to their children but who have limited time to do so, by suggesting that the emotional intensity which seems to characterize many father-child interactions compensates at least partially for the limited time spent in interaction.

What can parents expect to occur in the linguistic development of an infant bilingual? Firstly, there is no evidence that an infant who is exposed to two languages in the home will, in comparison with children living in a monolingual environment, be delayed in any way with regard to the production of his or her first word. In one study, for example, Doyle et al[57] compared thirteen young French-English bilingual children with thirteen monolingual children and found that the age at which the first word occurred was 11.2 months for the bilinguals and 12.0 months for the monolinguals.

Subsequent bilingual development will, again, vary with individual children and their particular circumstances, but generally, as found by Volterra & Taeschner[80] and Nygren-Junken,[115] they will pass through a three-stage developmental sequence:

Stage I

This stage lasts roughly from the beginning of speech until age 2;0. The majority of a child's sentences will be single-element ones (e.g. "Ball") until about 18 months, and then two-element ones (e.g. "Ball gone") until about two years. During this stage children really possess only one lexical system containing words from both languages. Their active vocabulary is very limited, and when they can give a name for something in one language, they will most probably not be able to do so in the other. This applies very much more to the production of words than to their comprehension. By age 1;4, for instance, Frank understood and responded to both *horse* and its German equivalent *Pferd*, these being very important words for him, since his bedroom overlooked a paddock where horses regularly grazed. But in his speech he used only *Pferd* (pronounced initially as [dɛət]), regardless of interlocutor, until he reached the age of 2;0. At age 1;4 *heiß* was the other German word in Frank's active vocabulary (but not its English equivalent, *hot*). At that same age he could say another eight words, all English. He could, of course, understand much more than he could say in both languages. But even in his receptive vocabulary there were some items he knew, or at least reacted to, in only one language. When asked in English at age 1;9 what noise a bird made, Frank would reply with a hearty "Ahk! Ahk!", this particular sound being a result of his being especially impressed by crows which frequently landed on a tree in his backyard. However, if his father asked him the same thing in German, he looked puzzled and made no response; the word *Vogel* (=bird) was obviously not yet part of his vocabulary. When asked the same sort of question about an ambulance, he would respond with siren noises only if the question were put in German.

Unfortunately, even at this early stage of what is called by Imedadze[116] "mixed speech" and referred to perhaps more appropriately by Oksaar[117] as an "overall code", where children seemingly unsystematically name things in one of their languages, rarely in both, some parents begin to worry that their children are acquiring neither language properly. (This is a fear which, as will be seen, will quite probably recur at later stages.) It is thus important to realize that what occurs in this stage is neither unusual nor cause for concern. It seems that for the moment the child regards the two languages as one system containing many synonyms, and in his or her small active vocabulary uses only one of the "synonyms". Thus Frank used *Pferd* from the possible choice of *horse* and *Pferd*. The same process also takes place in a monolingual environment, although in a less noticeable way: a child who hears and understands *horse*, *horsie* and *gee-gee* will initially most likely produce only one of them, say *gee-gee*. Since the child in a bilingual environment is at this stage not yet aware that he or she is dealing with two separate linguistic systems, he or she obviously cannot yet be expected to address adults only in the language heard from those adults. Towards the end of this first stage the child will gradually start to use a word from each language to refer to the same concept, but at first this will be done indiscriminately. At age 1;10 Frank had three words to express to his parents that his nappy was wet and needed changing: English *wet* (pronounced [wɛ]), German *naß* (=wet) (which he pronounced [na:s]), and also a form which could belong to either language, namely *piss*. He was not at all consistent as to which form he would use to which parent or even to other people. Only later, in Stage II, would he become fully aware that *naß* was to be used to his father, *wet* to most other people, and that the socially not quite acceptable *piss* was best used only within the family.

Stage II

This stage begins sometime around a child's second birthday. The child will have soon acquired an active vocabulary comprising words which designate the same item, action or function in both languages, and he or she will increasingly use the appropriate language when addressing different people. However, he or she may still produce utterances containing elements from both languages, since the same concept will not always be acquired simultaneously in the two languages and may continue to be bound to the context in which it was acquired. For example, Frank, aged 2;6, holding a short stick pointed at his mother said, "Look at my [vɛə] (= *Gewehr*, German for *gun*). Similarly, Thomas, aged 2;2, watching a flock of seagulls with his paternal grandfather, remarked, "Lots of *Möwen* (= seagulls), Granddad!" In both cases the children knew the corresponding English words and could produce them on request, but for a time they showed a definite preference for the German terms in their speech, irrespective of interlocutor. This preference is perhaps attributable to the fact that these particular words had featured much more prominently as topics of conversation in German with their father than in English conversations.

Some children go through an initial phase at this stage where they often refer to an object or activity in *both* languages. Frank, for example, at age 1;11, would frequently communicate to anyone willing to listen that he understood the dangers of touching the gas fire in the lounge room. Pointing at the fire, he would earnestly exclaim, "Hot heiß!" The child is here apparently becoming increasingly aware that there are two languages, that there are two words for everything, and that it is appropriate to address certain people in a certain language. but as yet he or she is unsure when or to whom to use which, so, to be on the safe side, resorts to both. As the child's awareness of the distinction between the two systems increases, the number of these double-barrelled terms will decrease. A similar use of synonyms to ensure understanding can also be observed in the speech of monolinguals: a small girl, aged 2;1, was heard urging her father to throw her up in the air yet again with the request, "More! Again!"

Even when a child begins to actively employ a term from each language appropriately, confidence that it is in fact the right term in the right language may take some time to develop. By age 2;0, for example, Frank would usually request a drink from his father with the word "Flasche!" (= bottle!) (pronounced by him [faʃa]) and from his mother with "Drink!" (pronounced [gɪŋ]). However, as can be seen in the following exchange, if no immediate acknowledgement of his request was madé, he would repeat it in his other language:

Frank (to mother): Drink! Drink!
Mother (failing to hear because of background noise): What?
Frank: Flasche! Flasche!

Oksaar[118] observed a similar strategy employed by her Estonian-Swedish bilingual son, Sven, between the ages of 2;4 and 2;10. When he asked his parents for something in one language and they did not react instantly, the request was repeated in the other language.

In fact, the parents in this study found the existence of two languages to

be quite an asset at this age when the child's pronunciation of words is not always readily intelligible. The child's spontaneous or elicited repetition of an unclear word in his other language gives the parents a double chance to comprehend (not unimportant if a child is prone to tantrums if not understood!). This is well illustrated in the following example:

Frank (age 1;11,17, comes up to his father in the lounge room): [ən bɛd], [ən bɛd].
Father (suspecting that Frank is using either English *bread* or *bed*, but unable to deduce which from the context): Was willst du denn, *Bett* oder *Brot* (*Now what do you want, bed or bread?*)
Frank: [bo:k]! (= *Brot*, i.e. *bread*)
Father: Brot?
Frank (extremely pleased): [a:]! (= *Ja!*, i.e. *yes!*)

During this second stage, the child's rapidly developing ability to keep his or her two vocabularies reasonably separate may not be matched by a corresponding flexibility in differentiating the syntactic rules of the two languages. One of the children in Volterra & Taeschner's[119] investigation, Lisa, for example, appeared for a long period of time, until the age of 2;9, to have acquired only one syntactic system for her Italian and German. This was observable in the case of Thomas and Frank only with regard to particular types of syntactic structure or on infrequent occasions. For instance, in English compound past tenses, the past participle is placed straight after the auxiliary verb (e.g. The dog *has eaten* the bone.), whereas in German the past participle is in the *final* position in the clause (e.g. Frank (2;5,15): Ich hab es allein *gemacht*. (Literally: *I have it by myself done*, i.e. *I did it myself*.) Frank made this differentiation between the two languages with the appearance of his first past tenses, although occasionally an utterance would be heard in German which followed the English pattern, e.g. Frank (2;10,19) (to father): Du hast vergessen das! (= *You have forgotten this!*); vergessen (= *forgotten*) should be last in the German sentence. But, as stated above, there was little evidence of a fused syntactic system. Where syntactic structures differed in the two languages, these differences were, on the whole, observed. To take one example: sentences with modal verbs (can, must, want, etc.) require the following verb to be placed at the end of the clause in German, but immediately after the modal verb in English. Frank's speech always showed this differentiation, as can be seen in the following dual language utterance to both his parents when he was aged 2;7,0:

Frank: I wanna *wash* my hands. [a: wɔnə wɔs mi hænz] (And then continuing after a barely perceptible pause:) Ich will meine Hände *waschen.* [is bil mai hɛna basən] (Literally: *I want my hands to-wash.*)

Stage III

In this final stage the child now speaks the two languages differentiated in both vocabulary and syntax, his or her speech revealing minimal interaction between the two languages. If being brought up in an environment where each language is bound to particular persons, the child will now consistently address interlocutors in the appropriate language. The transition from Stage II to Stage III is gradual, usually far from smooth, and may take considerable time. The time taken for this transition, as well as the degree to which the two languages are finally differentiated, will depend on many factors, such as the child's personality and natural ability, the parents' attitude, and the proportions of time of exposure to each of the languages. The child will attain relatively quickly an almost uncanny ability to speak to people only in the appropriate language. However, as many researchers into bilingualism (e.g. Leopold;[13] Haugen;[120] Clyne[25]) have clearly shown, it is very rare to find a bilingual person, child or adult, who can completely avoid one of his or her languages influencing the other in some way or other.

With regard to the separation of the two languages by conversation partner, it will be seen in the present study that it was not really until the age of 3;9 that Thomas was addressing his father predominantly in German (98%), whilst Frank reached this point much sooner, already speaking 95% German to his father at age 3;0 (see chapter 6 for further details).

The children's communication strategies

In the present study, a fairly stable communication routine has developed in the family: the father and the two boys communicate with each other in German, the mother and the two boys use English to one another, the father and the mother speak English to each other, and between themselves the boys speak predominantly English.

Since all family members understand both languages, no-one is left out of a conversation. The children switch with apparent ease from one language to the other depending on who it is they are speaking to. The following examples show how harmoniously the two languages co-exist in the family and how communication in a variety of situations is in no way impaired by the parents using different languages; if the family were monolingual, communication would most probably take place in much the same way:

Thomas (6;10,18) is looking at the cut-and-paste page in a German children's magazine, SESAMSTRAßE (*Sesame Street*).

Thomas (to father): Können wir die Rolltreppe machen? (*Can we make the escalator?*)
Father (to Thomas): Wir brauchen aber Garnrollen. (*But we need cotton reels.*)
Mother (to Thomas): Yes, and I don't think I've got that many.
Thomas (speaking directly to his father, but at the same time countering his mother's reservation): Ah, ah, wir brauchen nur zwei. (*Ah, ah, we only need two.*)
Mother (to Thomas): Do you reckon it'll work?
Father (doubtfully): Oh —
Thomas (to mother, but to counter both parents' doubts): I think so.

The father enters the kitchen where Thomas (5;10,13) is busy ironing handkerchiefs for his mother.
Father (admiringly, and rhetorically, to Thomas): Oho, wer kann denn bügeln? (*Oho, who can do the ironing, then?*)
Thomas acknowledges this recognition with a contented smile.
Mother (to Thomas): And tell Daddy who did the washing-up for me.
Thomas (to father): Ich! (*I did!*)

Thomas (5;11,1), Frank (4;0,9) and their parents are sitting at the table having their evening meal. Thomas addresses each of the family in turn, switching languages appropriately when he speaks to his father:
Thomas: Mum, I bet when you're finished, und, Bert, wenn du fertig bist (*and, Bert, when you're finished*), and when you're finished, Frankie, then I'll still have some juice left.

The family is travelling by train, and, much to Frank's annoyance, the people a few seats away are making quite a din. He begins to voice his annoyance to his father in German, changes his mind and turns to complain to his mother in English, and then completes his expression of disapproval with another comment to his father in German:
Frank (4;6,3) (to father): Bert, sie machen — (*Bert, they're making —*) (to mother) I can hardly hear what you're saying to Thomas because they're making so much noise. (To father) Sie gehen mir auf die Nerven! (*They're getting on my nerves!*)

The family is having a meal and the father wishes to give the boys another cup of milk but cannot locate Frank's cup:
Father (to Frank): Wo ist deine Tasse? (*Where's your cup?*)
Frank (3;6,1) (to father): Da. Ich habe meine grüne Tasse, Bert. (*There. I've got my green cup, Bert.*) (To brother) Thomas, green's my favourite colour.

In such a household, however, the children do have to face some difficult decisions on choice of language which are barely discussed by Ronjat[78] or Leopold.[13] Some of these will be examined in some detail below.

Children addressing both parents simultaneously

There are occasions when a child may wish to speak to both parents at the same time. But which language is he to use? In this investigation, Thomas adopted, around his third birthday, a certain strategy to overcome this problem, a strategy later also adopted by his younger brother, Frank, at about age 3;6. Faced with such a predicament, the children's solution is to address one of the parents by name, establish eye contact with him or her, and then proceed in the language appropriate to that parent, knowing that the other parent will understand anyway. In the initial stages of establishing this routine, Thomas obviously felt somewhat uncomfortable in such situations and would avoid eye contact with the parent whose language he was not using. If he did happen to glance at the other parent, this would often cause him to falter in his delivery and switch to the other language, e.g.:

> **Thomas** (age 4;3,17) (holding one of his favourite storybooks about a cat called Charlie and telling the story to his mother. While he is doing this, his father comes in and sits down beside them to listen. Thomas continues with the story, looking at first steadfastly at his mother, but at one point he catches his father's eye, falters in his delivery, and switches to and completes the account in German): . . . And Charlie looks at him up on the big rubbish-tin, and, and the tomcat went away. Charlie went in there and further and further. And then a fire eng— (looking at father) — und dann hat ein Feuerwehrwagen gekommen. Und Charlie hat auf der Straße gegangen. Er hat einen Brunnen gesehen. Und . . . (— *and then a fire-engine came. And Charlie went on the road. He saw a fountain. And* . . .)

This uncomfortableness had practically disappeared by Thomas's fifth birthday. In fact, by that time he was beginning to use this strategy to his advantage. When having difficulty expressing himself or finding a word in one language, he would establish eye contact with the other parent and switch to his other language, often in mid-sentence. In the following example, Thomas (5;10,22) is relating what has taken place in "show-and-tell" at school. He begins his account in German to his father, but soon runs into difficulties because he does not know the German for *vampire*, a word just learnt in English. To extricate himself from this vocabulary predicament, he switches to English and addresses his mother:

Thomas: Bert, im "Zeige-und-Erzähle-Spiel" hat Justin über Dracula erzählt. Ah, er hat scharfe Zähne und er ist, und er – (*Bert, in "show-and-tell" Justin told about Dracula. Ah, he's got sharp teeth and he's, and he* —), ah, Mum, he's a vampire and he bites ladies' necks and sucks the blood out, um, and then he kisses them!

This switch to English would not have occurred if his mother had not been present. He would then have either used the English *vampire* in his German, most likely in a hesitant manner, showing that he realized the word was not German and suggesting a desire for assistance, or he would have interrupted his report briefly with a direct request such as "Wie heißt 'vampire' auf deutsch?" (*What's "vampire" in German?*).

The same procedure is employed by Frank, e.g.:

Frank (5;10,8) (listening to a radio report about a woman caught smuggling money into the Philippines): Mum, the police caught her. That must have been, ah (looking a bit perplexed as he does not know the English term, then glances quickly specifically at his father) — Falschgeld, Bert. (*Counterfeit money, Bert.*)

Seldom do the children persist with one language while looking directly at the parent with whom they do not speak this language. On these rare occasions they are usually very excited and forget momentarily which language they are using, for example:

Frank (4;0,14) is telling both parents about the film DAVY CROCKETT AND THE RIVER PIRATES. He begins in English to his mother, switches briefly to German to address his father, and then, turning back to his mother, continues very excitedly: Und ein Mann hat ein Loch in das Boot geschossen — PENG! — und Davy war in das Wasser und mußte schwimmen, und . . . (*And a man shot a hole in the boat — BANG! — and Davy was in the water and had to swim, and . . .*)

When one of the children is addressing both parents simultaneously in one language, each parent answers freely in the same language he or she would normally use to the child, e.g.:

Frank (4;1,0) (specifically to his mother, but glancing in mid-sentence at his father to indicate that he is included): Can we go for a walk?
Father: Aber das Abendessen ist doch beinahe fertig. (*But tea's just about ready.*)
Frank: Oh, blöder Mist! (*Oh, damn!*)
Mother: Perhaps we can go after tea.

Even when one of the children addresses a remark to one parent only and the parent does not hear or for some reason does not reply immediately, the other parent may answer in the other language, e.g.:

Thomas (4;1,23) (to father): Hat dein Hemd ein Loch da drin? (*Has your shirt got a hole in it?*)
Father: Ein kleines, ja. (*A little one, yes.*)
Thomas (to father): Flickt Mami das für dich? (*Is Mummy going to fix it for you?*)
Mother: Yes, Thomas, I've got a few things I have to do.

Or one parent may add information in the other language, e.g.:

Thomas (6;1,23) (to father): Wie hat Myrtle gestorben? (*How did Myrtle die?*)
Father: An einem Herzinfarkt, Ernie. (*Of a heart attack, Ernie.*)
Thomas: Oh, hatte sie eine Krankheit? (*Oh, did she have a disease?*)
Father: Ja. (*Yes.*)
Mother: Of the heart muscles.
Thomas: Oh.

When the father wishes to address the mother and at the same time one or both of the children, he generally speaks German, e.g.:

Thomas (4;1,19), who has not been feeling well, is sitting with his father.
Mother (entering room, to father): Does Thomas feel better now?
Father (to mother, but including Thomas): Ja, viel besser. (*Yes, a lot better.*)

But he may instead use English and ostensibly address only the mother, this second alternative being mostly followed by some comment in German to the children to let them know they are included, e.g.:

Father (to mother): I think we might go to the beach a bit later on. (Then to the boys who are also present): Möchtet ihr das tun? (*Would you like to do that?*)
Frank (5;0,5): Ja, Bert . . . (*Yes, Bert . . .*)

Children addressing father plus monolingual(s)

Even more problematical for the children are situations where the children wish to address their father and a monolingual English-speaker simultaneously. The children then usually opt for English and address the monolingual, knowing the father will understand, e.g.:

Thomas (4;1,23), with his father, is watching his uncle skin a rabbit. He asks his father various questions in German and occasionally addresses his uncle in English. But when the family cat, Gingernuts, comes and sniffs at the rabbit, he excitedly addresses both men:

Thomas (to father): Warum muß Peter das aufschneiden? (*Why does Peter have to cut that open?*)
Father: Man muss ihm das Fell abziehen. Man kann das nicht essen. (*You have to skin it. You can't eat the skin.*)
Thomas (to uncle and father): Gingernuts's eating it!

However, whilst this is his usual solution in such cases, it is apparent that, being conditioned to using only German to his father, it does at times cause some conflict in his mind. As if to allay this conflict and to indicate to his father that he does not wish to break their arrangement of German only, he may occasionally use English to the monolingual English-speaker and then repeat basically the same information for his father in German, e.g.:

Thomas (4;1,18) (to an aunt): Cheppy said Mikie's feet are growing.
Aunt: Yeah.
Thomas (to father): Mikies Füße werden groß, Dad. (*Mikie's feet are getting big, Dad.*)
Father: Ja, sehr groß. (*Yes, very big.*)

This is done even more so by Frank.

Alternatively, the father may be addressed first in German and the information then be repeated in English for any monolinguals present, e.g.:

Thomas (4;2,6) has just returned from talking to a great-aunt and is telling his father and an aunt about the conversation.
Thomas (to father): Maria hat gesagt, sie glaubt, es wird regnen. (*Mary said she thinks it will rain.*) (Then to his aunt): Mary said she thinks it's going to rain.

Another possible, but very infrequent strategy is for the children to address the remark to their father in German and leave it to him to make any explanation necessary to monolinguals included in the utterance, e.g.:

Frank (4;11,0) (calling out to his father and his uncle): Abendessen ist fertig! (*Tea's ready!*)
Father: Ja, wir kommen. (*Yes, we're coming.*) (To uncle): Tea's ready, Peter.
Uncle: Oh.

Brother to brother communication

That English is the language predominantly used, even in private, between Thomas and Frank, is a situation which has developed naturally, that is, practically without parental intervention.

During the time until Frank's second birthday, that is, while his active vocabulary was still very small and he had not yet begun to differentiate between the two languages, Thomas tended to respond in the language Frank used to address him in. This was normally English, since most of Frank's utterances were in that language, a predictable result of his being exposed to it very much more than to German. In fact, many of the utterances Thomas directed at Frank at this stage were a mixture of English and German, particularly when they referred to their father or to activities engaged in with him. For example, Frank (1;4,4) was looking for his father and was assisted by his brother (3;2,27):

Frank: Dad dad dad.
Thomas: Dad dad's in the front room schreiben Bücher (*writing books*), Frankie.

Frank was thus not clearly classified as someone to whom only English was to be used. Thomas obviously realized that he understood German and also occasionally spoke it.

However, when Frank, at age 2;0, began speaking in more than one-word sentences, his utterances were at first largely in English, even to his father, from whom he continued to receive only German. Consequently, Thomas (3;10) spoke to him almost exclusively in English.

When Thomas was 4;0, the father tried to make one afternoon a week, when the mother was absent, a time when only German would be spoken by him and the children. This was more an attempt to encourage Frank (2;2) to speak more German than an attempt to induce the children to speak German to one another. This experiment worked reasonably well, Thomas accepting it cheerfully, but initially becoming frustrated with Frank's failure to speak only German. The following incident, for example, occurred in the second week of using German only during the mother's absence. Thomas protests at Frank's use of English in the presence of his father:

Thomas (4;0,15) (to father): Schorsch! Frankie spricht Englisch mit mir! Er kann noch nicht Deutsch. (*George, Frankie's speaking English to me! He can't speak German yet.*)

Father (trying to counter this objection): Doch. Was ist das, Frank? (*Yes, he can. What's that, Frank?*) (Pointing to a picture of a horse in a book.)

Frank (2;1,23): Das 'n Pferd. (*That's a horse.*)

Father (to Thomas): Siehst du! Er kann auch Deutsch. (*You see! He can speak German, too.*)

Thomas, in fact, took the idea of a German afternoon very much to heart and made disapproving remarks if he heard Frank speaking English to his father: "Frankie hat das auf englisch gesagt!" (*Frankie said that in English!*) On occasions he even went so far as to extend this disapproval to Frank's addressing *him* in English. He would then either voice his disapproval or refuse to answer his brother, e.g.:

Frank (2;6,22) (points out of the window at a car): What's that, Tom? (Thomas [4;5,4] ignores him. Frank repeats the question three times, but still no response is forthcoming. Finally he resorts to German):

Frank: Was ist das? (*What's that?*)

Thomas (visibly pleased, answers immediately): Das ist ein Auto, Frankie. (*That's a car, Frankie.*)

Indeed, even the father was not immune from chastisement for infringing against the rule of "German only" on these afternoons. On one occasion he was sitting at one end of the lounge room marking some university test papers while the children were playing at the other end. When adding up the marks students had obtained he calculated quietly, but aloud, to himself in English, little realizing that the vigilant ears of a young linguistic custodian would be tuning in to his words:

> **Thomas** (4;5,26) (accusingly, but somewhat amused by his father's "transgression"): Du hast Englisch gesprochen! (*You were speaking English!*)
>
> **Father** (quite taken aback, having been absorbed in the task at hand): Oh, oh —
>
> **Thomas**: Wenn du Englisch sprichst, dann werde ich auch Englisch sprechen. (*If you speak English then I'll speak English too.*)
>
> **Father** (amused and impressed by the logic of this argument): Das is wohl fair. Ich habe eben vergessen. (*That's fair, I suppose. I just forgot, that's all.*) (He returns to his calculations, this time making sure that he does them in German.)

Despite Thomas's initial despair, Frank did respond well to the setting aside of a regular time for German only, and his use of German on these occasions increased quite dramatically. The father's pleasure at this improvement was shared by Thomas who now began to offer his brother good-natured assistance in his efforts to express himself in German, e.g.:

> **Frank** (2;7,15) (rams two of his toy trucks together): Ein Unfalle! (a mixture of *Falle* meaning *trap* and *Unfall* meaning *accident*)
>
> **Thomas** (4;6,7) (in a kind tone of voice): Ein Unfall, Frank. (*An accident, Frank.*)

Eventually a situation developed where Thomas would, if he initiated the exchange and his father was in close proximity, but not necessarily a participant in the conversation, address Frank in German. If Frank was the initiator of an exchange to Thomas, he was not as consistent about using German in the father's presence; if he did this in English the reply from Thomas would usually also be in English. When the father was absent or not close by, the children would, with a few exceptions, to be discussed later, use English to each other. Thomas himself (4;10,15) summed up the situation succinctly when the father walked in on an animated conversation between the two brothers and jokingly commented:

> He, ihr zwei, heute ist doch unser deutscher Tag! (*Hey, you two, today's our German day!*)

Thomas's surprised, spontaneous reply was:

> Aber, Bert, nur wenn du da bist! Dann sprechen wir Deutsch! (*But, Bert, only when you're here! Then we speak German!*)

No attempt was made to interfere with this reasonable assessment of the situation.

Smolicz & Harris[121] show that this type of situation is by no means uncommon in Australian bilingual families. After questioning 838 children of various ethnic backgrounds (Polish, Italian, Greek, Dutch and Latvian), they came to the following conclusion:

> "In regard to active linguistic experience in speaking . . . the basic finding, which held for all ethnic groups in these surveys, was that even in those families where the ethnic language was spoken by the second or 1b generation[249] with ethnic elders, the language used with peers was almost invariably English."

Similar findings are reported by Clyne[122] and Bettoni.[123] Clyne questioned 74 children of German-speaking immigrants in and around Melbourne. The children, all of whom attended a German-language Saturday school, "generally spoke English among themselves". In her book ITALIAN IN NORTH QUEENSLAND, Bettoni says of the Australian-born children of Italian parents:

> "Among themselves they always speak English. They started doing that as soon as they went to school and saw no reason to change their habits later on. Only with their parents, their parents' friends and generally with first generation migrants who know little English do they speak their native Italian . . ."

After a period of approximately thirteen months (Thomas 4;0 to 5;1, Frank 2;1 to 3;2) opportunities for the father to be alone with the children decreased owing to the presence of playmates and also to the mother's no longer being absent for an eight-hour period each week as previously. Consequently their use of German to each other in their father's presence gradually declined. By the time Thomas was 5;11 and Frank 4;1 the children were using English to each other even if the father was alone with them, although, as will be seen, German has never completely disappeared from such communication. German is still used when one of the children addresses his brother but wishes at the same time to include his father in the remark. This is particularly the case when an attempt is being made to convince not only the brother of an argument but also at the same time to make an appeal to the father to recognize the validity of the argument, since in many cases it is he who has the final decision in the matter in question. In the following typical example, the children have been told that they must eat all their main course if they wish to have dessert. Thomas has not quite finished his main course when he reaches for his dessert:

Frank (4;1,23) (protesting to his father): Ernie hat sein Gemüse nicht gegessen! *(Ernie hasn't eaten his vegetables!)* (Implying that he therefore does not deserve dessert.)
Thomas (6;9,15) (turning to Frank): Das macht nichts! *(That doesn't matter!)*

German may be used by one brother to the other not just when seeking support from the father, but also simply to convey information to the father. This usually happens in the excitement of a game with the father, particularly when the majority of exchanges are between the father and Thomas or the father and Frank, that is, in German. In the following incident the father and the two boys are engaged in a rather hectic pirate game. The father, playing the part of the arch villain, is being assailed by two sword-wielding pirates.

Father (succumbing to a vicious sword thrust and slumping to the floor): Aua! Ooh!
Frank (4;10,1) (to father): Du blödes — *(You stupid —)*
Thomas (6;8,24) (to brother): Er ist tot! *(He's dead!)*

This remark by Thomas seems to be conveying both to Frank, to whom it is ostensibly directed, and to the father a stage in the game, that is, that the villain is dead (and should therefore pretend to be such).

In all these examples it is likely that English would have been the language employed if there had not been a definite need to include the father directly in the remarks.

In games where the father is a participant, the children do use quite a bit of German to each other, even when the father cannot be considered a direct addressee. Usually in such games the children are playing a certain role, assuming temporarily a different identity (see also p. 84). Often their voice is disguised to fit the part they are playing. Since they have become, as it were, temporarily different people, they can speak German to each other without any feeling of strangeness or sense that they are breaking the established pattern of communicating with one another in English:

Thomas (6;11,9), Frank (5;0,17) and their father are playing:
Frank (to father): Geh auf mein Bett! *(Go onto my bed!)*
Father (to Frank): Er läßt mich nicht durch. *(He won't let me past.)*
Frank (to Thomas): He! Lasse ihn durch! *(Hey! Let him past!)*

In these games there is seemingly no consistency about when the children will use German. German is simply one of two means of expression, encouraged no doubt by the active participation of their father and by the fact that they are acting out roles. The characters they portray are seemingly not bound to one language.

Other excerpts from the same day's play as that just quoted show, however, that even in such games the habits of normal communication are hard to break:

> Frank, playing a tough cowboy, approaches the saloon bar and addresses his father who is playing the role of barkeeper:
> **Frank**: Ich muß Bier haben! Ich bin durstig. *(I have to have some beer! I'm thirsty.)*
> **Father**: Bier? Frag deinen Freund, ob er auch Bier möchte. *(Beer? Ask your friend if he'd like some beer, too.)*
> **Frank** (to Thomas): Do you want beer?
> **Thomas**: Yeah.

If the father participates in a game and has to leave before it is finished, his influence may linger for some time after his departure. For example, on one occasion he had been playing cops and robbers with Thomas (6;11,9) and Frank (5;0,17), but had been called away. A tape-recorder left running revealed that the boys continued playing the game completely in German for about a minute.

When the father is not present at all, that is, when there is completely independent play involving only the two brothers, the use of German still does occur under certain circumstances. In role play, for instance, if the character in question is perceived as being a German-speaker, then that language will be used. One of the children's favourite stories in German was at one time a dramatic recording of ALADIN UND DIE WUNDERLAMPE *(Aladdin and the Magic Lamp)*. So German was the language chosen when the two of them played a game modelled on that story:

> **Thomas** (7;3,2): Ich bin der Geist der Lampe. Meister, dein Wunsch ist mir Befehl. *(I'm the Genie of the lamp. Master, your wish is my command.)*
> **Frank** (5;4,10): Hol mir ein interessantes Buch. *(Get me an interesting book.)*
> Thomas fetches a book and hands it ceremoniously to Frank.
> **Thomas**: Hier ist dein Buch, Meister. *(Here is your book, master.)*

Frank browses briefly through the book. After this interaction they move on to play something else, and their dialogue reverts to English. (Fantini[124] made a similar observation with his own Spanish-English bilingual children, Mario and Carla: "Roleplays were usually performed in the language of the person being portrayed, whether a playmate, a teacher, or Bionic Woman".)

Interactions in German between the two brothers may be associated with activities they frequently engage in with their father. For instance, as a means of improving Thomas's reading and writing of German, his father and he (beginning at age 5;3) would often write short letters to each other, frequently with Frank as an onlooker. Both children obviously came to associate this activity for quite a time with German, as shown by one occasion when they were overheard playing letter-writing:

Thomas (5;10,16): Let's write letters, Frank.
Frank (3;11,24): All right.
Thomas (pretending to write): Lieber Frank, willst du einen schwarzen Frosch? *(Dear Frank, do you want a black frog?)*
Frank (pretending to write a reply): Ja, Mutti und ich haben versucht, ein schwarzer Frosch zu kaufen, aber sie haben gesagt, sie haben keine schwarze Frosche. *(Yes, Mummy and I tried to buy a black frog but they said they haven't got any black frogs.)*

At times one of the boys may complete an utterance the father has begun to direct at the other but has had to interrupt for some reason, or he may repeat something said by the father which has not been heard by his brother, e.g.:

Father (seeing Thomas leave back door open on a breezy morning): Ah, Ernie, mach — *(Ah, Ernie, push —)* (Breaks off to attend to burning toast.)
Frank (4;8,23) (to Thomas): Mach die Tür zu. *(Push the door shut.)* (Thomas does so without comment.)

At times it is difficult to determine what motivates the choice of German between the two brothers when they are playing by themselves. German may be used for brief, high-spirited utterances of a teasing nature, e.g.:

Frank (4;4,22) (springs onto his brother's back, exclaiming): Du bist ein kleines Pferd! Hüh! *(You're a little horse! Giddy-up!)*

The incident culminated in a good-natured tussle, following which the conversation returned to English. An explanation for the temporary switch to German may be that both brothers enjoy teasing and wrestling with their father (but not their mother) in this way and thus associate this amusement with German, at least within the family.

Somewhat surprisingly, German is also used by the two brothers for a particular kind of teasing, namely the chanted taunt commonly heard in Australian schoolyards and quickly acquired by both children when they commenced school, e.g.:

Thomas (5;5): Frankie stinkt wie ein Stinktier, hahaha! *(Frankie stinks like a skunk, hahaha!)*

One would expect such taunts to be associated with the school and with the language of the school, English. A possible explanation may again be that, because at home the children have occasionally translated this kind of taunt into German and used it with great amusement in mutual banter with their father (but rarely with their mother), they have come to regard German as the family language for such teasing. If a monolingual playmate is present, such teasing is normally carried out in English.

On a few occasions the brothers have been observed using German to each other to reinforce a request which has already been made in English and which has been rebuffed, e.g.:

Thomas (6;8,8) (to Frank): Put the arrow back!
Frank (4;9,16): No!
Thomas: Steck der Pfeil zurück! *(Put the arrow back!)*

Evidently the use of German is seen as giving the request more authority.

Curious about how the children themselves viewed their use of German to each other, the mother questioned Thomas on one occasion about it and received a reply which demonstrated that he was reasonably aware of what went on:

Thomas (6;7,10) (to father): Frankie hat "Good morning, Thomas" gesagt. *(Frankie said "Good morning, Thomas".)*
Father: Auf englisch? *(In English?)*
Thomas: Ja. *(Yes.)*
Mother: Don't you talk German to one another?
Thomas: Sometimes, when we're playing a game. Not when we're just talking.

Whilst, apart from the exceptions discussed, English is the language predominantly used by the two brothers when playing by themselves, it is an English which frequently contains quite a number of lexical transfers from German, e.g.:

Frank (3;11,27) (teasing Thomas by greatly exaggerating the dire fate awaiting him if he did something particularly naughty): Then you would get a Klaps *(smack)* with the Gürtel *(belt)*, Thomas, and Blut *(blood)* would come out of your nose!

Since in most cases like this the brothers knew the corresponding vocabulary items in English, there is no linguistic necessity for their using German words. They seem rather to be deliberately endulging in a kind of linguistic game for their own amusement. This use of German words in English sentences does not occur if monolingual English speakers are present, unless it is a means of teasing the monolingual, and this occurs but rarely:

> **Frank** (3;6,16): I got a sausage at the butcher's!
> **Narelle** (a 6-year-old friend): Did Thomas get one too?
> **Thomas** (5;5,8) (smiling, to Narelle): No, I was at the schule *(school)*.
> **Narelle** (puzzled): Schule?
> **Thomas** (smiling mischievously): Yeah.

In a similar way, their occasional German utterances to each other do at times contain lexical transfers from English, usually well integrated ones (i.e. with the English words being adapted to the German sound and grammatical system so that they appear to be German), e.g.:

> **Thomas** (7;1,29) (assuming a tone of voice different from his normal manner of speaking): Was machst du? *(What are you doing?)*
> **Frank** (5;3,6) (also in a different voice from normal): Ich habe einen Stock. *(I've got a stick.)*
> **Thomas**: Oh.
> **Frank**: Kann ich das Kissen HITTEN? (cf. normal German SCHLAGEN) *(Can I HIT the cushion?)*
> **Thomas**: Ja, du kannst das HITTEN. *(Yes, you can HIT it.)*

This type of deliberate incorporation of English words is, again, apparently for the brothers' mutual amusement, there perhaps being some added appeal because they know they are doing something together which their father discourages in their speech to him (and which they nevertheless, sometimes deliberately make use of to tease him).

The much higher incidence of German lexical transfers and the occasional switches to complete German utterances in private, basically English communication between Thomas and Frank is most likely attributable to the fact that each boy knows very well that the other speaks German and, perhaps more importantly, that he will not, unlike the father, object to this type of linguistic behaviour. It may also be partly a result of their year of weekly German afternoons when they did speak quite a lot of German to each other. The presence or absence of the father has no perceptible effect on the number of lexical transfers or language switches contained in conversations between the brothers.

Another aspect of their relationship with each other and their two languages is the willingness of one to offer assistance, without any condescension, if the other should find himself in linguistic difficulties, e.g.:

Frank (4;0,20): Mum, Daddy's hungry.

Mother (preparing breakfast in the kitchen): Well, you tell your daddy that his porridge is just about ready.

Frank (going to convey this message to his father in the next room, but getting into difficulties because a normally easily recalled German word slips his mind): Bert, dein — ah — dein — *(Bert, your — ah — your —)*

Thomas (5;11,12) (calling out from the kitchen): Brei! *(Porridge!)*

Frank: Ah, Bert, dein Brei ist beinahe fertig. *(Ah, Bert, your porridge is nearly ready.)*

It seems very probable that English will continue to be the main means of communiation between the two brothers, but by no means to the total exclusion of German.

Brothers to sister communication

At the time of writing, Thomas's and Frank's sister, Katrina, is still an infant and has not begun to speak. From the start her mother has addressed her in English and her father has spoken to her in German. This caused Frank, on the day she was born, to express scepticism about a baby's ability to understand German, she being the only baby he had heard addressed in German. However, he readily accepted the explanation that his sister would be like the other children in the family and understand both languages. Thomas showed no surprise that his father addressed the new arrival in German.

As yet the boys have not established a specific language as the language to be used when speaking to Katrina, although the choice is determined to a large extent by who else is present. If they are playing with her and the only other person in close proximity is their father, they tend to address her in German, e.g.:

Thomas is playing with his sister on the floor and the father is sitting nearby reading.

Katrina (0;2,24) (babbling and smiling): E, e, ua (seizes Thomas's hair).

Thomas (7;5,28) (surprised and amused): Au! Du ziehst mein Haar! *(Ow! You're pulling my hair!)*

However, even when the father is present, the boys do not consistently address their sister in German, as can be seen in the following excerpts from a typical "conservation" between Frank and her:

Frank (5;7,11) (to Katrina): Du hast kalte Hände. *(You've got cold hands.)*

Katrina (0;2,29) (babbles): E, e, e
Frank (to father): Sie sagt, Hm! *(She's saying "Hm".)*
And a minute later:
Frank (to Katrina): Sag "Hm", Katrina. Sag "Hm". *(Say "Hm", Katrina. Say "Hm".)*

However, a few minutes later, when Katrina produces a succession of sounds, Frank comments on this to his father in German, but then addresses his sister in English:

Frank (impressed, to father): Sie ist ein guter Sprecher! *(She's a good speaker!)*
Father: Ja. *(Yes.)*
Frank (to Katrina): You're a good speaker.

When the father is absent and the mother or other English-speakers are present, the two boys address their sister predominantly in English. When alone with her, they still speak mostly English, although an occasional sentence in German is to be heard.

Thomas and Frank seem quite aware that they talk both languages to Katrina and even, very roughly, of the proportion of English and German they speak to her:

Father: Welche Sprache sprichst du mit Katrina? *(Which language do you speak to Katrina?)*
Frank (5;7,11): Englisch und Deutsch. *(English and German.)*
Father: Wann sprichst du mit ihr Deutsch? *(When do you speak German to her?)*
Frank (whose concept of numbers above twenty is just developing): Ein paarmal. Dreißigmal Deutsch. *(A few times. Thirty times German.)*
Father: Und wann Englisch? *(And when English?)*
Frank: Fünfzig-und dreihundertmal. *(Fifty and three hundred times.)*

Katrina's credibility as someone one can speak German to was strengthened when the first words, apart from people's names, which she responded to consistently were German: asked at age 10 months "Wo ist Katrinas Nase?" *(Where's Katrina's nose?)*, she would immediately point to her nose. Her brothers were particularly impressed because, initially at least, she would not respond at all to the same question in English.

It is hoped that when Katrina begins to speak the boys can be encouraged to continue speaking some German to her, at least when the father is present.

Private speech

Both children employ either English or German in their monologues, although from about their fourth birthdays the use of English for this purpose has increasingly dominated over German. In the early period, there sometimes seemed to be no particular reason for the choice of language, while sometimes the choice appeared to be governed by topic, e.g. if talking to himself about a game usually played with the father or about a conversation with the father, the child would be inclined to speak predominantly German, e.g.:

> Frank (3;5,24) is playing with a toy plane and talking to himself. He is re-enacting an incident just seen in an English-language television programme in which a light plane has crashed. Although the programme itself was in English, he has discussed it thoroughly afterwards with his father in German.
>
> **Frank**: Oh, oh, es hat abgestürzt! *(Oh, oh, it's crashed!)* Broke to pieces! Total kaputt! Verflixt noch mal! *(Completely wrecked! Damn it all!)*

Oksaar[125] reports on similar experiences with her Estonian-Swedish bilingual son, Sven. In an incident when he was aged 2;8, for instance, Sven was recalling aloud to himself the day's activities. He switched from Estonian to Swedish whenever he mentioned experiences which he had had during the day in a Swedish-speaking family. Leopold[126] also noticed much the same in Hildegard's monologues, her private speech in play being considered as an extension of games played with her monolingual peers. He made the following observation when she was aged 5;7,26: "When she plays alone, she speaks English because her solitary games continue her games with other children." Elwert[127] refers to this type of phenomenon as *Nachhallsprache* (=echo language), and describes how, having read a book in a particular language, he continues for a while to think about the book and discuss it with himself in the language in which it was written.

As found also by Ronjat,[128] Leopold,[129] Rūķe-Draviņa,[130] and Oksaar,[125] during monologues the children make appropriate language switches when pretending to address people, real or imaginary, who are associated with a particular language. This is illustrated in the following examples:

> Frank (4;3,10) is playing by himself and providing his game with a running commentary. He is talking about various taped stories, both English and German, which he owns. When he pretends to address his father, he switches to German:

Frank (to self): Where are my cassettes — oh, there they are — KING BASIL'S BIRTHDAY and THE CHRISTMAS PANATA. (To imaginary father): Bert, du hörst diese Geschichte. Nein, du mußt DIE DREI BÄREN hören. Willst du das hören? . . . *(Bert, you listen to this story. No, you have to listen to "The Three Bears". Do you want to listen to that? . . .)*

Thomas (6;4,21) is playing cowboys with his father, in German. However, a switch to English is made to address an imaginary shopkeeper, few of the shopkeepers in his experience being able to speak German.

Thomas (to father): Zieh! Peng! Peng! Ich habe dich getroffen. Oh — ich habe alle meine Patronen verbraucht. Ich muß neue kaufen. *(Draw! Bang! Bang! I hit you. Oh — I've used up all my bullets. I'll have to buy some more.)* (He leaves the room and goes to a make-believe shop): Thirty-six bullets, please. Ten bucks. (Returns to the game.) Jetzt kann ich wieder schießen . . . *(Now I can shoot again . . .)*

In solitary games where the children act out the parts of actual or made-up people, they assume the language of the person whose role they are playing. (See also pages 84–87 for additional details on role playing.) The process involved is practically the same as in games played by monolingual children where each imaginary character is given an appropriate tone of voice, accent, etc. A bilingual child simply extends this to have characters speaking more than one language. A typical example of both language and accent switching to suit the characters in a game is given in the following excerpt from a tape transcript. Thomas (7;5,24) is playing alone with a set of toy soldiers, consisting of American, Australian, German and Japanese troops. In the course of the game he gives each group of soldiers the language and/or accent appropriate to their nationality, including even a short stretch of invented Japanese:

Thomas (holding an Australian soldier and speaking with his normal Australian accent): It doesn't work. It's out of control. (Picking up a Japanese soldier and using invented Japanese): Encha masha shemewa mashema washemawe. PCCH! PCH! (= sound of guns). (Australian accent): Anything — Ich muß *(I must)* — (Australian accent): Shoot anything that comes around this way. PCCH! PCCH! AAH! (Holding an American G.I. and using an approximation of an American accent): Hundreds of men are dead. We'll get 'em. PRRRT! (Australian accent): We watched the men as they got shot. PCCH! PCCH! The bullet takes him. (Now holding two German soldiers): Was machst du? Du kannst nicht jetzt schießen, sie werden uns sehen. *(What are you doing? You can't shoot now,*

they'll see us.) (Australian accent): If I come round here I'll shoot and destroy them. I'm coming down. PSSCH! Shooting missiles everywhere. PETSCHIU! Ah! I'm shot! (Holding German soldier): Gut, daß du einen geschossen hast! Wo ist noch – da, gut. *(A good thing you shot one of them! Where's another — there, good.)* (Australian accent): The Australian troops. We fear the Germans because they've got a cannon . . .

Another factor which could affect a child's choice of language in private speech is the presence in the same room of one parent, even though the parent is otherwise occupied and does not speak to him. Ronjat[128] writes that his son, Louis, behaved in much the same way. His monologues were in either French or German depending on the subject which inspired them or the persons who were within earshot. It was Ronjat's impression, therefore, that his son's monologues were more often in German than in French since they generally took place in the presence of the mother and/or the maid, with both of whom Louis spoke German.

This effect of a parent's presence on the choice of language for monologues was much more noticeable with Thomas than with Frank. Until about the age of four years, for instance, his father's presence would frequently cause Thomas's remarks to himself to be expressed in German. Frank, on the other hand, until about age 4;6, mostly became so engrossed in his play and in his monologues that he seemed oblivious of anyone's presence.

Frank's monologues also do not always fall clearly into any of the categories outlined above. They are uttered generally very rapidly and with few obvious changes in tone of voice, the language switches occurring almost imperceptibly and often for no obvious reason, as in the following example, where Frank (4;5,11) is playing alone with playdough and acting out a particularly violent game. It is, of course, possible that the switches from one language to the other may be due to his assuming different roles in the game, but this could not be detected or verified on the tape:

Frank: Ein paar Menschen waren getötet. PCCH! Kaputt hat sein Kopf gegehen! *(A few people were killed. PCCH! His head breaked!)* PCCH! BRRM! Too old, too — Und dann war ein Mensch angezündet und getötet. Sein Kopf war aufgeschnitten! *(And then a man was set alight and killed. His head was cut open!)* Er muß straight to Krankenhaus gehen. *(He has to go straight to hospital.)* PCCH! He cut his belly off. Seine Hosen haben abgefallen. *(His trousers have fallen off.)* He's got no arms, he's got no legs. Brrm! . . .

It seems that in an examination of the children's private speech, a difference needs to be made between situations where they are pretending to address or assume the roles of other people and those situations where they are *conversing with themselves*. In the first type of situation, the language chosen is determined by the language perceived as appropriate for the imaginary people in question. However, which language does one use to address *oneself* when one speaks and understands two? From quite an early age, both children seem to have preferred English for this purpose. This preference reflects the fact that English is the dominant language of their environment and that, with the exception of communication with the father, the children are practically always addressed in English. The presence of the father can cause a child's remarks to himself to be in German, but this paternal influence has gradually diminished with each child after about age 4½. Even before that it was apparent that even in the father's presence English was preferred for private comments to oneself, e.g.:

> Thomas (4;3,25) is playing mechanics with his father and speaking German. But in an aside to himself he switches to English.
> **Thomas** (to father): Ich habe diese Räder abgenommen. *(I've taken these wheels off.)*
> **Father**: Warum? *(Why?)*
> **Thomas** (engrossed in his game, does not seem to hear his father's question, and talks to himself): I try — they sort of push in and out.
> **Father**: Was? *(What?)*
> **Thomas** (suddenly realizing his father is there): Sie kommen raus . . . *(They come out . . .)*

Fantini[131] has made similar observations. His children, bilingual in Spanish and English, use Spanish in most cases of private speech or thinking aloud, and this occurs even in the presence of English monolinguals, e.g.:

> **Mario** (6;1) (showing an English-speaking friend his book of drawings): Here it is. The one you didn't saw. His name is Shazam. (Then thinking aloud to himself): Algo 'sta mal. *(Something's wrong.)* (Turns again to his friend): Wait a minute.
> **Friend**: That's OK.

By age 4;7 Thomas had obviously established English as the language for speaking to himself, as is borne out by the following incident. His father, passing by his bedroom, heard Thomas playing by himself and giving himself a running commentary in English. Interested in his reaction, the father entered the room and jokingly asked, "Was?" *(What?)* Thomas's somewhat surprised response was, "Ich spreche mit *mir!*" *(I'm talking to ME!)*, the definite implication being that, since he was not speaking English to the father, the reprimand implicit in the father's question was unjustified. Just after Thomas's fifth birthday his father said the same thing to him again in a similar situation. Again his reaction was the same, indicating not only a clear awareness of the language of his private speech but also a conviction that this was entirely appropriate and should not be questioned:

> **Thomas** (5;0,9): Ich spreche mit mir selbst Englisch, Bert. *(I speak English to myself, Bert.)*
> **Father** (curious): Warum? *(Why?)*
> **Thomas** (surprised and perplexed by the question): Ah, ah, ich weiß nicht, Bert. *(Ah, ah, I don't know, Bert.)*

Under similar circumstances, Frank, at age 4;0, did not object in this way, but simply told his father in German what he was doing and then went back to talking to himself in English. However, when his father questioned him again at age 5;7,11, his reaction now closely resembled that of Thomas, although the reaction in this case is probably attributable more to Frank's annoyance at being interrupted in a private conversaton than to any desire to defend his use of English to himself:

> **Frank** (playing alone): . . . And I'll put that up there and —
> **Father** (entering the room): Was? *(What?)*
> **Frank**: Nichts. Ich spreche nicht mit dich! *(Nothing. I'm not talking to you!)*
> **Father** (feigning innocence): Mit wem sprichst du? *(Who are you talking to?)*
> **Frank**: Mit mir selbst. *(To myself.)*
> **Father**: Oh. Welche Sprache sprichst du mit dir selbst? *(Oh. Which language do you speak to yourself?)*
> **Frank**: Englisch. *(English.)*
> **Father**: Warum? *(Why?)*
> **Frank**: Ich weiß nicht. *(I don't know.)*

However, despite these observations, there are still occasions, admittedly infrequent, when the children do address themselves in German and when the motivation for doing so is by no means clear. For example, Thomas (6;0,2), on a walk with his mother and brother, sees a boy, with a large bandage around his leg, being pushed in a wheelchair.

> **Thomas** (to himself): He's got a – er hat ein gebrochenes Bein. *(He's got a broken leg.)*

Thomas's father is not present, he has been speaking only English with his mother and brother, and the injured boy and his friends are also talking English, yet for some reason a switch is made to German for his private comment.

Apart from a few casual remarks, such as those mentioned above, made by the parents expressly to elicit the children's reactions and opinions, no attempt has been made to interfere in this private sphere.

A particular type of private speech occurs in sleep. Which language does a bilingual use in his or her dreams? Elwert[132] scoffs at what he calls the widespread naive belief that a person dreams only in his "mother tongue": "Als ob man nur in einer Sprache träume!" *(As if you dream in only one language!)* Because the children in this study have talked but rarely while asleep and because of the difficulties of observing them when they do, examples of this type of speech are not plentiful. However, it seems that in general the language used by a child in his dreams is determined in much the same way as when awake. In this case, this means that the language used is English, unless the father (or someone else classified as a German speaker) appears in the dream, in which event he is addressed in German, e.g.:

Thomas (5;9,23) (in his sleep): I can get him under the arms. (Short pause) Das ist altmodisch, Bert. *(That's old-fashioned, Bert.)*

Similarly, Elwert,[132] reporting on his own experiences with dreams, writes that if people occur in a dream, they are addressed in the language in which they would be spoken to in a real life situation. Rūķe-Draviņa[130] also comes to the conclusion that the choice of language in a dream depends on the persons and circumstances occurring in the dream.

Communication with animals

As a general rule the children assume that animals understand only English, a reasonably logical assumption in a predominantly English-speaking society where they almost always hear animals addressed in English. This assumption applies to both live and imaginary animals. In the following example, Thomas (4;9,11), during a game with his father, switches to English to address an imaginary horse:

Thomas: Ich gehe, um Milch zu holen. *(I'm going to get some milk.)*
Father: Okay. Wo holst du die Milch her? *(All right. Where will you get the milk from?)*
Thomas: Ah, von Kühe. *(Ah, from cows.)* (Pretends to mount a horse.) Giddy up, horsie, giddy up. Da sind meine Kühe. Da ist eine. *(There're my cows. There's one.)*

On one occasion Frank (3;9,21) even attributed a cat with the power of speech and quoted it (but not himself) in English:

Frank: Eine weiße Katze war auf des Baum, und ich habe gesagt: "Komm runter, Katze!", und das Katze hat gesagt: *(A white cat was on the tree and I said, "Come down, cat!", and the cat said:)* "I'm coming down." Und dann hat sie runtergekommen. *(And then she came down.)*

This tacit assumption that animals can understand only English persists unless the children are confronted with an experience which suggests that the assumption needs to be revised as far as a particular animal is concerned. (This is practically the same procedure adopted as when meeting people for the first time.) An amusing example of this occurred when Thomas (5;6,20) and Frank (3;7,28), on a walk with their father, passed a house with a white cockatoo in a cage on the verandah, and attempted to coax it to talk to them. When their efforts (in English) met with no success, their father jokingly suggested that the cockatoo might respond to German. Much to the children's surprise (not to mention the father's!) there was an almost immediate response from the cockatoo:

Thomas: Hullo, cock. Hullo cocky. How're you?

Frank: Good day, cocky. Hullo, cocky. (To father): Er kann nicht sprechen. *(He can't talk.)*

Father: Vielleicht versteht er kein Englisch. Versuch's mal auf deutsch. *(He might not understand English. Have a go in German.)*

Frank (visibly amused by this suggestion, but doing it anyway): He, Kakadu! Guten Tag! Sag etwas! *(Hey, cockatoo! Good day! Say something!)*

Cockatoo: Hallo, hallo.

Thomas (amazed): Du hattest recht, Bert! Er versteht Deutsch. *(You were right, Bert! He understands German.)*

Frank (also astonished and delighted): Er hat "Hallo!" gesagt. *(He said "Hullo!")*

From that time on, this particular cockatoo was, to the father's amusement, identified as understanding German and was addressed accordingly. Their father did not have the heart to spoil their obvious delight and excitement at discovering a German-speaking cockatoo by pointing out that its responding to their overtures in German was purely coincidental.

The assumption that animals were to be addressed in English even carried over into games where the father assumed the role of an animal. The fact that he was assuming a role (see p.84) meant that he had temporarily changed identity and was to be addressed according to this new identity. However, since the father persistently insisted on being able to understand nothing but German in any animal role the children persuaded him to adopt, they quickly learned that they needed to use German to achieve the results they wanted, e.g.:

> **Thomas** (4;9,0) (to father): Du bist mein Pferd, Bert. Ein sehr schnelles Pferd. *(You're my horse, Bert. A very fast horse.)* (Climbs on his father's back) Giddy up! Giddy up! (The "horse" does not budge.) Ah, ah, hüh, hüh! *(Ah, ah, giddy up, giddy up!)* (The "horse" neighs and sets off at a reckless gallop, Thomas clinging on for dear life.) Whoa! Whoa! Ah! Stop! Ich meine Brrr! Brrr! *(I mean Whoa! Whoa!)* (The "horse" obeys, to Thomas's amusement — and relief.)

A few animals well-known to Thomas and Frank seem to have been classified by them as belonging to the same category as themselves, that is, able to understand both German and English but spoken to in German by their father and in English by most other people. One such animal, their maternal grandmother's dog, Jock, had, for instance, usually been addressed in German by the father in their presence, although they themselves addressed him in English. When, on one occasion, the father spoke English to the dog, Thomas (5;1,17) was clearly puzzled, indicating by his reaction and comments that he thought that Jock, like himself, shoul be spoken to in German by the father:

> The family is walking through the bush when Jock discovers and attacks an echidna which immediately takes evasive action, burrowing quickly and powerfully into the ground, its protective spikes presenting an almost impenetrable barrier.
>
> **Father** (calling the dog away): Come on, Jock. Here, boy. We're going on. Here!
>
> **Thomas** (somewhat perplexed, to his mother): Daddy talked English to Jock.
>
> **Father** (noticing Thomas's puzzlement): Jock! Laß den Ameisenigel doch in Ruhe! Komm doch! Wir gehen weiter. *(Jock! Leave the echidna alone! Come on! We're going on.)*
>
> **Thomas** (looking much happier): Come on, Jock. (To father): Er kommt nicht, Bert. *(He's not coming, Bert.)*
>
> **Father**: Ich hole ihn . . . *(I'll get him . . .)*

Communication with toys

Toys such as dolls, teddy bears, etc., are normally considered by the children to speak the same language as their owners. Their own toys are thus usually seen as being, like themselves, bilingual in German and English, whilst the toys of other children they know are regarded as English speaking.

For instance, when Thomas was very young, he frequently played with a green cloth doll who was, appropriately, called Greenie in English and Grüni in German. She was clearly bilingual, as can be seen in the following examples:

Mother: Did Greenie like her biscuit?
Thomas (3;10,13): Yes. Her said, "A nice biscuit".

Thomas (3;10,16) (arriving at the beach): Wir sind jetzt hier, Grüni. *(We're here now, Greenie.)* We're here now, Mum.

Interestingly, Greenie had special status in that she could be addressed in either German or English by Thomas. In fact her linguistic ability went beyond this:

Father: Grüni kann also Deutsch *und* Englisch? *(So Greenie knows German and English?)*
Thomas (3;10,12): Ja, und sie kann auch Französisch und Malaiisch. *(Yes, and she knows French and Malay, too.)*
Father: Sie ist aber eine kluge Puppe! Was kann sie denn alles sagen? *(She is a clever doll! What sort of things can she say?)*
Thomas: Wie geht's? Danke, gut. *(GERMAN: How are you? Well, thanks.)* Apa kabar? Baik. *(MALAY: How are you? Well.)* Ça va? Bonjour. *(FRENCH: How are you? Good day.)*

The choice of language used by the children to their toys and which they make the toys produce seems at present to depend very much on the situation created for a particular game and the toy's role in that game, and also on what other persons are present. An example is given in the section on private speech (p.67) of a game in which toy soldiers are assigned the language appropriate to their nationality. The father's direct participation in a game can cause a switch to German as the language used to and "by" the toys, unless it is important for the purpose of the game that the toys be identified as English speakers.

4 Departures from normal language choice in the family

Introduction

As in communication with each other (see p. 61), and in contrast to communication with monolingual English-speakers, the two boys have always been inclined to employ a number of German words (i.e. lexical transfers) in their English when addressing their mother. The frequency with which this occurs and the apparent motives for it have varied both with the individual child and with time.

Until he was aged about 3;8, Thomas had a small number of German words which he consistently used when speaking English to his mother, words such as *Ersatzrad* (= spare wheel), *Müllwagen* (= garbage truck), *Maschendraht* (= wire netting) and *Krankenwagen* (= ambulance). His mother not only accepted the use of these words but at times employed them herself when speaking to him. Despite this, he still obviously considered English to be the appropriate language for his mother to speak to him, as can be seen in the following example, where the mother, prompted by Thomas's use of German *wo* instead of English *where*, attempts to address him in German, and he steadfastly sticks to English:

Thomas (3;8,18): Wo's the cows?
Mother: Was? *(What?)*
Thomas: Where's the cows?
Mother: Was? *(What?)*
Thomas: Where's the cows? Where's the cows?

His tone of voice indicated that he was not simply repeating his question but also making a very conscious choice of language.

In communication with English-speaking monolinguals Thomas did not always remember to use English equivalents for the German words he normally used to his mother. It was apparent that he was beginning to regard them as belonging to both languages. As a result, his mother began pointing out that these words were in fact German and that most people outside the family could not understand them. He quickly and quite consciously modified his English speech, reducing significantly the number of German lexical transfers. Within a month he was criticizing his mother if she happened to forget the "new arrangement", e.g.:

> **Thomas** (3;9,22) (looking in boot of car): What's that?
> **Mother**: That's the ERSATZRAD.
> **Thomas** (very emphatically): No, you say spare wheel, not ERSATZRAD.

Whereas before he had been reasonably tolerant of his mother's occasionally addressing him with a German phrase, although seldom responding in German himself, he now begins to object to that also, e.g.:

> **Mother**: Was ist das? *(What's that?)*
> **Thomas** (3;9,18): You not say: Was ist das? You say: "What's that?"

However, this period of linguistic vigilance lasted only for about a month. He then again began using German words occasionally when speaking to his mother, though rarely to English-speaking monolinguals when he would use the corresponding English terms. It seems that he did this more or less unconsciously, sometimes realizing in mid-sentence what was happening, e.g.:

> **Thomas** (3;11,18): Mum, at the hardware shop you can buy nails, screws, MASCHENDRAHT *(wire netting)*, lawnmowers, saws, WELLBLECH *(corrugated iron)*, DACHZIEGEL *(roof tiles)* — (pauses momentarily and chuckles) I talkin' a bit of German!

Leopold[243] reports a similar reaction by Hildegard (4;7,14): "When she says a sentence with too much admixture of English she often comments: That is funny German."

Thomas's preference that his mother use only English to him continued, e.g.:

> **Thomas** (3;10,27) (looking with his mother at the pictures in LITTLE COTTONTAIL,[133] a favourite story book): What's this animal called, Mum?
> **Mother**: That's a WALDMURMELTIER.
> **Thomas**: I like it on *(sic)* English.
> **Mother**: It's a woodchuck.

Yet on rare occasions he would actively encourage his mother's use of German for no apparent reason, e.g.:

Thomas (3;11,21) is playing with a cake of soap in the bath.
Mother: When you're finished with the soap put it up on the little shelf on the bath.
Thomas: I know what you're talking about. You say it to me on *(sic)* German.
Mother (surprised but complying): Leg die Seife auf die Seite des Bads, wenn du fertig bist. *(Put the soap on the side of the bath when you're finished.)*
Thomas: Yes. I know what you're talking about.

This situation has basically continued through to the present time (Thomas 8 years old), with him from time to time deliberately inserting a German word in his English to his mother, as if simply to indicate to her that he realizes they both have another means of expressing themselves. The lexical transfers from German are generally clearly marked off by a change in tone of voice, which shows that he is aware that he is using them. She may accept them without comment, ask him if he knows the English equivalent, or, to his surprise and/or amusement, respond in kind, e.g.:

Thomas (6;0,19) (to mother): Can I have my NACHTISCH? *(dessert)*
Frank (4;1,27) (to mother): Why did Thomas say NACHTISCH, Mum?
Mother: I don't know. He often does that. (Gives Thomas his dessert) Sag: "Danke schön, Mutti". *(Say: "Thank you, Mum".)*
Thomas: Danke schön, Mutti. *(Thank you, Mum.)* (Then, somewhat bemused): Mum, why did you say that in German?
Mother (smiling): Well, you asked for NACHTISCH.
Thomas: Ah. (Smiling too, as if to say "touché!")

Asking him if he knows the English equivalent serves a dual function. Firstly, it acts as a check on the increase of such words in his English (although this can only really be considered a problem if they are used when speaking to monolingual English-speakers). Secondly, it helps reveal those concepts for which he knows only the German term, a situation which can then be rectified, as in the following example:

Thomas (5;11,27) is swinging round and round a tent pole.
Thomas: Mum, when I do this I get schwindlig.
Mother (laughing): What's that in English?
Thomas (ponders for a few seconds): I don't know.
Father: DIZZY oder GIDDY heißt das auf englisch. *(It's called DIZZY or GIDDY in English.)*

In the case of Frank, deliberate use of lexical transfers in his English when speaking to his mother occurred quite frequently between the ages of approximately 3;6 and 5;2. After 5;2 their use declined noticeably, most probably due to the influence of the long summer holidays occurring then, during which time he rarely had occasion to speak to his mother without monolingual English-speakers being present, a definite inhibiting factor; and secondly, because of his commencing school at age 5;4, immediately following the holidays, which reduced substantially his contact with his mother.

When Frank did deliberately insert German words in his English sentences or even use complete German sentences, he usually did so as an amusing way of teasing his mother, as in the following typical example:

Frank (3;10,23) out walking with his mother, passes by a letter-box.
Frank (with a big grin): Haben wir Briefe? *(Have we got letters?)*
Mother (smiling broadly): What?
Frank: Haben wir Briefe? *(Have we got letters?)*
Mother: What language are you speaking, Frank?
Frank: I'm speaking Deutsch. *(German)* Haben wir Briefe? *(Have we got letters?)*
Mother: Was denkst du? *(What do you think?)*

As usual, when his mother responds in German, Frank loses interest and reverts to English. The surprise and humorous effect brought about by using German has subsided and there is little point in continuing with the game.

This type of deliberate lexical transference is seldom used when speaking to the father, most probably because he has always discouraged this practice, mainly because of the weaker and particular position of German in the children's lives. If the father accepted the use of English words in their German, it was felt that, without the counterbalancing effect of any monolingual German speakers who would not understand such words, the children could come to regard them as *German* as well as English. The father's aim, however, is for the children to acquire a variety of German which would be easily intelligible to someone who knows only German. The mother, on the other hand, can afford to be much more tolerant of the children's occasionally using German words to her in their English and, in fact, as she does, at times to employ certain German words and phrases herself when addressing them. Because of the influence of a predominantly English-speaking environment there is, at least after commencement of schooling, little danger that German words will become fixed as part of their English. The children are, as a rule, fully aware that they are employing German words and that such a speech style would be inappropriate when addressing a monolingual speaker of English. As a result, there exists a mutual tolerance of occasional lexical transference from, or even brief switches to, German between the children and their mother.

In a videotaped experiment carried out when Thomas was 5;5,7, his mother switched without warning to German several times in the course of the conversation with him in order to observe his reactions. The conversation took the form of a quiz, with Thomas being the contestant, his mother the quiz master, followed by a casual conversation. We join the conversation after the mother has already asked and received answers to four questions in English:

Mother: Was ist ein Friedhof? *(What's a cemetery?)*

Thomas (no perceptible change in his facial expression or tone of voice to indicate surprise or even that he has noticed the language switch): Um, it's, it's a paddock with, um, graves, um, stone things in it and, and they've got a box under the ground and, and, and dead people are in there.

After five more questions in English and some general conversation also in English, the mother again put a question in German, which Thomas again simply answered in English, apparently either unaware of the language switch or perhaps if conscious of it, not considering it worthy of comment:

Mother: Wie war das Wetter, als ich im Bett war? *(How was the weather when I was in bed?)*

Thomas: Um, ah, when we first got up it was nice. It was just sunny.

However, in similar experiments carried out by his father, Thomas's reaction was quite different. For example, in a situation very similar to that described above with the mother, that is, with the father and Thomas (5;4,8) pretending to be on a television quiz show and the father switching unexpectedly to English:

Father: . . . Gut. Du hast schon sieben Fragen richtig beantwortet. Und nun Nummer acht: *(Good. You've answered seven questions correctly. And now number eight:)* Why is it dangerous to go outside during a thunderstorm?

Thomas (his facial expression changes quickly to one of annoyance and he responds in quite an offended tone of voice): Ah, sag das auf deutsch! *(Ah, say it in German!)*

Father (feigning innocence): Oh, oh — warum ist es gefährlich . . . *(Oh, oh — why is it dangerous to . . .)*

Thomas's reactions are no doubt a result of his father's more puristic attitude towards language mixing. He has consequently come to consider any use of English with his father taboo (except for quotational switching and for seeking linguistic assistance, discussed on pages 98 and 142–145, and role play, see page 84), and obviously feels upset if this arrangement is broken.

An interesting aspect of the type of experiment just described was the effect it had on the father. So accustomed was he to speaking only German to Thomas that he felt quite strange when addressing him in English, a definite sense of incongruity being created. Leopold[100] voices similar sentiments: "I sometimes say something in English to (Hildegard) when other children are present; but I have a feeling of constraint and unnaturalness when I do."

Thomas's attitude to unexpected language switches by his parents (which have been few and far between), remained very much the same over a period of two and a half years (5;0 – 7;7). At age 7;7, he showed no reaction when his mother unexpectedly addressed him in German, yet his father's attempt to address him in English was firmly rebuffed:

Father: Are you going for a walk, too, Tom?
Thomas (jerking his head around irritably): Was? Ja. *(What? Yes.)*
  (Turns away, obviously uncomfortable.)

Around Frank's third birthday he began to object to his mother's occasional use of German lexical transfers, even though he was prone to such words himself, e.g.:

Frank (3;2,0) (to his mother): I want to play with SPIELTEIG. (SPIELTEIG itself is a word coined by Thomas and used by the family, it being a literal translation of English PLAYDOUGH, a home-made substance similar to plasticine.)
Mother: What?
Frank: SPIELTEIG — playdough.
Mother: Oh, playdough. You want to play with Spielteig.
Frank: You don't say that. You say "playdough".
Mother: Oh. Who says SPIELTEIG?
Frank: Daddy does. He says it in German.

Amusingly, this period of vigilance with regard to his mother's speech, which lasted only a few months, included instances where she was not "guilty", Frank interpreting replies such as *Hm*, which could belong to either language, as being German only, e.g.:

Frank (3;1,25): Can I go outside?
Mother (giving an affirmative answer): Hm.
Frank: You have to speak English, Mum!

At age 4;0 Frank also paid no apparent attention to an unexpected switch to German by his mother in the course of a conversation, simply replying unconcernedly in English, whilst an unexpected switch to English by his father resulted in his looking somewhat ill at ease. When Frank was aged 4;4,5, the father repeated the experiment during a family meal, and the mother, when she saw how the situation was developing, joined in with her own language switch, with the following results:

Father (to Frank): What are you eating?

Frank (glances quickly up at his father with a look of amused annoyance on his face): Aah!

Father (pretending not to know the reason for Frank's flabbergasted exclamation): Was? *(What?)*

Frank: Du bist nicht Mutti! *(You're not Mummy!)* (The clear implication being that the only parent who should be addressing him in English is his mother.)

Father (feigning innocence): Oh, oh.

Frank (pointing to his mother): Sie ist Mutti. *(She's Mummy.)*

Father: Oh.

Mother (to Frank): Was ißt du? *(What are you eating?)*

Father (to Frank): What are you eating?

Frank (taken aback, with an expression of amusement on his face, looks from one parent to the other, realizing that he's been tricked): Aaah! (He laughs, and parents join in the laughter.)

Mother: What did we do, Frank?

Frank: What?

Mother: Did I pretend I was Daddy?

Frank (a little sheepishly): Yes. And Daddy pretended he was Mummy.

Mother (smiling): Are we teasing you?

Frank (smiling too): Yes.

In this incident it is much more the father's use of English than the mother's use of German which strikes Frank as unnatural, undoubtedly because such an occurrence is highly unusual. At the end of the meal he attempts to play the same trick on his father, but when the father does not act surprised and simply replies in English, Frank is unable to sustain what he feels to be an unnatural interaction:

Frank (grinning, looking directly at his father): May I leave the table?

Father: No.

Frank (still smiling): Why?

Father (jokingly): Because you're a naughty boy.

Frank: Aah! Nein, Bert, nein. Du bist nicht Mutti. *(Aah! No, Bert, no. You're not Mummy.)*

Fifteen months later, in spite of the relative scarcity of such "inappropriate" language switching by the parents in the meantime, Frank's attitude had changed somewhat. The quiz experiment carried out with Thomas at age 5;5,7 and already described, was repeated with Frank when he was 5;7,22. Again on the fifth question the mother switched to German:

Mother: All right then. Ah — was ist ein Friedhof? *(What's a cemetery?)*
Frank (no change in facial expression or tone of voice to indicate that he has noticed the language switch or, if he has, that he is at all distressed by it): Don't know.
Mother: Come on, think hard: Was ist ein Friedhof? *(What's a cemetery?)*
Frank (again answering perfectly normally): Eine Schule? Ich weiß nicht. *(A school? I don't know.)*

A month later, the quiz experiment was repeated, this time with the father. As in the case of Thomas he switched unexpectedly from German to English to ask the eighth question:

Father: Die nächste Frage ist — ah, fertig? *(The next question is — ah, ready?)*
Frank (5;8,19): Ja. *(Yes.)*
Father: Why is it dangerous to go outside during a thunderstorm?
Frank (giving no perceptible indication that he has noticed his father's unusual switch to English): Because the lightning could struck *(sic)* you and kill you.
Father (returning to German): Gut. Was ist der Unterschied zwischen einem Krokodil und einem Waran? *(Good. What's the difference between a crocodile and a goanna?)*
Frank (makes no comment about the language switch, simply answers the question in a normal tone of voice): Ein Krokodil geht in das Wasser, und ein Waran geht auf Land. *(A crocodile goes in the water and a goanna goes on land.)*

Differences from Thomas's reactions can be observed. Firstly, although it is rare for the father to address Frank in English, he shows no surprise or unease and simply replies in English. Secondly, whilst like Thomas he seems unaware of his mother's switch to German, he does himself switch to German to attempt an answer, whereas Thomas's reply was in English, the language normally used to his mother. The explanation for these differences may, at least in part, be due to the children's different experiences in the family due to their position in the family. Being first in the family, Thomas at age 5;0 and 5;4 was relatively unaccustomed to having his father direct questions at him in English. So when he did so, it came as a shock. However, by the time the experiment was conducted with Frank at ages 5;7 and 5;8, two years had passed, and he was quite used to hearing his father help Thomas with homework projects, which were of course in English, as well as with quizzes and the like in English-language magazines. In such cases, the question itself might be discussed in German but since the answer was required in English, it would often be necessary to state the question in its original English form in order to formulate an appropriate answer, e.g.:

> **Thomas** (7;4,14) (doing homework): Ich muß die Lücken füllen, Bert. Ich muß das richtige Wort finden — hier. *(I have to fill in the spaces, Bert. I have to find the right word — here.)*
> **Father**: Hm. Das sieht schwierig aus. *(Hm. That looks hard.)* (Reads aloud.) "Another name for steam is — ?"
> **Thomas**: Another name for steam is, ah, water vapour. (Begins to write it in.)
> **Father**: Richtig. *(Right.)*

Frank was also used to hearing Thomas sometimes ask his mother, on occasions when the father was absent, for assistance with short German writing exercises set by the father (for more details on these, see chapter 8), e.g.:

> **Thomas** (7;3,18): Mum, this one's a bit hard: Was ist ein Synonym für SCHROFF? *(What's a synonym for "precipitous"?)*
> **Mother**: That *is* hard. I don't think I know that word.
> **Thomas**: It's when a mountain's like that (indicating a perpendicular wall with his hand).
> **Mother**: Oh, real steep?
> **Thomas**: Yeah. Oh — I could put STEIL. *(steep)* That's nearly the same: Ein Synonym für SCHROFF ist STEIL. *(A synonym for PRECIPITOUS is STEEP.)*
> **Mother**: Good.

Frank probably saw the quiz experiment, in which the questions were read from a sheet of paper, as similar to this type of situation, a situation no longer unusual in the family.

As in the case of Thomas, the parents also carried out experimental language switches in free conversation with Frank (5;8,19) to compare his reactions with those of Thomas at a similar age and with his own reactions in the quiz experiment:

Mother (to father): I'm going to take Katrina for a walk in the pram. (Then switching to German and addressing Frank): Willst du mitkommen? Mit mir und Katrina? *(Do you want to come, too? With me and Katrina?)*

Frank (giving no indication that he has noticed the language switch): No, Mum.

Mother: Spazierengehen? *(For a walk?)*

Thomas: I'll come.

Frank (to mother): Where?

Mother: Nur durch die Straßen. *(Just around the streets.)*

Frank (still not commenting on his mother's use of German and answering quite normally): No, it might rain.

Mother: Oh, all right.

A few minutes later, just as the family is about to set out on the walk, Frank changes his mind:

Frank: I'll come and bring my bike.

Mother: And you reckon you can bring it back up the street without me carrying it?

Frank: Hm.

Mother: Oh, well, if you think so.

Frank (to father): Ich gehe mit, Bert. *(I'm going too, Bert.)*

Father: Ja. *(Yes.)* (Switches to English): But you've got to carry your bike if it's too steep.

Frank: Hm, ja, Bert. Tschüß. *(Hm, yes, Bert. See you.)*

As in the quiz experiment, Frank registers no surprise at his father's use of English and makes no comment on this, despite the fact that this would be a most unusual occurrence in these circumstances. It is as if he is, in this case and in the case of the language switch made by his mother in free speech, genuinely unaware that a language switch has taken place, as evidenced by his replying in the language normally used to the particular parent, rather than in the language of the language switch itself, as happened in the quiz experiment. In contrast, in both the quiz experiments and the free speech language switches, Thomas did not seem to notice that his mother had switched to German, and he replied in English, whilst in both situations he definitely objected to his father's use of English to address him.

Role-Play

The only circumstances in which both children are happy to accept their father's speaking English to them and to address him also in English is in role-play. If the father, for the purpose of a particular game, assumes the identity of an English-speaker, he can then speak English to the children without any protests from them and without their feeling ill at ease. However, for such a situation to be accepted by the children, the father must disguise his appearance or at least his voice and announce his "new" identity, i.e. the illusion has to be created that it is not really their father who is speaking English to them, e.g.:

> The father and the two boys are pretending to make a television show.
> **Father**: . . . und welche Geschichte hat dir am besten gefallen? *(and which story did you like best?)*
> **Thomas** (5;7,1): Ah, die letzte. *(Ah, the last one.)*
> **Father**: Und wir dürfen unsere Englisch sprechenden Zuschauer nicht vergessen — wir könnten ihnen auch kurz mal etwas über das Buch erzählen. Ich verwandele mich jetzt in ein Englisch sprechendes Monster. *(And we mustn't forget our English-speaking viewers — we could tell them a little bit about the book, too. I'll change myself now into an English-speaking monster.)* (Puts hood over his head and speaks in a gruff voice.) Now, Thomas, I see you've got a book there. Who read you that book?
> **Thomas** (answering unconcernedly and naturally): My mum.
> **Father** (alias the "monster"): Does she read it to you in German?
> **Thomas** (a little incredulously): No, you silly monster! She reads it in English . . .

This type of role-play, in which the father assumes the role of an English-speaker, began shortly after Thomas's fifth birthday and has occurred ever since, although only infrequently. As can be seen in the example just given, Thomas willingly speaks English to his father under these circumstances. In fact, if, after assuming his English-speaking role, the father should forget and lapse into German, he will most probably be pulled up by Thomas for speaking the wrong language! This occurs in the following example:

> **Thomas** (5;7,1): Bert, kannst du dich jetzt in der *(sic)* Englisch sprechende Monster verwandeln? *(Bert, can you change yourself now into the English-speaking monster?)*
> **Father**: Ja. *(Yes.)* (Picks up hood.)
> **Thomas**: Abracadabraca! Psch!
> **Father** (now with hood concealing his face): Ah, guten Tag. *(Ah, hullo.)*
> **Thomas**: Ah, auf englisch. *(Ah, in English.)*
> **Father**: Oh, hullo! Good day!
> **Thomas**: Hi.

Sometimes it is Thomas who assumes a new identity whilst his father remains himself, e.g.:

Thomas (5;6,16): Bert, ich werde Herr Givins sein. *(Bert, I'll be Mr Givins.)* (i.e. Thomas's physical education teacher at school.)
Thomas (putting cloth on his head to disguise his appearance and disguising his voice): Ah, how — good morning, George.
Father: Good morning . . .

Frank also accepts his father's use of English to him for the purpose of the game. However, for a time (about age 3;2 to 4;2) he found it difficult to divorce role-play entirely from reality and replied to his father only in German. Since about age 4;2, however, he has addressed his father in English if the latter has been playing the part of an English-speaker.

Despite their acceptance of their father as an English-speaking interlocutor for the purpose of role-play, it is apparent that there is still some sense of strangeness about it, for neither boy is keen for such a game to persist for very long.

Fantini[176] similarly reports how his son Mario (3;7), who normally spoke Spanish to his parents, assigned himself and his father the roles of English-speakers for a particular game and spoke English to him:

Mario: I'm Jerry. You David.
Father: Oh, do you want to play?
Mario: Unhuh.
Father: What do you have?
Mario: Motorcycle, boat . . .

Mario even addressed his mother in English when she called him and his father for breakfast while the game was in progress:

Mario (to mother): Wait a minute.

But the moment the game was over, Mario returned to being himself, and not the English-speaking Jerry, and thus reverted to Spanish:

Mario (entering kitchen, to mother): Mamá, cheyo ese ceyal. *(Mum, I want that cereal.)*

Normally Thomas and Frank do not insist that their father use English when he is playing the role of an English-speaker in a game with them. Indeed, when the father is participating in the game, both boys will generally still address him in German, even though the characters they are portraying (e.g. from a favourite television show) are normally clearly identified as English-speakers only. This may be due in part to the fact that the characters whose roles they and their father assume are usually from television programmes or stories which they have discussed with him in German. In addition, they are, in any case, accustomed to his quoting English-speakers in German.

The mother's knowledge of German

We have seen how the children and their mother sometimes use German words when conversing with one another. Despite this, they occasionally seem to forget that she knows German, perhaps because in their minds she is so closely associated with English, e.g.:

Frank (4;4,20) is being tucked into bed by his mother.
Mother: Good night! Schlaf gut! *(Sleep well!)*
Frank (surprised): How can you speak that?
Mother: Speak what?
Frank: Speak that? Speak Deutsch *(German)*?
Mother: What did I say?
Frank: You said, ah, "Gute Nacht". *(Good night)*
Mother: I learned it from you and Daddy. Did it sound good?
Frank: It sounded funny.
Mother: Why did it sound funny?
Frank: Mummies don't speak Deutsch *(German)*.
Mother: What do they speak?
Frank: English.

This type of generalization recalls that made by Hildegard Leopold[99] at almost the same age:

Hildegard (4;9,30): Mother, do all fathers speak German?

Otherwise, as can be seen in other sections of this study (e.g. see pp. 99 and 106), the children are obviously aware that their mother has a good knowledge of German. Both children, for instance, at times ask her for assistance in remembering an English equivalent of a German word or phrase (or *vice versa*), e.g.:

Thomas (5;6,1) (pointing at a large amount of litter left on a football ground): Mum, that's ah, ah — what do you call Umweltverschmutzung? *(environmental pollution)*
Mother: That's pollution, isn't it?
Thomas: Yes. That's what that is there.
Mother: It certainly is.

If the father happens to be absent when the children are doing short German writing exercises he has prepared for them and they encounter difficulties, they have no qualms about seeking their mother's assistance.

However, by age 6;9, Thomas was not accepting uncritically advice on German offered by his mother, particularly with regard to grammar. He considers her suggestions and then either accepts them gratefully or, if he is dubious about the accuracy of what she says, prefers to wait and confirm the point in question with his father, e.g.:

> **Thomas** (7;4,29) has just written a sentence to describe a picture: Dieses Mädchen spielt Musik auf einen Klavier. *(This girl is playing music on a piano.)* See, Mum.
> **Mother** (questioning the case ending): Shouldn't that be "auf eine*m* Klavier"?
> **Thomas** (says the sentence out aloud): No, Mum, that sounds right.
> **Mother** (doubtfully): Oh.
> **Thomas**: I'll ask Daddy when he comes home.

Later, when he asked his father and discovered that his mother had in fact been right, he accepted the correction readily. Thomas thus trusts his own linguistic intuition more than he does his mother's. However, he usually accepts unquestioningly his father's advice on German usage, as indeed he does both parents' advice on English usage. The occasional scepticism about his mother's German is probably in large part due to his having heard his mother at times asking his father about points of German usage. Frank, at least still at age 5;11, did not share this scepticism and willingly accepted his mother's suggestions.

Thomas's realization that some aspects of German give his mother difficulties has also been evident on a few occasions when he has helpfully corrected her pronunciation of certain German words, e.g.:

> Thomas (6;9,3), Frank (4;10,13) and their mother are looking at an Asterix comic together:
> **Frank** (to mother): Has Asterix got a knife?
> **Mother**: He's got a sort of knife-sword.
> **Thomas**: A Dolch *(dagger)*, Mum.
> **Mother**: Dolsch. (Not being familiar with the word, pronounces it [dɔlʃ] instead of [dɔlç].)
> **Thomas**: No, leave out the "sch" — Dolch [dɔlç].
> **Mother**: Oh – Dolch [dɔlç].
> **Thomas**: Yes, that's right.

Leopold[134] reports that his daughter Hildegard (5;2) also assisted her mother with German:

> "Hildegard feels already superior to her mother in the handling of German, helps her along, or takes a hand in her search for

articles . . . Her (Hildegard's) interferences are friendly helps, and they occur only sporadically."

Storytelling by the parents

At bed-time each day the children are read a short story or a chapter of a book by each of their parents. As a general rule, this means that the father reads to them in German and the mother in English. Exceptions to this are infrequent, but do occur nonetheless.

The father has rarely read to the children in English. If asked by them to read something printed in English, he has almost always translated it into German, something which the children have not only accepted but have come to expect. This applies also to magazines, books, etc. present in the household in other languages such as French, Dutch, Afrikaans — a German rendition is expected. Although at times it would be easier for the father to read the children particularly more technical types of literature in the original English, he has been reluctant to do so, mainly because this would take away precious contact time with German.

However, under certain circumstances, the father may read to the children in English. One such instance occurred when Thomas was aged 7;2 and Frank 5;3. The birth of their sister was imminent and because of this and the effects of the scorching forty degrees Celsius summer heat, their mother was often too exhausted come bed-time to read to them. As a consequence, the father first read them their German story as usual and then, taking the mother's place, read in English the English story she would have read had she been feeling well enough. This was appreciated by the children as being a special occasion brought about by the particular circumstances. If the children had difficulties with understanding any part of the story, explanations were given in German, e.g.:

Father (reading from *The Bobbsey Twins at Snow Lodge* by Laura Lee Hope[135]): "I do hope Papa will be home for Christmas," sighed Nan, for Mr Bobbsey's business trip, in relation to lumber matters had kept him away —"
Frank: Was ist LUMBER? *(What's lumber?)*
Father: Bauholz. Das ist amerikanisches Englisch. In Australien sagt man meistens TIMBER. *(Timber. That's American English. In Australia we usually say "timber".)*

From age 7;3, Thomas showed a marked increase in interest in a variety of written material which he would attempt to read to himself. If he found the going difficult, he would, regardless of the language involved, ask whichever parent was available for help. Such assistance could be given in both languages. For example, the father could help Thomas with reading difficult English words and then perhaps give a translation of them in German, following this up if necessary with an explanation, also in German. The following is a typical example:

> **Thomas** (7;6,18) (reading a MANDRAKE THE MAGICIAN comic aloud): ". . . You understand our terms for re—, re— was ist dieses Wort, Bert? *(what's this word, Bert?)*
> **Father**: Zeig mal her. *(Let me have a look.)* Release — Freilassung *(Release)*.
> **Thomas** (re-reading that particular section): "You understand our terms for release of your brat, mighty Emperor of the Central Galaxy?" Was bedeutet das, Bert? *(What does that mean, Bert?)*
> **Father** (translating): Verstehst du unsere Bedingungen für die Freilassung deines Kindes? *(Do you understand our terms for the release of your child?)*
> **Thomas**: Was sind Bedingungen? *(What are terms?)*
> **Father**: Das bedeutet: Verstehst du, was wir wollen, wenn wir deine Tochter freilassen? *(That means: Do you understand what we want if we release your daughter?)*
> **Thomas**: Ich weiß, was die Rattenmänner wollen: *(I know what the Rat Men want)* (quoting from the next caption): "50,000 humans for our food pens!"

The only slight difference between the attitudes of Thomas and Frank in this regard is that, between the ages of about 4;9 and 5;6, Frank sometimes found it very humorous to ask his father to read in German a new English library book which his mother had not yet had a chance to read to him. Such requests were accompanied by giggles and amused comments from Frank such as: "Wir klauen eine von Muttis Geschichten!" (=*We're pinching one of Mummy's stories!*)

The attitude of the children towards their mother's reading to them in German or to her reading German material to them in English is not so clear-cut and has changed in the course of time.

Until age 4;11, Thomas preferred his mother to read him only stories written in English. On the rare occasions he did ask her to read a book he knew was in German he requested that she do so *in German*. If he wanted a particular book read to him and did not realize it was not in English and the mother's translation into English was not fluent, he would become some-what impatient, e.g.:

Thomas (4;11,11): Can you read me this, Mum?
Mother: But it's in French.
Thomas: Read it in English.
Mother: All right, I'll try. (Begins translating): Towards the middle of
   March spring arrived. It came during the night with — ah, ah,
   bouffées — oh, what's that mean? Wait a minute — I think it means
   something like wind, and ah, let's see —
Thomas (a little impatiently): Why can't you read it like Daddy reads me
   the Afrikaans magazines?
Mother (amused at this criticism): Well, he can translate Afrikaans into
   German better than I can translate French into English . . .

However, at age 4;11,15, for some reason, Thomas had a change in
attitude. He discovered an attractive nature book in the bookshelves and
asked his mother to read it to him. When she pointed out that it was in
German and, remembering his reactions to her previous translation
attempts, that she would have to read it slowly if she did so in English, he was
still keen for her to proceed. At times she sought his assistance with certain
words, e.g.:

Mother: What's ELSTER, Tom?
Thomas: That's a MAGPIE.

Sometimes, when neither of them knew a word, a dictionary was needed:

Mother: This is about a bird called a FELDLERCHE, but I'm not sure what
   that is in English.
Thomas: I don't know either.
Mother: Well, I'll just get Daddy's dictionary. (Does so.) Oh, it's a
   SKYLARK.

Despite these interruptions to the reading, Thomas showed no sign of
discontent. Later the same day he even asked her to read him in English a
German story he knew well. Since that time Thomas has seldom asked his
mother to read him anything German, but when he has, he has been happy
for her to translate it into English.

Like his brother, Frank preferred his mother to read him only stories
which he identified as English stories. If he did ask her to read him a German
story he was (unlike his brother at a similar age) far from happy, as can be
seen in the following example:

Frank (3;9,22) (handing his mother the book DIE TANTE UND DER SEE-
   HUND *(The Aunt and the Seal)* by Gina Ruck-Pauquèt[136]): Can you
   read me this story?

Mother: All right. (Reads two paragraphs in German.)

Frank (interrupting suddenly): Can Daddy read me this story? (Without waiting for an answer, he clutches the book and goes over to his father): Bert, kannst du das lesen? Kannst du Deutsch lesen? *(Bert, can you read this? Can you read German?)*

Father: Warum kann Mutti es nicht lesen? *(Why can't Mummy read it?)*

Frank: Mutti kann Deutsch nicht sprechen. *(Mummy can't speak German.)*

His reaction shows that he regarded his mother's reading in German as very unusual and conflicting with the usual language arrangements in the family. By a year later, Frank (4;9) was occasionally asking his mother to read him favourite German stories, usually during the father's absence, but he requested that she do so in English, and this attitude has continued until the time of writing.

Code switching and triggering

In this study most switches from one language to the other are (as seen on pp. 48ff.) attributable to the fairly clear-cut patterns of communication which have developed within the family. That is, they are predominantly dependent on who the person being addressed is and which language has been established as being appropriate to speak to that person in. Some exceptions to the normal pattern have been discussed in the sections on brother to brother communication (pp. 54ff.) and on parents and children (pp. 50–53), and the particular use made of switching from one language to the other for the purpose of directly quoting utterances in the original language is to be described in the next section (pp. 98ff.).

Other reasons for switching from one language to the other in discourse may be linguistic ones. Stolt,[137] in an analysis of language switching in Martin Luther's *Tischreden* (=Table Talks), identified certain "linguistically neutral" words, that is, words which could belong to either language, which caused the speaker to lose his "linguistic orientation" and to continue his discourse in a different language from that in which he started. Clyne[25] gave the name *trigger word* to this kind of word since it triggers a switch from one language to the other, a switch of which the speakers themselves are often, initially at least, unaware. Clyne[138] lists five types of words which may act as trigger words: *lexical transfers* (i.e. words from one language used in the other but which are not normally considered part of the other, e.g. Frank's (5;5) continued use of *Panzerwagen* (=armoured car) in his English), *proper nouns* (e.g. Sydney, Adidas), *homophonous diamorphs* (i.e. words having the same meaning and sounding the same or similar in both languages, e.g. German *Glas* and English *glass*), *loanwords* (i.e. words originally belonging to only one of the languages but now also considered part of the other, e.g. *kindergarten*), and *compromise forms* between the two languages (i.e. forms which may arise in a bilingual's speech which strictly speaking belong to neither language but are close to the equivalent word in both, e.g. [ɪs] for German *ist* [ɪst] and English *is* [ɪz]). Clyne found that trigger words caused about 30% of his German-Australian informants to switch from one language to the other when they were being interviewed.

To this list of trigger words we can add a quoted word (or phrase) from the other language which triggers a language switch either in the speaker himself or in a listener, e.g.:

Frank (5;6,26) (showing his mother some German writing he has just done for his father): Look what I wrote, Mum.
Mother: Gee. Can you write HUND *(dog)*?
Frank: Ja. *(Yes.)*

Here the quoting of the German *Hund* causes Frank to reply in German, rather than, as usual to his mother, in English.

Examples of switching languages due to triggering are quite rare in the speech of Frank and Thomas. One possible reason is that their phonological systems are, unlike those of many of Clyne's informants, quite distinct for English and German. This decreases the number of potential trigger words, since in their speech most loanwords, proper nouns and homophonous diamorphs are, as far as pronunciation is concerned, clearly assigned to one language or the other, e.g. their pronunciation of *Poster* (now also a common German word) is quite distinct for German [po:stɐ] and for English [pʌustɐ]; they are felt to be different words. Another reduction in the number of potential trigger words is caused by the relatively low number of lexical transfers in the children's speech, in turn a result of their father's encouraging them to avoid them unless absolutely necessary.

Clyne[139] isolates four types of triggering: *consequential triggering* (i.e. following a trigger word), *anticipational triggering* (i.e. in anticipation of, before a trigger word), *sandwich words* (i.e. words "sandwiched" between two potential trigger words), and *contextual triggering* (i.e. triggering not because of a trigger word but because of the context of the situation). The trigger word setting off a language switch need not occur in the speaker's own speech but may be used by somebody else who is present (including voices on radio and television). A closer look will now be taken at these types of triggering, using examples from the children's speech.

(a) Consequential triggering

The speaker reaches a trigger word and then, becoming momentarily disoriented and forgetting which language (s)he is speaking, continues in the other language. It is almost a reflex reaction, which in the case of Thomas and Frank is usually detected immediately and laughingly corrected, but which can go unnoticed by some bilingual speakers and result in a switch to quite lengthy stretches in the other language.

Examples:

(i) **Thomas** (4;3,17) (praising his mother's home-made bread, to his father): Der Ladenbrot ist nicht so gut wie Mammis BREAD, ah, Brot. *(The shop bread isn't as good as Mummy's BREAD, ah, bread.)*

Here, the word *Mammi*, the pronunciation of which is practically the same as its Australian English equivalent, *mummy*, has acted as a trigger, causing Thomas to be momentarily confused about which language he is speaking; he associates *Mammi* with *mummy* and utters the next word in English. However, as is often the case, he realizes his mistake and quickly re-orients himself to German.

(ii) Frank (4;6,12) is pretending to be Big Foot, a large anthropoid creature he has seen in a television show. The proper noun Big Foot triggers a switch from German into English:
Frank (to father): Du mußt laufen, weil Big Foot IS AFTER YOU! *(You have to run because . . .)*

(b) Anticipational triggering

This type of triggering takes place when a speaker is thinking ahead to what he or she is about to say and, anticipating the imminent occurrence of a trigger word, switches from one language to the other just before reaching the word in question, e.g.:

Frank (3;6,7) (talking to his father about a gift he has received from a family friend): Das war nett *of* Jim. *(That was nice . . .)*

Here, the name Jim, belonging as it does to both English and German, functions as a trigger and induces Frank to switch to English just before it.

Sometimes a trigger word can be anticipated prior to commencing a whole sentence or clause, causing this to be uttered entirely in the other language. For example, Thomas (4;4,0), during an otherwise all-English conversation with his mother, forgets the English word *saucer*. He can recall the German equivalent, *Untertasse*, and wishes to ask his mother for the English equivalent. However, he obviously plans the sentence in advance and the effect of the anticipation of the trigger word *Untertasse* on the sentence proves so strong that at his first attempt he utters it all in German:

Thomas (to mother): Weißt du, wie ,,Untertasse" heißt auf englisch?
(Do you know what "Untertasse" is called in English?)
Mother (surprised at being addressed in German): What?
Thomas: Do you know what "Untertasse" is in English?
Mother: That's a saucer, isn't it?

(c) Sandwich words

This type of triggering is in effect a combination of consequential and anticipational triggering. When a word is sandwiched in between two potential trigger words, particularly if they are loanwords or proper nouns, this word may be said in the language with which the trigger words are identified by the speaker at that moment rather than in the language (s)he began in and/or continues in. For example, Thomas (7;6,23) is telling his father about two television programmes he will watch that evening:

Thomas: Ich werde mir "Grange Hill" AND "The Changes" ankucken.
(I'll watch "Grange Hill" AND "The Changes".)

The word "and", because of the powerful effect of the two trigger words surrounding it, namely the titles of two English film series, is said in English. Thomas is, to use Clyne's[140] words, "unable to switch in and out of German quickly enough to avoid adapting the sandwich word to the two trigger words."

However, generally both Thomas and Frank do manage to cope with keeping such sandwich words in the appropriate language, albeit often with some noticeable effort, indicated, for example, by hesitation in the flow of speech.

Triggering of any kind has been observed only very rarely in the children's communication with monolingual English speakers, the following being one of the few examples recorded:

Thomas (6;1,25) (showing an aunt his new running shoes which are made by the German company Adidas, a word he pronounces in the German way even when speaking English): Roxanne, look at my runners — (pointing at the brand name) Adidas. Do you know, Adidas *ist* — ah, Adidas *ist* — oh! (Amused and slightly frustrated by his failure to continue in English after *Adidas*, he makes another concerted effort): Adidas — is — a German name. It . . .

The reason for the low incidence of triggering when speaking to monolingual English speakers is that in such communication there are many fewer potential trigger words than in communication within the family; lexical transfers scarcely occur and proper nouns and loanwords are usually distinctly anglicized, thus reducing the chance that they could be associated with German and trigger a switch to that language.

(d) Contextual triggering

This type of triggering, which is the most common type occurring in the speech of Thomas and Frank, is not brought about by a particular word or expression as shown in the first three types, but rather by the context of the situation. A certain activity or situation is closely associated with a particular language and this may trigger a switch to that language, a switch which appears to be more or less unconscious, although sometimes detected and corrected by the speaker. Examples:

(i) Frank (3;11,17) and his mother are alone in the kitchen. Frank is being a bit silly and squirts some juice on his mother.
Mother: Now those ants will crawl on me and bite me.
Frank: They haven't got mouths.
Mother: Yes, they have. How do you think they eat?
Frank (with an incredulous expression on his face): Du scherzt nur!
   (You're just joking!)
Mother: I mean it. They've got mouths.

Frank gives expression to his disbelief that creatures as small as ants could really have mouths by means of an exclamation in German. He mistakenly thinks that his mother is teasing him with an outlandish claim. However, it is normally the father who teases him (in German) with incredible assertions, a game greatly enjoyed by both and in which Frank's usual retort, once he catches on, is "Du scherzt nur!" Associating this activity with his father and thus with German triggers a switch from English to German.

(ii) On school mornings a certain routine operates in the household. On four out of five mornings the father sees that the children's hair is brushed. This activity consequently seems to be closely associated with speaking German, which explains the unexpected switch to German in the following example:

Mother (calling from bathroom): Come and get your hair brushed, Thomas.

Thomas (7;5,15) (who is in the kitchen): Ja, ich komme. *(Yes, I'm coming.)*

(e) Blocked switching

The same kind of words which can trigger a switch from one language to another can at times also cause a speaker to bypass a normally expected language switch, e.g.:

Frank (5;7,14) (about to go to bed): Gute Nacht, Bert. *(Good night, Bert.)*
Father: Gute Nacht. Schlaf gut. *(Good night. Have a nice sleep.)*
Frank (heading for his bedroom, glances over his shoulder and addresses his brother): Tschüß, Ernie. *(See you, Ernie.)*

Although, as has been seen elsewhere, the two brothers do sometimes use German to each other, but usually in a special tone of voice and as part of a game or for amusement, the above was uttered in a normal, tired tone of voice. Normally at this age a switch would automatically have been made to English. It seems that the effect of Frank's brief exchange in German with his father is still being felt and blocks the expected switch to English. Examples of blocked switching are uncommon in the children's speech and the children usually become immediately aware of what is happening and then make the appropriate switch. Blocked switching virtually never occurs in communication outside the immediate family, and when it does, it is nipped so quickly in the bud that the addressee remains unaware of it, e.g.:

Frank (5;2,26) (to father): Hat Graeme Fische gefangen? *(Did Graeme catch any fish?)*
Father: Ich glaube ja. Frag ihn. *(I think so. Ask him.)*
Frank (to his uncle): *Ha—*, did you catch any fish, Graeme?

Here, there is a slight carry-over effect from the German remarks immediately preceding the question to the uncle which temporarily checks the switch to English. *Ha-* is the first syllable of the same question in German: *Ha*st du Fische gefangen?

The reason the children detect so quickly such failures to switch when talking to monolinguals seems to be that they are both very much aware that these people cannot understand German. Inside the family it is not so crucial if this happens, as everyone will still understand.

(f) Triggered switches in style in the one language

Triggering is not confined to switching between languages but may also occur between varieties of the one language. The trigger involved may be the use of a certain lexical item (e.g. "Bloody oath!" used as an affirmative answer to a question such as "Do you like it?" rather than "I certainly do" or the like), a certain pronunciation (e.g. *'ouse* instead of *house*), a grammatical construction (e.g. "That *ain't* fair" instead of "That *isn't* fair"), or the context of the situation and the person being spoken to. The following is a typical example of such style switching. Thomas (6;9,25) is talking to a great-uncle, a tin miner and skilled raconteur who embellishes his anecdotes with many colourful expressions and expletives, particularly the so-called Great Australian Adjective *bloody*, and to whom Thomas listens with obvious pleasure. Normally Thomas uses *bloody* sparingly in his speech, probably because it meets with disapproval at school. However, as can be seen in the conversation, his great-uncle's use of *bloody* quickly triggers off a switch by Thomas to this style of speech. But it is not only the word acting as a trigger but the whole situation. Just as it seems appropriate to switch to German to address his father so it also appears appropriate when addressing his great-uncle to switch to the style of speech he associates with him. In the last line of the excerpt it can be seen that Thomas corrects his speech, changing Standard English *those* (which he normally says) to *them*, the form appropriate to this variety of English, a switch set off no doubt by a similar use of *them* by his great-uncle a few seconds before:

Thomas (seeing his great-uncle for the first time for several months): Good day, Georgie!
Great-uncle: Good day. How are you, mate?
Thomas: Good.
Great-uncle: By bloody oath you're growin'!
Thomas (smiling, excited): Georgie, in Sydney we went to this beach and saw these hang-gliders fly off these bloody cliffs.
Great-uncle: Yeah?
Thomas: Yeah. Remember you said we could go up to Scamander and practise flying on the sandhills? (A standing joke between the two is that the great-uncle can fly, a joke supported by a trick photo showing him doing exactly that.)
Great-uncle: On them beaches, yeah, when we get up on them sandhills.
Thomas: Yeah, those beaches.
Great-uncle: We'll have bloody fun then.
Thomas (chuckling): Yeah. It's bloody good at those beaches — them beaches.

Quotational switching

When monolingual speakers wish to quote directly what someone has said, they may reproduce the person's tone of voice, accent, dialect, choice of vocabulary and the like. Something of the original is injected into the quotation, and it is thus made to sound more credible. If this is not done, at least partially, then the quotation can sound out of place or even unauthentic, as, for example, if the Queen of England were quoted verbatim in a broad Australian accent.

In communication between *bilinguals*, the decision as to how to quote someone is a little more complex, since often a choice has to be made between translating an utterance for the purpose of quotation or leaving it in its original language. According to Haugen,[141] reporting on Norwegian-English bilinguals in America, Timm,[142] writing about American Spanish-English bilinguals, and Kouzmin,[143] discussing Russian-English bilingualism in Australia, the desire of bilingual speakers to quote in the original language is perhaps the main factor promoting language switching. Fantini[144] also reports that his children, when speaking Spanish to him and his wife, switch to English to quote English-speakers.

In this study, both children, when quoting a person or a section of a story, etc., *verbatim*, usually do so in the language in which the original was made, regardless of which parent they are addressing, as can be seen in the following example:

> **Thomas** (7;4,18) (has just watched with great amusement an episode of the slapstick comedy NONSTOP-NONSENS, starring Didi Hallervorden, shown in the original German on Channel 0/28, the multilingual television station in Sydney and Melbourne, and is now gleefully recounting some of the incidents to his mother): Didi was in the bath and these men were after him and the woman said, "Untertauchen!" *(Dive!)*, and he went under all the soap and water . . .

However, when the children report in *indirect* speech what somebody has said (e.g. She said *that* . . .), the language used is the one normally used to the particular parent, e.g.:

> **Thomas** (5;10,9) (telling his father that his headmaster informed the school at assembly that a boy had had a lucky escape from serious injury in an accident): Herr Cahill hat gesagt, daß Mathias über die Straße gelaufen ist, und ein Auto hat ihn umgefahren. *(Mr Cahill said that Matthew ran across the road and a car knocked him down.)*

The children's wanting to quote someone in the original language seems to be motivated by one of three factors (or, in certain cases, by a combination of these factors):

- A feeling of incongruity at quoting someone in a language he or she does not speak.

- A desire to capture the flavour of the original utterance(s).

- To extricate oneself from a vocabulary difficulty.

The most important motivating factor is that the children have a definite feeling that it is incongruous to quote someone in a language they know he or she cannot speak; it would be inappropriate to portray the person as being a speaker of that language. In this particular study this applies particularly when the children wish to quote an utterance by a monolingual English-speaker to their father. The sense of incongruity seems to be especially strong if the person is quoted in the first person. It is as if the children then temporarily assume the role of that person, a role for which only one language is seen as appropriate.

When quoting what they themselves have said in a particular situation, there is nowhere near as much reluctance to present the quotation in a translated form and not in its original form. Since they speak *both* languages, there is not the same feeling of strangeness and incongruity about doing this; they are not depicting themselves as being capable of something of which they are not, even though it does not give a true picture of a conversation, as can be seen in the following example:

> **Frank** (5;6,0) (telling his father about life at the primary school where he started two months earlier): Bert, ich habe einen neuen Freund. Er heißt John. Er hat gesagt: *(Bert, I've got a new friend. His name is John. He said:)* "What's your name?" Und ich habe ,,Frank" [fraŋk] gesagt. *(And I said "Frank".* [pronounced as in German]) Und dann habe ich gesagt: ,,Was ist dein Name?" Und er hat gesagt: *(And then I said, "What's your name?" And he said:)* "My name's John."

The new friend, John, knows only English and is depicted as such; to have quoted him in German may have given the father the impression that he could speak German. When quoting himself, Frank feels free to use German, the language he uses with his father, since by quoting John in English he has already placed the conversation in an English-speaking setting, i.e. the father will realize it was a conversation conducted in English.

If the children do present a quotation in translated form, the feeling of incongruity is difficult to escape, and this often leads to their making an explanatory remark indicating that the actual words used in the original were in the other language, e.g.:

Frank (4;5,10) (telling his mother about an incident which took place two hours before): And Daddy said, "Where's your shoes?" (Slight pause.) IN GERMAN.

This strategy of switching languages to quote people in the original has not been acquired from the parents, since they both practically always translate quotations into the language they speak to the children. By about age 3;9, this was obviously beginnning to puzzle Thomas and was beginning to be felt to be not quite appropriate. Questions such as "Hat sie Deutsch gesprochen?" *(Did she speak German?)*, for example, were a common reaction to the father's quoting some English-speaker in German. Eventually he did accept translated quotations from his parents without comment, although he was not happy about doing this himself. Consequently, more and more of his direct quotations to his parents (and brother) came to be in the original language.

Frank, perhaps in imitation of his brother, adopted a similar strategy to when the need arose for direct quotation, although, as will be seen, his attitude to whether to quote in the original or in translation does differ in some cases.

Besides the desire to avoid a feeling of incongruity, another reason for the children's wanting to quote in the original language is the wish to capture accurately the flavour of the original utterance which they feel may be lost in translation. For example, at age 4;10, 15, Thomas was speaking to his father about the American children's television programme SESAME STREET and wished to quote one of the characters, Cookie Monster. In order to capture the effect of this character's deviant English phonology and syntax, he switched to English.

Thomas: Und dann hat Krümel gesagt: Ich — ah, auf englisch hat er gesagt: *(And then Cookie said, I — ah, in English he said:)* Ah, me not real understan dat. (Uttered in a gruff voice.)

As in the above example, the quotation is often preceded by a switching marker in the form of an expression such as "Ich sage das auf englisch." *(I'll say this in English.)*, which warns the listener that the other language is going to be used briefly and that the speaker is not really violating the usual language arrangement. Hasselmo,[145] in a study of the speech of Swedish-English bilinguals in America, identifies a similar desire on the part of his informants to explain a language switch. One informant, in a stretch of discourse in Swedish, switches to English to quote an English-speaker, explaining in Swedish: "För hann talte ängelska, vet du." *(For he spoke English, you know.)*

The flavour of the original which the children wish to preserve when quoting does not necessarily consist in deviant pronunciation or sentence structure as in the last example. The speaker may have used particular words or a particular accent, the effect of which would most probably be lost in an attempt at translation. Indeed, this desire to recapture the particular effect of an utterance may also manifest itself when the children are told in translation what someone has said, e.g.:

Thomas (7;1,20) (on a fishing expedition with his parents, brother and grandparents) (to father): Blutet Omas Finger? *(Is Grandma's finger bleeding?)*

Father: Ja. *(Yes.)*

Thomas: Was hat sie gesagt? *(What did she say?)*

Father: Sie hat gesagt: ,,Dieser verflixte kleine Brassen hat mich doch gestochen!" *(She said, "This damned little bream spiked me!")*

Thomas (amused): Was hat sie auf englisch gesagt? *(What did she say in English?)*

Father: "This bloody little bream spiked me!"

The request to hear the original version seems here to be motivated by a desire to savour the effect of his grandmother's actual words, there of course being something tantalizing about the grandmother's use of a mildly taboo expression as suggested by the German *verflixt* (=damned, bloody).

A third reason for the children's quoting someone in the original language is to extricate themselves from a vocabulary difficulty. That is, they are uncertain about how the original utterance should be rendered in the other language. Haugen[146] mentions a similar strategy by second generation Norwegian-English bilinguals in the U.S.A. who felt no hesitation at switching to English when their Norwegian vocabulary was inadequate. In the following example, Frank (4;0,9) is called upon to relay two messages from his mother to his father. With the first, telling his father what time it is, he encounters difficulties because the task is beyond his conceptual development at this stage, being more than a matter of simple translation; he cannot tell the time in either language. To circumvent this problem, he therefore quotes this message in the actual words of the original. The second message is much more straightforward and is easily and confidently reproduced in translation:

Father (to Frank): Frag mal Mutti, wieviel Uhr es ist. *(Ask Mum what the time is.)*

Frank (runs to his mother): What's the time, Mum?

Mother: A quarter to three.

Frank (returning to his father): Mutti hat, "It's a quarter to three" gesagt. *(Mum said . . .)*
Father: Oh gut, danke. *(Oh good, thanks.)*
Frank (going back to his mother): Does Daddy have to get Thomas?
Mother: Yes. Tell him it's just about time for him to get him.
Frank (again to father): Mutti hat gesagt, du mußt Thomas jetzt abholen. Ich komme mit. *(Mum said you have to get Thomas now. I'm coming with you.)*

Normally the parents give assistance when they foresee any linguistic difficulties in relaying a message (see p. 145), but in this case the mother was not aware that the time information was to be passed on to the father.

Walburga von Raffler-Engel[79] also observed that a satisfactory translation depends on whether a child has a clear conceptualization of the message. Ronjat[147] similarly reports that his son Louis (aged about 4;0) could normally translate messages very well, but: "It can be seen that his skill as a translator sometimes fails in the face of an expression which is a little abstract." (Translated from the French.) Sometimes what starts out to be a report in the third person is converted to a first-person account and quoted in the original language, in the following case because of something which Thomas sees as virtually untranslatable. Again he realizes this in advance and warns his father of the necessity to switch to English:

Thomas (7;3,22): Bert, weißt du, Kevin — er ist mein Freund — er hat eine Geschichte geschrieben und — ah, ich muß das auf englisch sagen. Das ist sehr schwer. In seiner Geschichte hat er geschrieben: *(Bert, you know, Kevin — he's my friend — he wrote a story and — ah, I'll have to say this in English. It's very difficult. In his story he wrote:)* "I'll chuck wheelies in the best dragster races and I'll be the best dragster in town."

The expression "chuck wheelies", i.e. the act of putting one's foot down hard on a car's accelerator and releasing the clutch suddenly so that the car's tyres spin rapidly with a loud screeching noise before they finally grip the surface of the roadway and propel the car rapidly forwards, is seen (not without reason!) as an obstacle to translation, as is the term "dragster", which is a low car built to race at full speed over short distances. By quoting in English, Thomas has avoided having to use the English terms as lexical transfers in his German.

Another means of extricating oneself from a vocabulary predicament in one language is to quote what someone else (or even oneself) says (or would say) if speaking the other language. This strategy can be seen operating in the following example, where Thomas (4;6,22) is on a walk with his father and they come to a section of roadway where water is trickling through the surface. Thomas begins to explain what he thinks the cause of this is, but realizes in mid-sentence that he does not know how to say "leak" in German. He neatly circumvents the difficulty by quoting a remark his mother has made to him on a previous walk:

Thomas: Siehst du? Kuck mal! Wasser. *(Do you see? Look! Water.)*
Father: Ja, Wasser auf der Straße. *(Yes, water on the road.)*
Thomas: Ich glaube, das, das, das — Mami sagt auf englisch: *(I think it, it, it — Mummy says in English:)* "I think it's leaking under the road."
Father: Ach so, ja. Es läuft unter der Straße aus. *(I see, yes. It's leaking under the road.)*
Thomas: Ja. Vielleicht ist ein Rohr kaputt. *(Yes. A pipe might be broken.)*

Almost the same strategy is used by Frank (3;1,14) in the next example. Water in a whistling kettle on the stove begins to boil and the kettle emits a piercing whistle. When his father asks what it is, Frank forgets how to say it in German:

Father: Oh, was ist dieses laute Geräusch? *(Oh, what's that loud noise?)*
Frank: Das, das, ah, auf englisch sagt man: *(The, the, ah, in English you say:)* "The kettle's boiling."

A very rare method of circumventing a problem with vocabulary which is related to the above type of quotation switching is to actually request to be permitted to say something in the other language, that is, to quote what one would ask the other parent if he or she were present. In the following example, Thomas (7;3,6), interested by discussions with his mother about the births of babies to various friends and relatives, has obviously been thinking about what he has heard and wishes to clarify some points. His mother, however, is not present, so the query has to be directed to his father. Unfortunately, the question contains a medical expression *(induce)* which at the time is unknown to him in German:

Thomas: Bert, kann ich dich etwas auf englisch fragen? *(Bert, can I ask you something in English?)*
Father (surprised at this unusual request): Was denn? *(What then?)*
Thomas (rather bashfully, because he has to use English, not because of the nature of the question itself): Can you get induced if the baby's a boy?
Father: Oh. Ja, ja, es ist doch egal, ob es ein Mädchen oder ein Junge ist. Ja, es ist schwer, das auf deutsch zu sagen. Ich glaube, man könnte sagen: Kann die Geburt eingeleitet werden, wenn das Baby ein

Junge ist? *(Oh. Yes, yes, it doesn't matter if it's a girl or a boy. Yes, it is hard to say that in German. I think you could say: Can the birth be induced if the baby's a boy?)*

When the children switch from one language to the other for the purpose of quotation, the original utterance is sometimes not given in its entirety, only significant elements of the original version being cited. (This was also observed in the speech of bilinguals studied by Clyne.)[148] In the following example, the phrase quoted in the original English is thus quoted because of the need to reproduce the feeling of the mother's joking, but in Frank's eyes slightly risqué, reference to his father:

> **Frank** (4;1,23) (gleefully to his father): Ich habe Mutti gesagt, du hast dasselbe Eis gehabt wie mir *(sic)*, und Mutti hat gesagt, du bist *(I told Mummy you had the same ice-cream as me, and she said you're)* A BLOODY COPYCAT!

It will be noted, however, that this is not a direct first-person quotation. If a first-person quotation had been made, it is most probable, judging from other examples recorded, that it would have been completely in English: Mutti hat gesagt *(Mummy said)*: "I think he's just a bloody copy-cat!"

Another aspect of quotational switching occasionally observed in the speech of both children is that a section of discourse which is not part of the quotation unit itself may also occur in the language of the quotation, a phenomenon which Hasselmo[149] refers to as "morphological raggedness". The quotation unit itself has a triggering effect,[150] i.e. it triggers off a language switch either before the quotation unit (called by Clyne[25] "antici-pational triggering"), or after the quotation unit (Clyne's "consequential triggering"), as in the following example:

> **Frank** (4;4,16) (telling his father about an incident which occurred during his Christmas holidays): . . . und ich hab zu Erni gesagt: *(and I said to Ernie:)* "What can we do first? We might go up to Peter and Roxanne's tent," I SAID, SO WE DID. (He realizes almost immed-iately that he has switched to English for more than the quotation of his utterance and corrects himself): Und wir haben das gemacht. *(And that's what we did.)*

An amusing, but very rare, kind of quotational switching, which is really a double switch, occurs when the utterance quoted is not the actual original utterance but a translated version of it which has been heard from one of the parents, e.g.:

Thomas (7;4,20) (drawing a cartoon and wanting one of the characters in it, a Roman soldier, to be speaking Latin): Bert, wie schreibt man "Du Blöder" auf lateinisch? *(Bert, how do you write "you idiot" in Latin?)*

Father (struggling to recall his rusty Latin): "Tu demens es." *("You are mad.")* (Spells it out and Thomas writes it down.)

Later, when showing his mother his work, she comments on the Latin utterance and asks what it means. Instead of translating it, as expected, into English, he gives the meaning in German, the language he originally used to elicit the Latin version:

Mother: That's a nice drawing. What's this mean here: "Tu demens es."? Does that mean: "Don't do that."?

Thomas: No, it means "Du Blöder". *(You idiot.)*

Mother: Oh, does it?

Thomas: Yes. In LATEINISCH. *(Latin)* Daddy told me how to write it.

The use of the German lexical transfer *Lateinisch* for "Latin" can be attributed to the fact that most of Thomas's discussions about languages have been with his father and he has rarely heard the English equivalents of some language names. However, he can, if need be, come up with the English equivalent, as can be seen in the discussion below which he had with his friend Shane about the same cartoon. This conversation also confirms other observations that even verbatim quotations are always translated for the benefit of monolingual interlocutors; the expression *"Du Blöder!"* is unhesitatingly translated into a very colloquial equivalent:

Thomas (7;5,2): Shane, he's saying "You dummy!" to that man — ah, that's *Lateinisch* — (a two second pause) — Latin, I mean. My dad can write Latin . . .

Quotational switching in storytelling

With regard to quoting sections of stories to their parents or other bilinguals in the original language, the two children have somewhat different attitudes, showing again that even when growing up in the same family under basically the same conditions, children do not necessarily acquire bilingualism in exactly the same way.

(a) Thomas

Thomas has always been, up to the time of writing (i.e. eight years of age), quite prepared to retell in one of his languages a story he has heard only in the other. If, while doing so, he does code-switch, it is usually for only some direct quotations of characters' utterances. It seems that he attempts to tell the whole story in one language but, particularly when reporting characters' utterances, the pull of the actual wording and language of the original at times proves too strong. This can be seen in the following example where he is telling his mother in English about a dramatized radio version of a favourite German story, MÜNCHHAUSENS REISE NACH RUSSLAND (*Münchhausen's Journey to Russia*):

> **Thomas** (6;10,24): Münchhausen tied his horse to a post and when he woke up the snow had melted and his horse was on top of the church. And he said, "Ich kann ihn mit meinen Pistolen herunterschießen." *(I can shoot him down with my pistols.)* And he shot and his horse fell down to the ground . . .

It does not seem, in all cases, to be the exact wording of a character's original utterance which has made an impression, but rather the sense of the utterance and the language in which it was said, e.g.:

> **Thomas** (6;3,0): Mum, in ELTERN (PARENTS, the name of a German magazine) there's a boy who says, "Oma, diese Schokoladekekse tun mir gut!" *("Grandma, these chocolate biscuits do me good!")*, and he's got chocolate all over his face. I'll get it and show you.

The actual words said by the boy in the magazine were:

> ,,Oma, diese Schokoladeplätzchen sind einfach Klasse!" *("Grandma, these chocolate biscuits* [with, however, PLÄTZCHEN being the word for "biscuits", not the near-synonym employed by Thomas, KEKSE] *are just great!")*

Occasionally Thomas does switch languages in narration when he is not quoting a character's utterance. In these cases, the switch seems to be made to quote a crucial line in the story, as in the following example, where he is showing his mother a German book entitled DEUTSCHE MÄRCHEN UND SAGEN[151] (*German Fairy Tales and Legends*):

> **Thomas** (5;11,18): I know this one, Mum. It's called DIE WILDE JAGD (*The Wild Chase*). It's about some kids, and their mugs get filled up all the time by the ghost, but he tells them not to tell anyone. But they tell their mother and father, und die Gläser werden nie wieder gefüllt. *(and the glasses are never again filled.)*

This, the last sentence and the climax of the story, is similar to what Haugen[152] calls the "untranslatable and inimitable punch line", for which many of his Norwegian-English bilingual informants switched to Norwegian in anecdotes they had begun in English. Hasselmo[153] observed much the same in the speech of Swedish-English bilinguals in America. However, in

Thomas's case Haugen's explanation seems to be applicable only if a not too strict interpretation is made of "inimitable" and "untranslatable". For the climactic sentence used by Thomas is not a word-for-word quotation of the original, which reads: ". . . und im gleichen Augenblick waren die Krüge leer und füllten sich nie wieder." *(and in the same moment the mugs were empty and never again filled up.)* But, despite its not being a verbatim quotation, the final sentence has obviously made quite an impression on Thomas, and in recalling the story, it is as if he receives an acoustic image of this sentence, an image which is clearly German. The line is not "untranslatable' in the strict sense, but rather preferably not translated. If necessary, Thomas *can* provide an English equivalent, as he would do if talking to a monolingual and as can be seen in a continuation of the same conversation, when the mother, out of curiosity, actually asks him to translate it:

> **Mother**: Oh, und die Gläser werden nie wieder gefüllt. What's that in English?
> **Thomas**: Um, the glasses wouldn't fill themselves for ever and ever.

Interestingly, this elicited English version, with its *fill themselves* (cf. German "füllten sich") is, in a way, a closer literal rendition of the original than his own German version.

(b) Frank

Frank's attitude to storytelling differs considerably from that of his brother. He has always been very reluctant to retell a story, in part or in whole in anything but the original language. That is, he associates a story he has usually or only heard in a particular language closely with that language. It is not that he has memorized the actual wording of a story and is simply reproducing it, since each story is recounted using his own particular style of expression. Nevertheless, he obviously does have a strong feeling that a particular story is a German story or an English one. This feeling that a story belongs to a particular language manifests itself clearly in the following incident:

> **Frank** (4;2,12) (coming to his mother with a German storybook called MONSTER GEHT IN DEN ZOO[154] *(Monster Goes to the Zoo)*: I'll "read" you a story, Mum. It's called MONSTER GEHT IN DAS ZOO *(Monster Goes to the Zoo)*. . . . Sie spielen Karten. Sie kucken aus das Fenster. Sie machen ein Hubschrauber. Sie fliegen über das Stadt. Sie fliegen zu das Zoo. *(They play cards. They look out of the window. They make a helicopter. They fly over the town. They fly to the zoo.)* (Then changing from his narrating tone of voice to a

conversational tone of voice, and at the same time switching from German to English): Look, Mum, snakes. A big one and a little one. (Then back again to his narrating voice and German): Sie gehen zu die Gorillas . . . Monster und der Junge kaufen Fritten und ein heißes Würstchen. Dann gehen sie nach Hause. *(They go to the gorillas . . . Monster and the boy buy some chips and a hot dog. Then they go home.)* Was that a nice story?

Frank's reproduction of the story is in German, the language he has always heard it in. However, it can be seen that comments *about* the story, which are directed at his mother, are in English; these are not *part of* the story itself.

Stories for Frank are very similar to what Hasselmo[149] calls a "preformulated sequence", in which a speaker finds it very difficult to depart from the language in which the particular sequence was formulated. One of Hasselmo's informants, even when asked in English to retell a certain story, switches to Swedish to do so, although an aside to the interviewer during the narration is in English.

Just how strong the influence of the language associated with a particular story can be, became very evident when Frank's father tried to get him to retell several of his favourite stories in English and German. He found no difficulty in doing this if he was familiar with the story in both languages, e.g. *The Three Pigs*, even though his two versions still reflected the slight differences between the English and German versions he had heard. However, faced with the task of retelling a popular story about an Eskimo boy heard only in German, OOTAHS GLÜCKSTAG *(Ootah's Lucky Day)* by Peggy Parish,[155] Frank (5;5,14) was very insistent that German was the only language in which it should be told:

> **Frank** (rather pathetically): Ich will das in Deutsch . . . Ich kann das nicht in Englisch. *(I want to do it in German . . . I can't do it in English.)*

His reactions to being asked to retell in German a story heard only in English have been the same.

In fact, stories which Frank has heard in only one language, are so closely associated with the language of the original that if a monolingual speaker of the other language asks him to retell it, he either refuses to do so or tells it in the original language, even though his listener cannot understand. This last alternative, for instance, was observed when his friend Shane picked the German book OOTAHS GLÜCKSTAG *(Ootah's Lucky Day)*, already mentioned above, out of the bookshelf:

Shane: Is this a good story?
Frank (5;5,20): Yeah, real good. I'll tell it to you: Ootahs Glückstag.
Ootah wacht sehr früh auf . . . *(Ootah's Lucky Day. Ootah wakes up very early . . .)*

He continued to tell the story in German, Shane's interest being sustained by the pictures in the book. Frank's only departures from German were several short comments in English about the story.

Not all listeners are as patient as a child friend, however. This means that Frank usually refuses to tell a German story to someone he knows understands only English. However, he is prepared to make comments *about* the story, which may, in fact, amount to a résumé of the story. It is only when he feels he is *retelling* the story that he cannot depart from the language of the original.

Similar findings are reported by Hasselmo.[153] He shows what happens when a speaker is forced to render a Swedish preformulated sequence in English:

"Very strong prompting of English, viz., a direct request that English be used, was required in order to get the informant to retell the story in English. The poor performance, as far as story telling is concerned, is in flagrant contrast to the informant's normal performance. . . . (He) . . . is involved in something that is quite difficult, viz., breaking the rules of his private speech economy by rendering in English a sequence which is preformulated in Swedish only, and that is . . . a reason for the poor performance."

Even Thomas, who, when asked to retell in one language something preformulated in the other, usually does so willingly and with a surprising degree of confidence, does not perform as fluently as when retelling in the original language, particularly in the initial stages of his narration. At age 7;5, for example, Thomas was asked to retell in English the story of OOTAHS GLÜCKSTAG *(Ootah's Lucky Day)*, until then heard only in German. The pictures of the book were used as a visual stimulus, the text being concealed so as to avoid his reading it and translating. His narration of the first four double pages is given below together with, for the sake of comparison, a German version recorded two weeks later. (More of his version is given in chapter 7.) As can be seen, his English rendition begins rather laboriously and clumsily, with frequent hesitation pauses (with pauses of 0.5 second and more being indicated), as he struggles to reproduce a familiar story in an unfamiliar form:

I

Ootah's (1.0 sec), Ootah wakes up. (0.8 sec) There's no things (0.5 sec) in the pot (1.0 sec) to eat (0.7 sec) or (2.3 sec), ah (3.9 sec), or there's no oil (1.2 sec) for the fire.

Ootah wacht früh auf. (0.6 sec) Er ist sehr hungrig. (0.9 sec) Er hat kein Fleisch und kein Öl zum Kochen. *(Ootah wakes up early. He is very hungry. He has no meat to cook and no oil to cook with.)*

II

Ootah (3.6 sec), Ootah (0.5 sec), Ootah's dad and all the other (0.7 sec), um, (1.0 sec) hunters (1.5 sec) come, and go away.

Ootah will auf die Jagd gehen, aber sein Vater sagt nein. (1.8 sec) Seine Leute brauchen Fleisch, und sie werden nicht vor Hunger sterben. *(Ootah wants to go hunting, but his father says no. His people need meat, and they won't die of hunger.)*

III

Ootah wants to go (1.6 sec) too. He puts his (1.6 sec) people, his, um, his (1.8 secs) dogs on his sled. (0.7 sec) Then he goes off.

Ootah spannt seine Hunde an, und die Hunde bellen vor Freude. (0.6 sec) ,,Hoffentlich ist dieses ein Glückstag für mich," sagt er. *(Ootah hitches up his dogs and the dogs bark with delight. "I hope this is a lucky day for me," he says.)*

IV

Soon he sees (2.4 sec) a little black dot. "Maybe it might be a seal. (0.7 sec) Seal meat is very nice."

Ootah sieht ein schwarzer Fleck. ,,Vielleicht ist das ein, ein Eis— (0.8 sec), ein Seehund," sagt er. ,,Seehundfleisch schmeckt gut." Der Fleck wird größer und größer. *(Ootah sees a black speck. "Perhaps it's a, a polar—, a seal," he says. "Seal meal tastes good." The speck gets bigger and bigger.')*

However, as Thomas's telling of the story in English progresses, his confidence and consequently his fluency improve noticeably; by the end of it his narration is flowing as easily as in his German version. Nevertheless, Thomas himself showed that he was aware of the difficulties involved in this type of task; on being asked what it was like telling the story of Ootah in English, he remarked:

Thomas: Das war okay, Bert, aber nicht so leicht wie auf deutsch. *(That was all right, Bert, but not as easy as in German.)*
Father: Warum? *(Why?)*
Thomas: Ah, ich bin an die deutschen Worte gewöhnt. *(Ah, I'm used to the German words.)*

Another example of Thomas retelling a story in a different language from that of the original was recorded when he was aged 5;7,1. He was asked to tell in German JACK AND THE BEANSTALK, a story he had previously heard only in English. He handled this task reasonably well, although he did have difficulty remembering not to quote characters in English (as already mentioned), and his rate of delivery (64.5 words per minute) was much slower than for the English version (89.4 words per minute) and also somewhat slower than his normal storytelling in German (ca. 72 words per minute). As well, the German narration contained more filled pauses, repetitions and vocal hesitations than when retelling a story he had already heard in German (see pp. 165–166 for exact statistical details), indicating again that a definite conscious effort is required to divorce a story from its familiar form in one particular language and reproduce it in another.

5 Influences from outside the immediate family

Attitudes of monolingual English-speakers

Usually Thomas has seemed quite at ease speaking German to his father in the presence of monolingual English-speakers. However, he has appeared able to sense when a person has a negative attitude towards German being used in his or her presence. His reaction has been to avoid speaking German as much as possible while such people are within earshot.

Unfortunately, bilingual children in probably any bilingual situation will be exposed at times to even overt hostility from people who (usually monolingual themselves) are so intolerant that they cannot bear a language other than the majority language being spoken in their presence, even if the people speaking the other language are engaged in a completely private conversation. This antipathy is typified in a letter by a Mrs R. C. Miller to the editor of the SYDNEY MORNING HERALD (13.2.1981, p.6):

> "Nothing annoys me more than two or more 'ethnics' jabbering away in their native language in the company of English speaking people, particularly in a work environment. Is it really too much to ask them to observe simple politeness by refraining from resorting to their native language in the company of English speaking persons."

Accompanying this view is undoubtedly a fear that things are perhaps being said about one in a language one cannot understand. People who hold this view fail to realize that even in a completely monolingual environment we do not expect to hear and understand everything said by people who are not speaking specifically to us. Nor do we in such circumstances by any means always speak loudly and distinctly so that all present will understand us. Why should the use of a foreign language be any different? It is surely only

113

impolite if a person is linguistically excluded from a conversation in which he or she is a definite participant. However, there seems little justification in objecting to people who share a common language using that language for their private communication simply because it is not understood by other people who are within earshot.

Hesse,[156] in an article reflecting on her own experiences as a German-English bilingual in Australia, makes a pertinent observation on this aspect of bilingualism:

> "Socially I found that it was not always rude to use a foreign language in the presence of monolinguals; it could be courteous to mark out areas of privacy and turn a private conversation into a mere background noise. Most people are grateful if they cannot understand what does not concern them."

Thomas's awareness that someone is not favourably disposed towards the use of German developed with age. It was not present at age 3;8, but had appeared by 4;3. By age 6;6, whilst he may still have sensed such antagonism, he seemed to have ceased to be intimidated by it, perhaps influenced by his younger brother Frank's complete lack of concern. Frank has always remained blissfully ignorant of any such covert or overt disapproval of his use of German and happily speaks German to his father wherever they may be or whoever may be present.

Often the attitudes of people in positions of comparative prestige and authority, such as teaching and medical personnel, can have a decisive influence on how children and also their parents view their bilingualism. A negative attitude can obviously have an adverse effect on a family's resolve to raise its children bilingually, particularly if this attitude is expressed in the guise of helpful advice with the children's welfare in mind. Parents, who naturally wish to do the best for their children, may be inclined to accept such advice from people they regard as experts. Unfortunately such adverse opinions may be based on personal conjectures or prejudices rather than on any objective evidence.

The family in this study was warned by a child health doctor just after Thomas's third birthday that speaking two languages was too great a burden on him and was impairing his acquisition of English, and it would be in his best interests for him to be addressed in English only. This pronouncement was made after a fifteen minute examination. Thomas's failure to perform adequately on several verbal tests, due in part to his being shy of performing in front of a stranger, was attributed immediately to his being bilingual. The unfortunate part about this particular case was that the doctor in question worked in a clinic which was located in an area where a considerable proportion of the population which she would be required to advise came from non-English speaking countries. One wonders whether this sort of advice was also given to such families in which the parents' ability in English would usually be far less than in their mother tongue. Abandoning the mother tongue, particularly for another in which the parents lack proficiency, could have far-reaching consequences on parent-child communication and rapport.

Medical personnel may attribute problems children may have with speech development, such as unclear speech or stuttering, to their bilingualism, and advise the parents to expose their children to only one language, or at least to delay the exposure to two languages (such advice being mentioned, for example, in articles by Métraux[157] in 1964 and by Berthoz-Prouz[158] in 1976). There is, however, no evidence that bilingualism *per se* causes stuttering or disfluent speech. Wendell Johnson,[159] Professor of Speech Pathology and Psychology at the University of Iowa, for example, in a 100-page discussion of research into stuttering and its causes, does not even mention bilingualism. What does become clear, however, from his work on disfluency in speech, is that *all* children speak disfluently to some degree, but it usually only becomes a problem for the child when it is seen as such by adults. Johnson writes that ". . . in case after case, stuttering as a serious problem developed after it had been diagnosed. The diagnosis of stuttering — that is, the decision made by someone that a child is beginning to stutter — is one of the causes of the stuttering problem, and apparently one of its most potent causes."

Johnson stresses the importance of the attitude of parents and others towards a child whose speech is not always fluent. To label him or her a "stutterer" will only aggravate the problem, whereas to accept him or her as a "normal" or "good" or "acceptable" speaker will most likely lead to quite a different kind of behaviour.

When a bilingual child has difficulty in expressing him- or herself in one of his or her languages and has to grope for words or struggle with various grammatical constructions, resulting in a certain amount of repetition and hesitation, it is quite possible that this will attract the attention or even arouse the impatience of listeners and perhaps be considered stuttering. The child's self-consciousness and anxiety about his or her speech, or more exactly, about listeners' possible negative reactions to it, are the most likely causes of such disfluency, or at least the causes of its becoming a problem. Indeed, the disfluency may be conspicuous in only one of the child's languages, in the one which has to be used in circumstances causing uneasiness.

Attributing the problem to the child's bilingualism and trying to solve it by removing one of the languages would seem to be not at all satisfactory. In fact, such an action could have the opposite effect, merely increasing the child's anxiety, especially since, in most cases, it would be the language of the home which would be the one to go. If the child is suddenly told he or she cannot use the familiar home language, the language associated with the warmth and security of the family, perhaps even the language in which he or she feels most confident and at ease, he or she cannot fail to become aware that people consider he or she has a speech problem, undoubtedly a serious one at that for such drastic action to be taken. It is very doubtful that such an experience and realization would lead to improvement in fluency in the language remaining.

The solution lies rather in the attitude of the listener, and much of the advice given by Johnson[160] to parents, teachers, etc., who have contact with children with disfluent speech applies equally well to people coming into contact with bilingual children:

(i) "Make talking enjoyable. See to it that the child has as much a feeling of success as possible in speaking. (One) should do all (one) can to make the child's speaking enjoyable and rewarding. Certainly (one should) not make a point of criticising him for mistakes in grammar and pronunciation . . . or for other things about his speech that are not important in relation to the fun and satisfaction he gets from speaking as well as he can."

(ii) "Try to be the kind of listener (the) child likes to talk to . . . when he is "talking over his head" be patient, and now and then supply him with a new word which he has not yet learned but which he needs at the moment. To a reasonable extent and in meaningful ways help him to add to his vocabulary — preferably at those times when he needs words he hasn't learned in order to tell you things he has never tried to say before."

(iii) "Read to (the child) whenever you can. In reading or speaking to him, enunciate clearly, be interested in what you are reading and avoid a tense, impatient, or loud voice. Enjoy this reading and make it fun and companionable. Do some of it every day, (if a parent) preferably just before bedtime, if possible."

As can be seen, this advice, if followed, reduces the child's anxiety about speaking and makes it an enjoyable experience for him or her. Whilst

Johnson mentions these steps specifically as effective means of building confidence in the disfluent speaker, they would seem to be a sound procedure for assisting also the bilingual child who is having difficulty in expressing him- or herself.

During bilingual children's education they and their parents may have the misfortune to encounter members of the teaching profession who are intolerant of bilingualism. Most of this intolerance is fortunately not as vehement as an example mentioned by Eve Isaacs[161] in her 1977 study of Greek-speaking children in Sydney: "I heard one teacher advise a soap-and-water mouth rinse for those using other languages (i.e. not English) within the school grounds." Nor is the intolerance usually rigidly institutionalized as set out in the rules of a French high school in Truchtersheim in East Lorraine, a school attended by many pupils whose home language is German (and mentioned in Hoffmeister's[162] 1977 report on the language situation in that region):

Article 5 — General Discipline
French must be the usual language of all pupils, in their games
and their conversations, in the playground and in the buildings,
as well as on the school buses.
(Translated from the French)

Generally, this sort of antagonism seems to be based on the mistaken belief that the children's acquisition of, and competence in the majority language, and hence their overall level of participation in school affairs will be improved by outlawing the language of the home. Besides not being supported by research evidence, this view again entirely ignores the harmonious functioning of the family unit. In such cases firm action should be taken by parents to protect the interests of their children.

From all this it would appear to be essential that health workers and teachers who have to deal with children from bilingual homes should have basic, factual information about bilingualism incorporated into their training programmes.

In this study both Thomas and Frank have had the good fortune to encounter only teachers who have simply accepted, usually even without comment, the fact that they also speak German. Perhaps their attitude may have been different had the children not been able to function linguistically as well as their monolingual English-speaking classmates. (Further details on the children's schooling are given on pages 134–137).

Relatives and Friends

There have been very few problems with monolingual English-speaking relatives and friends accepting the children's bilingualism, perhaps for the simple reason that both children are able to function linguistically in a way which is practically indistinguishable from that of their monolingual Australian-English-speaking peers. These relatives and friends accept good-naturedly the children's use of German to their father in their presence, and occasionally ask, often teasingly, for an English translation, which is usually given readily and with good humour, e.g.:

> Thomas (5;2,0) and Frank (3;3,8) are talking to their paternal grand-mother who, not feeling well, is resting in bed. Unfortunately, they begin to squabble and Frank cries. The father intervenes.
> **Father** (to Frank): Wein nicht in Omas Schlafzimmer. *(Don't cry in Grandma's bedroom.)*
> (Frank stops crying.)
> **Grandmother** (amused by his reaction): What did your Dad say to you?
> **Frank**: He said, "Don't cry in here."
> **Thomas**: He said in German (speaking very slowly and distinctly): Wein nicht in Omas Zimmer.
> **Grandmother**: And what does that mean?
> **Thomas**: That means, "Don't cry in Grandma's room."

Sometimes a translation is forthcoming unsolicited when the children remember that someone present will not have understood something in German and it is wished to include him or her in the conversation, e.g.:

> Frank (3;7,22) informs his father of the fate of a biscuit he has just dropped and then repeats his statement in English for the benefit of a great-aunt:
> **Frank** (to father): Das hat kaputtgegehen. *(That breaked.)* (Then immediately to his great-aunt): Dot, that did broke to pieces.

Usually the parents make an effort to prevent a monolingual speaker of English, who is participating in a conversation with the family, from being excluded from those sections of the conversation conducted in German. Being used to the linguistic situation in their own family, the children may forget that the German segments of their conversation are not intelligible to others present. If this happens, either parent will briefly inform the English-speaker about what has been said, e.g.:

> Thomas (6;1,20) is watching an aunt breastfeeding her baby daughter.
> **Aunt** (to Thomas): Madeline's having her tea.

Thomas: Oh. (Looks on with great interest, then turns to his father): Ich will etwas zu trinken, Bert. *(I want something to drink, Bert.)*
Father (amused, to aunt): He wants something to drink, too, Maree.
Aunt (laughing): Does he?
Thomas (to father): Ich will schwarzen Johannisbeersaft. *(I want black-currant juice.)*
Father: Okay. *(All right.)* (To aunt): He doesn't want milk, though, he wants blackcurrant juice.

Or the children may be reminded by a parent that someone present cannot understand German and be asked to repeat or explain something in English, e.g.:

Thomas (5;1,12) is questioning his father about a childhood incident involving a tiger snake. Two relatives with no knowledge of German are present:
Father: . . . und ich bin durch die Brombeeren gegangen, und plötzlich habe ich etwas gehört. Ich habe mich umgekuckt, und da war eine große Tigerschlange . . . sie hat mich gejagt. (. . . *and I was walking through the blackberries and suddenly I heard something. I looked around and there was a big tiger snake . . . it chased me.)*
Thomas: Bist du sehr gesaust? *(Did you really zoom along?)*
Father: Ja, und ob! Erzähl jetzt mal Maree und Graeme, was passiert ist. Sie können nichts verstehen. *(Yes, I'll say! Now tell Maree and Graeme what happened. They can't understand anything.)*
Thomas (to relatives): Ah, ah, do you know, when Daddy was a little boy, he was going in the blackberries, when he heared something and he looked around and there was a big snake . . .

When the children were younger, it was necessary to formulate carefully such requests to help monolinguals. The children, whilst quite willing to do this, revealed that they did not really fully appreciate the difficulties monolinguals had in following German conversations. This is clearly illustrated in the following incident which occurred when Thomas was aged 3;11,28. Walking around the town with his father and a visiting uncle, he chattered away in German to his father and in English to his uncle. The father would tell the uncle what Thomas said in German but occasionally he would suggest that Thomas do such explaining himself. Passing a paint factory, the father explained to Thomas what was manufactured there, and seeing the uncle's puzzlement, asked Thomas to explain:

Father: Sag Peter, was man in dieser Fabrik macht. *(Tell Peter what they make in this factory.)*
Thomas: Paint, Peter.

This remark startled the uncle and only added to his puzzlement since he had understood none of the remarks preceding it. Thomas was simply answering the German question in English in the same way he would do to his mother (who, however, would have understood the preamble!)

To have elicited a more intelligible explanation in English, the father should have phrased his request in the following manner: "Sag Peter, daß man in dieser Fabrik Farbe macht." *(Tell Peter they make paint in this factory.)* Thomas would have reproduced in English the information of the question saying: "Peter, they make paint in this factory."

The various procedures described above appear to be an effective way of keeping monolingual listeners informed and preventing possible disharmony in such interactions. The only other solution would be for the children and the father to speak English to each other on such occasions, as Leopold[99] did with his daughter Hildegard when monolingual visitors were present. However, this would mean a fairly drastic reduction in the children's contact with German, especially during school holidays and as the children acquire playmates who visit regularly. It could also perhaps have the unfortunate effect of giving the children the impression that the speaking of German was something to be ashamed of and concealed.

Sometimes, being so accustomed to the situation prevailing within the family, where everyone understands both German and English, one of the parents, too, may forget that those present do not understand the German parts of a conversation. This usually occurs in relaxed, informal situations with relatives or friends. In the following incident, Frank (aged 5;3,24) comes out of his bedroom to inform his father that he cannot get to sleep because a mosquito is buzzing around his head. As his father goes off to dispatch the offending insect, his mother comments on Frank's predicament to a sister-in-law, her comment, however, assuming that her sister-in-law has understood the exchange between Frank and his father:

Frank: Bert, es gibt eine Mücke, und ich kann nicht schlafen. *(Bert, there's a mosquito and I can't sleep.)*
Father: Oh, ich komme. *(Oh, I'm coming.)*
Mother (to sister-in-law): He can't sleep when there's one in his room.
(The sister-in-law looks decidedly puzzled, understandably, since she has no idea what is being referred to. The father has overheard from the next room.)
Father (to mother): She won't know what you're talking about.
Mother (suddenly realizing what has happened): Oh, I'm sorry, Maree, I always think if I can understand everyone else can! Frank said he can't sleep because there's a mosquito in his room.

Sister-in-law (amused): Oh.

Of course, Thomas and Frank have been fortunate in that practically all relatives and family friends, most of whom are monolingual English-speakers, have been sympathetic to their acquisition and use of German. Such favourable, or at least non-antagonistic, attitudes certainly make it easier for both parents and children to establish and maintain a minority language in the immediate family. Opposition and negative reactions from relatives and friends with whom a family has regular contact could have a very damaging effect on the parents' resolve to continue raising their children bilingually and also, of course, on the children's confidence and desire to use the minority language.

A rather sad example of this is given in a recent article by Sønder-gaard.[163] A native speaker of Danish, he and his wife, whose native language is Finnish, failed in their attempt to raise their son bilingually in Denmark. There are several reasons why this attempt failed, with Søndergaard himself considering relatives' negative attitude one of the most decisive:

> ". . . during the whole experiment the parents were under sev-ere pressure from (monolingual Danish) members of the family who maintained that the boy would suffer, perhaps permanently, from this double acquisition of language."

Unfortunately, Søndergaard did not feel confident about countering this opposition:

> "It was difficult to resist this (pressure), because we could not consult any expert on bilingualism, and because at that time we did not know any families where bilingual children were being brought up."

This writer has found in the few cases where relatives and friends have expressed doubts about the advisability of the children's bilingualism, that a discussion of what is involved, including some reference to the research evidence on infant bilingualism, allays most of these doubts. Their doubts are really a fear of the unknown, but once they receive some sort of comprehensible explanation, much of the mystery, and consequently also the concern, disappears.

Playmates

Since about age 3;8, Thomas has, on the whole, been very much aware that playmates would not understand conversations between his father and himself, or between his father and his brother, and has usually mentioned this to his playmates when they first encounter a verbal exchange in German, as if to forestall any bewilderment on their part. For example, Thomas (age 6;1,20) is playing with a young cousin whom he seldom sees. His father approaches carrying his shoes:

> **Father**: Hier sind deine Schuhe, Ernie. *(Here are your shoes, Ernie.)*
> **Thomas**: Danke schön, Bert. *(Thanks, Bert.)* (Turns to cousin): Becky, do you know what language I talk to my father?
> **Cousin**: No.
> **Thomas**: It's German.

This awareness that few people of their acquaintance understand or speak German has been present in both children from about age 2;0. German was obviously classified by them even then as a language to be spoken only to their father, except in exceptional circumstances. In Thomas's case, this assessment of the division of the two languages was temporarily upset when he was aged 3;8. At that time he was enrolled in a German kindergarten in Melbourne which ran for two and a half hours on Saturday mornings. He was surprised to find that there were other children who could understand German. He did have several playmates before he started at the German kindergarten, all of whom he addressed only in English. But now he seemingly began to equate children he did not know with his new acquaintances at the German kindergarten, that is, children capable of understanding German. Thus, when an acquaintance of his mother's visited her with two monolingual English-speaking children, Thomas immediately began talking to them in German, much to their bewilderment. His mother had to explain to him that the children could not understand German. From then on he endeavoured to speak to them only in English, although he did still occasionally inadvertently switch to German. However, he would then remember almost immediately and quickly give an English translation, e.g.:

> **Thomas**: Das ist ein kaputtes Rad — that's a broken wheel.

He subsequently distinguished carefully between children at the German kindergarten and other children.

If a monolingual child is playing with Thomas or Frank and the father wishes to include the friend directly in his remarks, he usually gives the message in German and English, e.g.:

The father sees Thomas (6;11) and Frank (5;0) with a friend looking at the web of a dangerous redback spider.

Father (to Thomas and Frank): Faßt die Spinne doch nicht an! *(Don't touch the spider, will you?)* (To friend): Don't touch the spider, will you, Shane?

If the father does not do this and Thomas considers that something he says is also relevant in some way to his monolingual playmates, he will supply them with an explanation in English. For example, the father catches sight of Thomas (7;0,1), Frank and a friend Shane, playing on the roadway in front of their house and calls them back:

Father: Das ist zu gefährlich. Spielt doch hier auf dem Rasen, sonst müßt ihr reinkommen. *(That's too dangerous. Play here on the lawn or else you'll have to come inside.)*
Thomas (to Shane): If we go on the road again we have to go in.

Even when the information does not affect a playmate directly, Thomas tends to keep him or her informed, particularly if it is a close friend, e.g.:

Father (to Thomas) (7;3,3): Ernie, ich muß nochmal schnell zum Laden runterfahren. Ich habe vergessen Saft zu kaufen. *(Ernie, I just have to drive down to the shop again. I forgot to get some juice.)*
Thomas: Okay, Bert. Tschüß. *(Okay, Bert. See you.)*
Father (getting into car): Tschüß. *(See you.)*
Thomas (to Shane): My dad's going back down the shop to get some juice for us. He forgot it the first time.

If a friend asks out of curiosity what has been said because no English explanation has been forthcoming from the father or Thomas, Thomas happily explains, e.g.:

Thomas (7;3,8) is playing in a neighbour's yard and his father calls to him through the fence to tell him that he will be gone for a few minutes.
Father: Ernie, ich fahre schnell mal zur Post. Ich bin gleich wieder da. Okay? *(Ernie, I'm just going to duck down to the post-office. I'll be right back. All right?)*
Thomas: Ja, Bert. *(Yes, Bert.)*
12-year-old neighbour (who has never heard the father speak German before): What did your Dad say?
Thomas: He said he's going to the post-office. (And then explaining with a certain amount of pride.) But you wouldn't understand because he said it in German.
Neighbour: In German? Can you speak German?
Thomas: Yes. Frank can, too.
Neighbour: Say something in German for me.

Thomas: All right: Mein Vater spricht Deutsch. *(My father speaks German.)*
Neighbour: What's that mean? . . .

Frank has not been as conscious of the fact that playmates will find the use of German, initially at least, strange and he rarely attempts any explanation, although he will translate important information which obviously affects him and his playmate, e.g.:

Father (to Frank (4;10,9) who is playing with a friend): Frankie, sag Shane auf Wiedersehen. Wir fahren jetzt zum Strand. *(Frankie, say goodbye to Shane. We're going to the beach now.)*
Frank (to Shane): See you, Shane. We're going to the beach.

However, in the excitement of play, Frank is inclined to forget that his friends cannot follow what is said in German, e.g.:

Frank (5;3,26) is excitedly telling his father about an incident involving his friend, Shane, and another boy, Fred. (For comment on quotational switching, see pp. 98ff.)
Frank: . . . Und Shane hat zu Fred gesagt: *(And Shane said to Fred:)* What d'you want? Und Fred hat gesagt: *(And Fred said:)* Do you want to come out and play? Und Shane hat ,,Nein!" gesagt. *(And Shane said "No!")*
Shane (who has been listening attentively): Who did?
Frank (somewhat bewildered): You did, Shane, remember?
Shane (uncertainly): Yeah.

This situation is understandable, because this particular friend, Shane, had by this stage been an almost daily visitor to the family's home for eight or nine months since their move from Victoria to New South Wales. Frank at least was beginning to regard him practically as one of the family. This and possibly also the fact that Shane frequently seemed to (or pretended to) understand much of what was said in German, caused Frank often to forget to offer an explanation, even when he was not excited, e.g.:

Father: Hast du meine Schlüssel gesehen, Frankie? *(Have you seen my keys, Frankie?)*
Frank (5;5,7): Nein. *(No.)* (To friend): Did you, Shane?
Shane: No.
(Both children return to their game. It is very doubtful that Shane understood the father's question to Frank in this case.)

Shane's initial reaction to the use of German, his first close contact with a language other than English, was one of surprise and curiosity. It took him quite some time to accept that Thomas and Frank were "Australians":

> **Thomas** (6;7,13) (to his mother): Shane's asked me a hundred times where I come from and when I tell him Tasmania he wants me to say Tasmanian words for him.

It was apparent that Shane, who only vaguely knew where Tasmania was, thought that the language used by Thomas and Frank with their father was that spoken in Tasmania. Thomas's reaction to this naiveté about language was also interesting. He had just moved from a neighbourhood where many of the neighbours spoke a language other than English and where a quarter of his class at school did not speak English with their parents. In fact his best friend at school had been a girl who spoke Greek with her parents. She had taught Thomas some Greek phrases and he had reciprocated with some German ones. Finding himself now in a very monolingual English-speaking environment, it was difficult for him to reconcile himself to the fact that few children knew much about any language but (Australian) English:

> **Thomas** (6;7,13) (to his mother): Shane doesn't really understand about languages. He thinks they speak another language in America, like French. He doesn't know they just speak English with a few different words.

Shane quickly adapted to the linguistic situation in the family and was soon able occasionally to deduce the sense of much that was said from the context, e.g.:

> The father joins in a war game which Frank, Thomas and Shane are playing and pretends that he has taken over Frank's fort (=bedroom). The children plot his removal.
> **Shane** (holding a toy tank): I'll destroy your dad.
> **Frank** (5;4,0) (smiling): Bert, Shane wird dich zerstören. *(Bert, Shane's going to destroy you.)*
> **Father**: Mich zerstören?! *(Destroy me?!)*
> **Shane**: Yeah! PCHIU! (Shoots at father.)

Once when the children and Shane were playing with a toy soldier set and Shane stated that he wanted to be the German army, Thomas and Frank (6;11 and 5;0 respectively) insisted that he could not be because he did not speak German. Shane, however, was undaunted:

> **Shane**: Well, you tell me what to say, then.
> **Thomas**: Okay. For "Fire!" you say, "Feuer!"
> **Shane**: Feuer!

Thomas: That's good, Shane.
Shane: How do I say "Stick 'em up!"
Frank: Hände hoch!

Thomas and Frank were impressed by Shane's ability to pronounce very accurately the few phrases they gave him and he earned the right to play the part of the German army in the ensuing battle.

Occasionally the children have been observed teasing monolingual playmates by exploiting their non-knowledge of German, but such instances are rare and fortunately are quite without malice, e.g.:

Thomas (7;3,13) is listening to a German story, ALI BABA UND DIE VIERZIG RÄUBER *(Ali Baba and the Forty Thieves)* in the lounge room when Shane knocks at the back door. Thomas goes to let him in.
Thomas: Hi! My Dad and me are listening to a story on cassette. Do you want to hear it too?
Shane: Yeah.
Thomas (to father): Bert, Shane will die Geschichte auch hören. *(Bert, Shane wants to hear the story, too.)*
Father: Aber sie ist auf deutsch. *(But it's in German.)*
Thomas (a little sheepishly): Ich wollte ihn nur ein bißchen necken, Bert. *(I just wanted to tease him a bit, Bert.)*

This type of teasing is carried out only with some close friends or relatives, in other words only with people the children know intimately and who they know can take and appreciate a joke.

Thomas began using German as a means of teasing when he was aged 3;4,29. Realizing that a visiting uncle, who was good-natured and with whom he enjoyed skylarking, knew no German, he quickly exploited the situation to amuse himself at the uncle's expense. On one occasion he showed his uncle a book in German on foxes:

Thomas (smiling mischievously): This would be a good book for you, Graeme. This is the page Frankie likes. (He points to a picture showing a fox outside a fowl house and "reads" the commentary.) Fuchs kann nicht rein. Bauer hat Tor abgeschlossen. *(Fox can't get in. Farmer locked gate.)* (Then, highly amused by the trick he has played on his uncle, he kindly translates for him.) Fox can't get in. Farmer shut gate.
Uncle (ruffling Thomas's hair): You tricked me, didn't you?
Thomas (gleefully): Yes!

He continued this sort of teasing when his paternal grandmother came for a month's visit when he was 3;7. When she asked him whether he would like her to read him a story, he would often bring out a German book, knowing full well she could read no German, chuckling audibly in anticipation of the effect this trick would have on her:

> **Thomas**: Grandma, can you read me this book?
> **Grandma**: All right. (Opening book, feigning annoyance): Oh! It's in German! You know I can't read German, you little hound! Get me an English one.
> (Thomas giggles with delight, knowing his grandmother's anger is not at all genuine. The game is repeated on many occasions, providing him [and his grandmother] with much merriment.)

Fantini[124] mentions that his children Mario and Carla also amused themselves in a similar way: "To tease their grandparents, they rattled off words in Spanish."

Peer group pressure

In certain situations it does sometimes happen that bilingual children come in for teasing or aggression from monolingual children of their own age because they speak another language with their mother and/or father. This could cause sensitive children some anguish or even make them resentful of their home language. Mike and Marjukka Grover,[164] the parents of two Finnish-English bilingual children living in England, make, in a letter to the JOURNAL OF MULTILINGUAL AND MULTICULTURAL DEVELOPMENT, the following valid points on this subject:

> "All children will be teased by their peers and especially when they stand out from the group — 'four-eyes', 'carrot top', or after an accident, 'smelly pants' are all common. But if in the case of bilingualism children can be brought to understand that they have something that other children do not and that teasing is very often the manifestation of jealousy, then that is a large step in the right direction."

The realization that being bilingual *is* something special and an achievement to be proud of is a significant weapon against any antagonism from peers. If necessary, suggestions could also be given to the children of more practical ways to counter such teasing: a comment such as "Can you only speak *one* language?!", uttered in a suitable tone of disbelief, is usually quite an effective counter-attack.

However, Thomas's and Frank's experiences would suggest that most monolingual English-speaking children are not hostile to their knowing and using another language but simply very curious because it is something outside their own immediate experience. If parents, and particularly teachers, took time to satisfy this curiosity by giving even a brief, simple explanation, this would help monolingual children to realize that speaking two languages is nothing unnatural and nothing to be ridiculed.

Use of the "wrong" language

It is very rare that either child addresses a monolingual English-speaker in German, besides for the purpose of teasing as mentioned above. When this does happen, he is usually either very excited or has just broken off a German conversation and has become momentarily linguistically disoriented. The mistake is realized after a few words, e.g.:

> Thomas (5;1,23) is pretending to dig a ditch in the bedroom and is most anxious that no-one opens the door and disturb his game. His grandmother half-opens the door and he rushes to close it and prevent her coming in.
> **Thomas**: Niemand soll reinkommen! *(No-one is to come in!)* Nobody is allowed to come into this place because there's a big hole here!

Such momentary false language starts invariably occur when addressing people with whom he is completely at ease and who have demonstrated a complete acceptance of his bilingualism. In a similar vein, Fantini[165] reports that his children, who speak Spanish to both parents, use English appropriately to English-speakers, but if they are on especially intimate terms with an English-speaker, they are inclined to switch intermittently to Spanish.

Another factor which can cause children to use the wrong language is that the monolingual English-speaker is not directly visible and they are acting on suggestions given by their father in German, e.g.:

> Frank (4;2,25) wishes to fetch his toy guitar from a bedroom occupied by his aunt and uncle. He reports to his father how his first timid attempt has failed:
> **Frank**: Ich habe gesagt — ich habe das in Englisch gesagt: Darf ich reinkommen? — und sie haben das Tür nicht aufgemacht. *(I said — I said it in English — "Can I come in?" — and they didn't open the door.)*
> **Father**: Sag: Kann ich meine Gitarre holen? *(Say: Can I get my guitar?)*
> **Frank** (goes and calls through the bedroom door): Kann ich meine Gitarre holen? *(Can I get my guitar?)*
> **Father**: Auf englisch. *(In English.)*
> **Frank**: Ah, ah, I want to get — can I get my guitar?

In a face-to-face situation the choice of the wrong language would be much more unusual.

Both children have also experienced difficulties when making letter cassettes with their father to send to monolingual relatives. The fact that they are facing a microphone and not the actual people they are addressing, and thus receiving no response to their remarks, together with the presence of their father, often offering advice, makes it difficult for them to remember to speak only English, e.g.:

> **Father**: Komm mal her, Tom. Wir machen eine Kassette für Oma. *(Come here, Tom. We'll make a cassette for Grandma.)*
> **Thomas** (4;4,3) (holding microphone): Guten Tag. *(Hullo.)*
> **Father**: Ah, ich glaube, es wäre besser, wenn du Englisch sprechen würdest. Okay? *(Ah, I think it would be better if you spoke English. All right?)*
> **Thomas**: Hullo. How're you?
> **Father**: Grüß auch die anderen. *(Say hullo to the others, too.)*
> **Thomas**: Guten Tag, Marie — (2.5 second pause) — hullo, Maree, hullo, Grandad . . . . How are you? Ah, Timothy gave a tractor to us. See! (Holding the toy tractor up to the microphone) . . .

It is the lack of response rather than lack of visibility which seems to be the deciding factor in this type of failure to use the right language. In similar circumstances, but talking instead on the telephone, both children do not depart from the language appropriate to the person they are talking to, even when their father is present and suggesting things they could say. Interestingly, by their fifth birthdays both boys were able to switch into English to address non-present monolinguals on tape, undistracted by their father's presence and his making suggestions in German.

The Children and German-English Bilinguals

Although the children's contact with native speakers of German is sporadic, they have no difficulty in communicating with them in German, once they have overcome initial shyness. The nature of the first encounter with a person is crucial as far as determining which language will be used with that person on that first occasion and in the future. The children's initial shyness and reticence, for instance, are usually interpreted by German native speakers as an inability to understand or speak German (despite assurances from the parents to the contrary), and they immediately switch to English. However, once a person speaks to either child in English, particularly in an initial encounter, that person is classified as an English-speaker and, from that moment on, will most likely always be addressed in English.

The importance of the language used by an interlocutor in an initial interaction with the children can be seen in the following example. At age 4;1,11 Thomas first met M, a Swedish-German-English trilingual. He had been told in advance by his father that M could speak German well and spoke this language with her husband. She addressed Thomas in German only, and he responded in the same language. Eight months later, at age 4;10,19, he saw her for the second time. On this occasion M spoke to him in English, but he replied in German.

M.: Why did you get the day off?
Thomas: Because, ah, weil, weil ich nicht im Kindergarten bin. *(Because, ah, I'm not at kindergarten.)*

At first he begins to answer in the language he is addressed in, but then the pull of M's classification as a German-speaker proves stronger. Elwert[166] reports similar personal experiences. For instance, a German nurse-maid, engaged expressly to impart German to him and his sister in Italy, made the mistake of addressing them first in Italian:

> "By doing this she was classified by us as one of those persons one spoke Italian to. And, having got used to this, it would have seemed to us unnatural and affected to speak another language with her."
> (Translated from the German)

Even as an adult Elwert always preferred to speak to a person in the language in which they had had their first conversation.

The language used by interlocutors to the parents in the presence of the children need not be the language used between the interlocutors and the children. For example, even if a person addresses the father in English and receives English back, but speaks to the children in German, as is the case with M mentioned above, they seemingly do not regard this as anything out of the ordinary and are quite happy to communicate with that person in German. Actually, such a situation would in any case be little different from that already existing within the family.

Unfortunately, the children have had no contact at all with monolingual speakers of German. All the native speakers of German they meet have some proficiency in English. Many of these speakers incorporate numerous lexical transfers from English in their German, and/or they make frequent switches from one language to the other, a situation not unusual where there is language contact. Clyne,[167] for example, found that switching to English in the middle of a stretch of German discourse — and often in mid-sentence — occurred in the speech of thirty-six out of fifty pre-war immigrants in

Australia. Ironically, Thomas and Frank seem to classify such speakers as not proper speakers of German and, consequently, English is the language chosen for conversing with them. Fantini[165] similarly notes that his bilingual son, Mario, showed intolerance of language mixing by Mexican-American peers in a Texas kindergarten. Because, in his judgement, they did not speak Spanish convincingly, he spoke to them solely in English. (However, in a subsequent article Fantini[168] reports that by age 7;0, Mario had undergone a change in attitude: "If his interlocutors switched or mixed codes, he did likewise even though he normally maintained a rigid separation of his languages.")

Interestingly, in both cases it is the dominant language of the community which is chosen by the children when they consider an interlocutor's fluency inadequate. In the present study this occurs even when an interlocutor's English shows great phonological, lexical and syntactic deviations from the norm. There are several probable reasons for this. Firstly, their father's German, virtually their only model for this language, contains practically no lexical transfers from English. Secondly, both children are accustomed to encountering people from a variety of ethnic backgrounds (e.g. in many local shops) whose English deviates often considerably from Australian English. Thirdly, the television programmes, particularly the American children's series "Sesame Street", have influenced the children's acceptance of deviant English. Some of the characters in this show, particularly Cookie Monster, speak a type of English which deviates either phonologically and/or syntactically from that of native speakers of (American) English. The result of this continual exposure to deviant varieties of English is that they are tolerated by the children, whereas deviant forms of German are not.

Ronjat's[169] son, Louis, showed a more adverse reaction than any of the children already mentioned. He was upset by anyone who addressed him in an imperfect form of either of his languages when he knew that the person spoke the other language better. At age 2;3, for instance, Louis showed great distrust of a German visitor who addressed him in heavily accented French and also in German. Almost a whole day of urging was needed before he would talk nicely to the man. If, however, people were reasonably competent in one or both of his languages, he was quite willing to speak it with them. At age 3;7, for example, when addressed alternatively in French and German by a friend of the family, he answered her in the same way without showing any surprise or embarrassment. The crucial difference in this case was that this particular person spoke both languages approximately equally well.

To date, in the present study, only one exception to Thomas's and Frank's non-acceptance of a deviant form of German has occurred, namely when they met Mrs K who spoke German as a second language, fluently but with a distinct accent, and whose English was restricted to only a few words. A native speaker of Turkish, she worked in Germany for ten years before coming to Australia. Her daughter, Ilda, was in Thomas's class at school. Thomas's mother and Mrs K communicated in German, with the mother occasionally acting as an interpreter for Mrs K in dealings with school personnel. Although the children were somewhat puzzled by Mrs K's German:

Frank (4;0,9): Sie sagt komische Dinge. *(She says funny things.)*
Thomas (5;11,11): Sie spricht es komisch. In einem Akzent. *(She speaks it funny. In* [i.e. with] *an accent.)*

they soon realized that English was of no use when addressing her. They both obviously found the situation strange and were shy about speaking German to her, although they would eventually do so if urged by their mother. This strangeness was perhaps compounded by the fact that such occasions were the only times when they heard their mother conversing at length in German. When asked by his father to comment on his mother's German in such conversations, Thomas (5;11,11) said: "Das klingt ein bißchen komisch." *(That sounds a bit funny.)*, but then considerately added: "Aber es ist ziemlich gut, weil, ah, sie hat nicht viel geübt." *(But it's fairly good because, ah, she hasn't had much practice.)*

Despite the unusualness of the situation, the children were obviously willing to help the mother if she had difficulties with her German, e.g.:

Mrs K has just received from the school a letter which, being in English, she cannot read. The mother is translating it into German for her.
Mother: . . . und *(and)* — oh, ah — Thomas, how do you say "They'll let you know later on what's required"?
Thomas (6;4,2) (without hesitation): Sie werden dir später sagen, was man braucht. *(They'll tell you later what is needed.)*

Even when the sense of strangeness was compounded by the fact that the mother, caught up in a German conversation with Mrs K, occasionally addressed the children in German, they took it in their stride, e.g.:

The mother is talking with Mrs K about a proposed visit to the zoo the next day. Frank (4;0,8) interrupts to refer to a carton of flavoured milk, known as "Big M".
Frank: Mum, Mum — we bought a "Big M", but you forgot to buy a straw.

Mother: I know. I've got plenty at home.

(Mrs K laughs at Frank's earnest face.)

Mother (to Mrs K): Er hat gesagt, wir haben ein "Großes M" für morgen gekauft, aber wir haben diese Dinge vergessen — *(He said we bought a "Big M" for tomorrow but we forgot these things —)* (failing to recall the German for "straw", she demonstrates a sucking noise.)

Mrs K: Ja, ich weiß. *(Yes, I know.)*

Mother: — aber ich habe viele zu Hause. *(But I've got a lot at home.)* (Turns quickly to Thomas who is standing nearby listening): Thomas, wie heißen diese Dinge, die man braucht? *(Thomas, what are those things called that you need?)*

Thomas (5;11,0) (looking slightly amused): Ah, straws.

Mother: No, I mean in German, so Ilda's mother can understand.

Thomas: Ah, Trinkhalme. *(straws)*

When an English-speaker who knows some German tries out his or her German on the children, they are amused and pleased. Even a few words are viewed positively. But, unless the person can continue convincingly with the conversation in German, the children just treat it as a kind of game and fairly quickly revert to English, a language they consider the speaker to be more competent in. On such occasions Thomas and Frank tend to slow their rate of German speech and speak very distinctly, e.g.:

Grandfather (coming out of bedroom): Guten Morgen, Tom. *(Good morning, Tom.)*

Thomas (6;2,0) (smiling, always being impressed if his paternal grandfather uses one of about a dozen German phrases he knows, and answering slowly and clearly): Guten Morgen. Es ist schlechtes Wetter heute. *(Good morning. The weather's bad today.)*

Grandfather: I didn't understand that last bit.

Thomas: That means "The weather's bad today."

Grandfather: Yeah, it's not too good, is it?

Leopold[170] reports on a similar attitude of his daughter Hildegard (5;9,3):

> "My brother-in-law George, who knows very little German, insists on saying brief German sentences to her . . . She criticizes his defective German but always replies in German, as she does with the few other people who speak to her in German."

Ronjat's[169] son Louis was obviously distressed when confronted with such a situation. At age 3;4, for example, when a family friend, who had always spoken French to him, started to address him in rather primitive German, he refused to reply and turned his back on her. No amount of scolding by his maid could get him to answer the lady or shake hands with her as he normally would.

Fantini[165] shows that his son Mario's attitude changed with age:

". . . between his fourth and fifth years Mario met several individuals who had achieved varying degrees of fluency (in Spanish) through study. Yet because they did not speak Spanish convincingly, Mario went into English, despite their attempts to maintain conversation in Spanish."

But Fantini[168] reports that "by 7;0, Mario had learned to accept the attempts of others to speak to him in Spanish even if they lacked sufficient fluency and native pronunciation."

Kindergarten and school

Thomas began kindergarten at age 4;3, Frank at 3;4, both spending two hours three days a week in completely monolingual English speaking groups. Thomas became somewhat hesitant about speaking to his father, i.e. speaking German, in the kindergarten environment, but otherwise his year at kindergarten did not affect his willingness to speak German. Frank readily spoke German to his father at all times in the kindergarten. It was originally thought[171] that the age difference might explain the difference in the children's attitude towards speaking German at the kindergarten, since by age 4;3 Thomas was already developing an awareness that some people react unfavourably to the use of a language other than English in their presence. However, at age 5;7 Frank was still completely uninhibited about speaking German to his father whoever happened to be present. His beginning primary school in the preparatory class at age 5;3,27 did nothing to alter this situation. At age 5;2,29 Thomas began primary school in the preparatory class. This had an unexpected favourable effect on his bilingualism, since in his class there were a number of other bilingual children whom he heard speaking to their parents in the schoolyard in Greek, Turkish, Italian and Serbo-Croatian. He showed considerable interest in this and obviously took some pride in the fact that he, too, could speak a language other than English. His parents capitalized on the situation to portray bilingualism as something natural, but special. He showed no inhibitions about speaking German with his father in front of his classmates or teachers.

When Thomas was aged 6;5,12 the family moved interstate and he was enrolled at a school where he had some difficulty settling in and where he heard no other language but English. The trauma of the move and readjustment did temporarily affect the quality of his German (as discussed on pages 145–146), although he still freely spoke German to his father in the school precincts.

In some bilingual families, parents and children speak the language of the school when meeting in the school grounds and then switch to the other language once away from the school. This may be done for a variety of reasons, e.g. the school may be seen as a domain in which only the school language is appropriate; the children and/or parents may not wish to appear different from the other children and their parents; they may be apprehensive about the reactions of the other children or parents. The Dutch scholar Meijers,[246] in his book DE TAAL VAN HET KIND *(The Language of the Child)*, reports on a typical such situation involving some of his grandchildren:

> "One daughter, married to an Englishman, lives in England. In the home English is always spoken, to and of course also by the two children. The mother attaches importance to the children's also learning Dutch and they speak it pretty well, albeit with an English accent . . . In the home the children have no objections to Dutch when their mother speaks it to them. But the children have given her the emphatic instruction: 'Don't speak Dutch to us when you come to pick us up from school. The other kids think that's dumb.' "
> (Translated from the Dutch.)

However, if teachers and other children are tolerant of the use of other languages, it is unlikely that the children will feel uneasy or embarrassed about speaking to their parents in another language within the school precincts. If the parents use the language naturally and confidently in such situations, their children will be given the confidence to do likewise. From observation it would seem that the usual initial reaction of other children and teachers is one of interest and curiosity, which should be interpreted as such, that is, a natural inquisitiveness about something different, rather than a sign of hostility. (See also pp. 127ff. for further discussion of this point.)

The fact that their father speaks only German to them, has caused several minor dilemmas for both Thomas and Frank at school. One dilemma was at first hypothetical: out of curiosity the father asked Thomas (7;8,0) what he would do if his teacher asked the children in his class to write a letter to their father. He immediately recognized the predicament this would place him in, that is, as part of his school work the letter would need to be written in English, yet at the same time German should be used in a letter to his father, and he replied as follows:

Thomas: Ich weiß, Bert, ah, ich würde, ah, das in Englisch schreiben, und im Schulbus würde ich das in Deutsch schreiben. *(I know, Bert, ah, I'd, ah, write it in English and on the school bus I'd write it in German.)*

Six weeks later, however, this quandary became a reality. Thomas's teacher issued the children with a stencilled card which on its front cover had the message "Happy Father's Day" and a picture to be coloured in. The children were asked to think up and write appropriate greetings to their fathers on the inside of the card. At first Thomas wanted, and attempted, to leave the card blank so that he could fill it in later at home in German. (He did not think it would be acceptable to write in German in what was part of an English lesson.) But, being embarrassed about having to explain why he was not writing anything, he then wrote in pencil:

> To dear Dad
> Happy Father's Day
>   Thomas

However, when he arrived home, and before giving the card to his father, he carefully rubbed out this message and replaced it with the following:

> Lieber Bert
> Alles Gute zum Vatertag
>   Ernie XXX
> *(Dear Bert*
> *All the best for Father's Day*
>   *Ernie XXX)*

It is probable that Thomas would still have been faced with a difficulty if he and his father spoke English to each other but still had their respective nicknames, Ernie and Bert, since this, too, would clash with the expected "normal" forms of address between a son and his father.

As it turned out, Thomas's teacher proved to be very understanding when the incident was mentioned to her, making the comment, "He could have written it in German, it wouldn't have mattered."

To date, Frank's only moment of language conflict occurred on a school "Open Day", that is, when parents could visit their children's classroom and observe and help them with their work. As part of the activities, Frank's teacher wished the children to tell their parents a short story to go with a picture they had coloured in; the parents were then to write down the story underneath the picture:

Frank (5;10,17) (to mother): Can you write it for me, Mum?

Mother (holding Frank's 6-month-old sister): Oh, I'm sorry, Frank, I think I'll have to take Katrina out and change her. But Daddy will be able to help you.

Frank (looking worriedly at his father): Aber das muß in Englisch sein. *(But it has to be in English.)*

Mother: Yes, but you tell Daddy and he'll write it down in English for you.

Frank (looking relieved, he hands his father a pencil): Hier, Bert. *(Here, Bert.)* (He begins the story): Das Kaninchen hat spazierengegehen . . . *(The rabbit went for a walk . . .)*

The father then simply wrote down in English what Frank dictated to him in German, a procedure which satisfied Frank and resolved the problem. Otherwise he chatted unconcernedly in German with his father about his schoolwork.

When problems do arise at school because of a child's bilingualism, problems which cannot be resolved in discussion between parent(s) and child, it is important that parents get in touch with the child's teacher, as usually a solution can be worked out. Otherwise the child may begin seeing his or her bilingualism as a burden rather than as an advantage.

6 Further possible problems in establishing bilingualism

Children's reluctance to speak the home language

In trying to establish or maintain bilingualism in a family, the parents may at certain times become discouraged and be tempted to abandon the attempt. Such discouragement may come from outside the family (e.g. from teachers or medical personnel who may attribute any speech difficulties or learning problems to a child's bilingualism) (for a discussion of this, see pp. 113ff) or from within the family itself (e.g. through conflict caused by the parents unrealistically expecting the child to be not only bilingual but equally proficient in both languages, usually the language which is not the dominant language of the community). Discussions with Australian families, in which attempts to bring up the children bilingually have failed, indicate that it is mainly these periods when a child avoids using the language other than English, or speaks it with large numbers of lexical transfers from English, which persuade the parents that the attempt is futile. In addition, the child's English may contain a considerable number of transferences from the other language, e.g.:

> **Frank** (3;5,10) (to mother): Peter's dog Smoochie has got a GEBROCHENES BEIN. *(broken leg)*

In the face of such language mixing, the parents may fear that the child is acquiring neither language properly. This anxiety is understandable, but provided the parents persist with raising the child bilingually, such periods of language mixing should, if not disappear, be reduced to a minimum.

In some cases it may not be the mixing of the two languages which causes concern and doubts, but the failure of one of the languages to be used at all for some time. For example, Walburga von Raffler-Engel[172] reports that she addressed her son in Italian, whilst her American husband spoke to him in English, but that the boy at first spoke only Italian. He initially had only a passive knowledge of English and did not utter his first English words until age 2;8, but from then on used both languages, rewarding parental persistence. This demonstrates the advisability of parents' not giving up, if, at the onset of speech, or for some time thereafter, a child uses predominantly only one language. Continuing to talk to a child in the language he or she is reluctant to speak, will ensure that he or she is acquiring a passive knowledge of that language which will, in most cases, eventually be activated.

In the present study, both children have gone through short periods where they have shown reluctance to speak German to their father, preferring to address him in English. An analysis of the taped corpus reveals that at the age of 3;5,3 the percentage of all-English utterances used by Thomas to his father was a quite high 58%. Only 25% of utterances were completely German, while 17% were a mixture of English and German. The percentage of German words (tokens) directed at his father on this 45-minute tape was a mere 28%. The same problem did not arise with his speaking of English, most probably because virtually all linguistic contact at that stage, apart from with his father, was with English-speakers. At virtually the same age (3;5,0), for example, 95.1% of the utterances Thomas directed at his mother were completely English, 2.4% completely German, and 2.4% a mixture of English and German. 97.8% of words (tokens) spoken to his mother were English. When communicating with English-speaking monolinguals the percentage of English words used was even higher.

Frank's resistance to German occurred at around age 2;7, when his utterances to his father contained only 40.3% German words. But, as can be seen in Table 1 on page 142, by age 3;0, this percentage had increased to 95.1%, and by age 4;0 to 98.5%, below which it has never since dropped. Like Thomas, Frank has shown no resistance to speaking English; from age 2;6 to age 5;7, for instance, the *lowest* percentage of English words recorded when addressing his mother was 98.5%.

The figures just mentioned for Thomas's German at age 3;5,0 and for Frank's German at age 2;7,6 do not really give a true picture of their active ability in the language at those times, i.e. they show what they *did* produce, not what they *could* produce. The figures are more an indication of their willingness to speak German. This could be seen when their father pretended not to understand something they said to him in English. They then demonstrated that they were capable of producing predominantly German utterances:

Father: Und nun ist Schlafenszeit, Frankie. *(And now it's time for bed, Frankie.)*

Frank (2;7,5): Nein! *(No!)* I'm not going to bed.
Father: Was? *(What?)*
Frank: Ich geh nicht in Bett. *(I'm not going to bed.)*

Father (noticing Thomas searching in his toy box): Was suchst du? *(What are you looking for?)*
Thomas (3;5,3): A little pig.
Father: Was? *(What?)*
Thomas: Ein kleines Schwein. *(A little pig.)*

However, this period did mark the lowest point in the children's use of German. It is the father's impression that if he had relented at these points in time and spoken English to them, they would have been quite happy to have abandoned German. However, only a few months after these periods of resistance to German, judging from their adverse reactions when their father addressed them in English, they would have accepted a change to all-English communication with him only with some difficulty. It is also the father's impression that even if he had continued to speak German to Frank and Thomas but had not persisted in eliciting German responses from them they would have become receiving bilinguals only, with their knowledge of German confined to comprehension and their ability to speak the language limited. Such situations are not uncommon in immigrant families, where parents continue to address their children in the language of their country of origin but the children reply in the language of the new country. For example, Clyne's[247] 1968 investigation of seventy-four families with German-speaking parents and children either born in Australia or arriving in the country before the age of 5, showed that in fifty-six (75.7%) of the families the parents spoke only German to the children. Yet in only sixteen (28.6%) of these fifty-six families did the children speak only German to the parents. In twenty-seven (48.2%) the children spoke a mixture of English and German, and in thirteen (23.2%) the children always answered their parents in English. A similar tendency is revealed by the research of Smolicz and Harris[248] in 1976 into the linguistic behaviour of other immigrant groups in Australia: the percentage of Polish, Dutch, Italian and Greek-speaking parents using only their language to their children is considerably higher than the percentage of children responding in that language only.

When a child for some reason shows reluctance to speak the language of his parent(s) or begins to interlard his speech with numerous lexical items from the dominant language of the community, it would seem that the problem can be successfully overcome provided the parents are persistent, yet show understanding and good humour. In this, the child's personality obviously has to be taken carefully into account. It is important that the language does not assume any negative connotations for the child. With some children, for instance, to insist that they never resort to the dominant language of the community could cause frustration and resentment and have an adverse effect on their willingness to speak the other language. Instead, a child should be given every encouragement to speak the language and should be helped when his linguistic knowledge is not adequate to express his thoughts. When the child either consciously or unconsciously uses elements from the other language or, to avoid doing this, struggles to find an appropriate way of expressing himself, the parent(s) can casually supply the missing vocabulary item, help with an idiom, etc. If this is done in moderation it should not inhibit the child's desire to communicate. After a few gentle reminders of this kind the child will in most cases adopt the word or expression appropriate to the language in question. Of course, this will not always work immediately, and a particular word or expression may persist for some considerable time. For instance, at age 3;5 Thomas predominantly used English *her* instead of German *sie* and *ihr*. Five months later *her* was being used side by side with *sie* and *ihr*, e.g.:

Thomas (3;10,0): Warum HER gern singt? Hat SIE Musik für mich gemacht? *(Why her likes singing? Has she made music for me?)*

Isolated examples of *her* were still to be found in Thomas's German as late as age 3;11,7, but by 4;0,7 the word had finally disappeared. However, apart from such stubborn cases, most lexical transfers survived for only a very brief period.

As can be seen in Table 1, which is based on an analysis of the taped corpus, there was a steady increase in the percentage of German words Thomas spoke to his father, from a very low 28.0% at 3;5,3 to 59.0% at 3;5,22, 69% at 3;7,22, 74% at 3;8,8 and a very high 99.5% at 3;10,7. From 3;10,7 onwards the percentage of German words in Thomas's speech to his father has never gone below 98%. Table 1 also shows that the number of German lexical transfers present in his English to his mother has always been low. From age 3;10,7 he had about equal success in eliminating English words from his German as he did avoiding transferring German into his English. In the 17 month period from 3;10,7 to 5;3,6 Thomas used an average of 99.4% German words to his father and 99.6% English words to his mother.

It should be stressed that Table 1 shows only the degree to which the children used words from one language when speaking the other (discussed further under "lexical transference" on pp. 194–198). The transference of other features from one language to the other is examined on pp. 175ff.

TABLE 1

Age	THOMAS		FRANK	
	Addressing father Percentage of words in German	Addressing mother Percentage of words in English	Addressing father Percentage of words in German	Addressing mother Percentage of words in English
2;7			40.3	100.0
3;0			95.1	100.0
3;4			97.7	98.5
3;5,3	28.0	97.8		
3;5,22	59.0			
3;7,22	69.0			
3;8,8	74.0	99.5		
3;9	98.0	100.0		
3;10	99.5	99.5		
3;11	98.8	100.0	95.1	99.0
4;0	98.7	98.1	98.5	99.5
4;4	100.0	100.0	99.5	99.5
4;6	99.6	100.0	99.8	99.5
4;10	98.8	99.7	98.8	100.0
5;0	99.2	99.8	99.8	100.0
5;3	100.0	100.0	99.5	100.0

Thomas and Frank usually receive parental linguistic assistance gratefully, providing it is offered relatively unobtrusively. The children obviously wish to communicate with their father in German and naturally look to him for guidance when they are having difficulty expressing themselves. For example, at age 5;6,0, Thomas was showing his father how he could jump over a chair:

Thomas: Jetzt mache ich das — without tripping. *(Now I'll do that —)*

The tone of voice with which the switch into English was uttered was somewhat hesitant and uncertain, and, together with the slight break in the flow of speech, marked it as an "intruder". As he made the switch, he looked directly at his father, obviously seeking assistance. The difficulty Thomas has encountered here is not with vocabulary but with the syntactic construction required (which is different in German, literally "without to trip"). The conversation continued:

Father: Ohne zu stolpern. *(Without tripping.)*
Thomas: Hm, ich springe rüber, ohne zu stolpern. *(Hm, I'll jump over without tripping.)* (Satisfied, he proceeded to leap over the chair.)

The children's resorting to the other language in such predicaments is not discouraged, but when this happens both parents do ensure that they are provided with a suitable equivalent in the appropriate language. Nor are direct questions about vocabulary in the other language discouraged, e.g.:

> **Thomas** (3;9,22) (to mother): Dad drew me a — ah, what you say for LEUCHTTURM?
> **Mother**: Lighthouse.
> **Thomas**: He drew me a lighthouse.

Ronjat[173] states that he never supplied German vocabulary to his son with whom he spoke only French, since this would be an "infraction of the rule 'one person, one language'." When Louis (3;7) asks him how to say "lizard" in German so that he can tell his mother what they have seen on a walk, Ronjat does not give him the information.

Leopold[70] shows a similar attitude towards helping his daughter, Hildegard:

> "At first she did not know the names of the languages. 'How does Mama say it?' was her question for an English equivalent (*which, however, she could not wheedle out of me*)."

No such refusals of information are made in the present study because it is felt that this would not foster learning. The child could become caught up in a vicious circle if both parents adhered rigidly to this principle, making the obtaining of a term in one of the languages a very tedious process. Consequently, information is given to Thomas and Frank whenever requested, e.g.:

> Frank (4;9,30) has been questioning his father about any "wicked" things he did as a schoolboy and has listened to the somewhat embellished accounts with great amusement. He wishes to share his enjoyment with his mother who is in the next room.
> **Frank** (chuckling): Mum! Mummy! Hey, Daddy threw a snowball at the, Mummy, at the — (to father) was sagt man in Englisch? *(What do you say in English?)*
> **Father**: Headmaster.
> **Frank**: Ah. Mummy, Daddy threw a snowball at the headmaster.
> **Mother**: Oh, he didn't, did he?
> **Frank** (thrilled): Yeah!

At times, the children even seek assistance from their father with reading English, e.g.:

Thomas (5;9,10): Bert, ich brauche Hilfe. Was bedeutet s-o-n? (Spelt out in German) *(Bert, I need help. What does s-o-n mean?)*
Father: Son.
Thomas: [sʌn]
Father: Ja. *(Yes.)*
Thomas: Meinst du Sonne [zɔnə]? *(Do you mean sun?)*
Father: Nein, Sohn [zoːn]. *(No, son.)*
Thomas: Ah. Danke schön, Bert. *(Ah, thanks, Bert.)*

If their mother is not present, the children ask their father for explanations of unfamiliar English words they hear on the wireless or television or elsewhere. If they hear an unfamiliar expression in one language they may use the other to seek verification that they have correctly decoded it, e.g.:

Thomas (5;5,16): Warum hast du das benutzt? *(Why did you use that?)*
Father: Oh, nur zur Abwechslung. *(Oh, just for a change.)*
Thomas: For a change?
Father: Ja. *(Yes.)*

This sometimes happens even when the expression in question is clearly explained, e.g.:

Mother: In England there's a longer twilight than in Australia.
Thomas (6;8,1): What's that, Mum?
Mother: That's that sort of greyish, darkish time before it gets properly dark.
Thomas: Ah, DÄMMERUNG. *(dusk, twilight)*
Mother: Yes.

Leopold[98] reports on similar experiences with his daughter, Hildegard (8;0,6): "When she asks me for the meaning of an unfamiliar German word, which she does not do often, I give her as a rule not the English translation, but a simple explanation in German. Often she says then the more familiar English equivalent to show that she has understood."

Far from representing a danger to the maintenance of bilingualism, such requests for information demonstrate a desire on the part of the child to improve his or her knowledge of both languages, and as such they should be welcomed and every assistance given. These requests should be treated no differently from queries in and about one language (in fact, the type of request which would occur in a monolingual family), e.g.:

Frank (4;4,17) (searching for a toy bow and forgetting momentarily its name in German): Wo ist mein — ah — das Ding, das Indianer haben? *(Where's my — ah — the thing that Indians have?)*

Father (pointing): Da. *(There.)*
Frank (picking up the bow): Sag mir, wie das heißt, Bert, damit ich weiß. *(Tell me what it's called, Bert, so that I'll know.)*
Father: Oh, dein Bogen, Frankie. *(Oh, your bow, Frankie.)*
Frank (satisfied): Ah, mein Bogen. *(Ah, my bow.)*

Sometimes the parents anticipate such difficulties and supply the children with vocabulary which may be unfamiliar in the other language, e.g.:

Thomas (5;9,23): Ich werde Mutti sagen, was der Mechaniker gesagt hat. *(I'll tell Mum what the mechanic said.)*
Father: Okay. Lichtmaschine heißt "generator" auf Englisch. *(OK. "Lichtmaschine" is called "generator" in English.)*
Thomas: Ah, gut. *(Ah, good.)* (Said appreciatively. Runs to mother.) Mum, the mechanic said he has to fix the generator. It's broken.

Or if a child is discussing a subject in one language and is using vocabulary which it is felt he would not know in the other language, the parent with whom he speaks this other language will usually join in, using the vocabulary the child lacks. All this saves the child from a feeling of frustration which could lead him to avoid a particular topic in one language because he lacks the appropriate vocabulary, which is often just one crucial word.

In this study the significant effect which emotional factors can exert on a child's acquisition of bilingualism become apparent. As can be seen in Figure 1 on page 173, in a speech sample recorded at age 6;3, Thomas made 3.6 errors per 100 words in his German, yet in a speech sample taken at age 6;6 there was a sudden upsurge in the number of errors, an all-time high of 7.5 errors per 100 words of German being made. This special sample was taped approximately one month after the family had moved from Melbourne to Sydney. Although the whole family regretted having to make the move, it affected Thomas particularly. He missed his former friends and school greatly and had difficulty in adjusting to a much larger, more impersonal school where the other children unfortunately reacted aggressively to him as a newcomer. Since the move to Sydney had been made so that the father could take up new employment, Thomas seemed for a while to blame him for the unhappiness he had been plunged into:

Thomas (6;6,0) (agitatedly, after a day of bad experiences at school, to father): Warum hast du uns bloß zu dieser blöden, verflixten, verdammten Stadt gebracht? *(Why ever did you bring us to this stupid, damned, bloody town?)*

This time of upheaval and unhappiness clearly caused the decline in the accuracy of his German. The parents did as much as possible to help Thomas over this difficult period, for example by visiting his school and discussing the matter with his teacher (who proved very understanding and helpful), by giving him additional attention and sympathy at home, in short, by showing him that they understood his feelings and cared very much about his well-being.

These actions, plus the natural healing effect of the passing of time, helped him return to his normal cheery self quite quickly, so that one month later, at age 6;7, he was making only 3.5 errors per 100 words of German, having returned to his former accuracy. The whole experience demonstrates the more precarious position of a language relying on only one source of input and indicates the importance of a stable, secure environment for such language acquisition.

Effect of the father's not being a native speaker of German

The most unusual aspect of the case of bilingualism under study is that the father is not a native speaker of the language he is passing on to the children. This, expectedly, has certain disadvantages, but there are also some advantages.

The main disadvantage is that in certain areas the father does not feel as confident about vocabulary in German as he does in his native English. But in seven years fortunately only a few incorrect vocabulary items have been passed on to the children. If such errors are detected quickly they are easily eliminated. However, late detection can mean that the word or expression has already become firmly established and will be difficult to eradicate. For example, when Thomas was aged 3;10,14, his father discovered, much to his chagrin, that the word *Wellenblech* for "corrugated iron", which he and Thomas had been using for nine months and which, to make matters worse, was one of Thomas's favourite words, should in fact be *Wellblech*. He had forgotten that whilst compound nouns formed with *Welle* (=wave) normally began with Well*en* (e.g. *Wellenreiter*, "surfer", literally "wave rider"), they did not if the texture of materials was being described. It took much explanation and gentle persuasion before Thomas would accept *Wellblech*. After three days he would accept it as a synonym of his beloved *Wellenblech*, but still insisted adamantly:

Thomas (3;10,17): Ich sage *(I say)* Wellenblech!

Fortunately, this resolve was quickly forgotten, and he was soon using the correct *Wellblech* in his own speech, apparently unconcernedly. Just how firmly entrenched the form *Wellenblech* had been, however, was demonstrated some thirteen months later when Thomas recalled that he and his father had once said *Wellenblech*. However, it is some consolation to find documented in great detail in Clyne's[174] work that even native German speakers born in Germany and residing in Australia are often very uncertain about German vocabulary. For example, the following was heard in an interview on Radio 2EA, the multilingual radio station in Sydney:

> ". . . und wir haben den Hühnerstall aus CORRUGATED IRON gemacht." *(. . . and we made the chook-house out of CORRU-GATED IRON.)*

As Clyne[175] shows, second generation speakers consequently use many lexical and semantic transfers (see glossary or pp. 180–200 for explanations of these terms) as well as neologisms which they have heard in their parents' speech and which they believe to be German. A non-native speaker is perhaps more conscious of this danger and takes greater precautions to avoid it.

The other few incorrect forms passed on by the father were mainly minor pronunciation errors. These were words which he knew from reading but whose pronunciation he had not heard or learnt, e.g. *Kokosnuß* (=coconut), the first vowel of which he mistakenly pronounced as short [ɔ] instead of long [o:]. Fortunately, errors like this were promptly detected by checking in a dictionary in cases of doubt. The father then presented the children with the correct form in another conversation as soon as possible, explaining, if questioned, that he had unfortunately made a mistake and had pronounced the word wrongly when he had previously used it. Within a day or two the incorrect pronunciation would disappear from the children's speech. The children readily accepted that it was not possible for anyone, including their parents, to know what every word meant or how every word should be pronounced, be it in German or English. They knew from an early age that both parents frequently consulted books to obtain or verify information on various subjects. The following is a typical example:

Thomas (3;11,1): Was sagt du für WALLFLOWERS, Dad? Sagst du Wand-blumen? *(What do you say for "wallflowers", Dad? Do you say WANDBLUMEN?)* (A literal translation, *Wand*=wall, *Blumen*= flowers.)

Father (scarcely a gardening expert in any language, but doubting that such a literal translation would be correct): Ah, ich weiß nicht recht. Ich muß das mal nachschlagen. *(Ah, I don't really know. I'll just have to look that up.)* (He does so in a dictionary): Goldlack. *(Goldlack*, literally *gold varnish*, the German name for *wallflower*.)
Thomas: Goldlack.

The well-known German picture dictionary, DUDEN BILDWÖRTER-BUCH, proved to be a particularly invaluable aid to the father and because of its thousands of pictures and interesting information a favourite reading book of the children. There, at a glance, can be found the names of the most esoteric objects a child might ask about. For example, at age 4;4 Thomas, looking at a drawing his father had done for him of an electric train, wanted to know the name of the two poles which carry the electricity from the overhead power lines to the train:

Thomas: Wie heißen diese Stromdinge? *(What are these power things called?)*
Father (baffled, knowing this in neither German nor English): Oh, keine Ahnung. *(Oh, no idea.)*
Thomas: Ich hole unser Bildwörterbuch. *(I'll get our picture dictionary.)* (Does so.)
Father (finding the word): Stromabnehmer.

(Interestingly, the English equivalent could not be found in any dictionaries owned by the family and Thomas had to ask a train-driver the next day at the station to learn that the English word was *pantograph*.)

On another occasion, Thomas (5;8,10) persuaded his father to play cards with him. His father, who rarely plays cards in English, let alone in German, had to consult a dictionary to check on a few card-playing terms in German. Later, Thomas was telling his mother about the game:

Thomas: Mum, Daddy and me had a game of cards.
Mother: Did you? Was it good?
Thomas: Yes. Daddy needed a dictionary.
Mother: Did he? Why?
Thomas: Because he didn't know what everything's called in German.
Mother (feigning surprise): Dearie me.
Thomas (defensively): But he does now.

Another disadvantage of the father's being a non-native speaker of German is that he virtually represents the children's sole source of German; there are no German speaking relatives to provide linguistic support through regular contact with the children. The children are used to communicating in German with only one person, their father. His variety of German assumes, therefore, a much greater importance for the children than their mother's English, since they are constantly engaged in communication with other English speakers of various ages and speaking various types of English.

Although the children had sporadic contacts with other German speakers in their first five years, it became apparent that during that time they tended to look on German as a unique family possession. An encounter with someone who addressed them in German, particularly if unexpected, was usually greeted with amazement, amazement that someone else spoke "their" language. In the following example, Thomas (3;10,7) and his father are in a foreign-language bookshop looking at children's books in German. All the while Thomas chatters on excitedly in German about the various books and the view from the 9th floor window. Eventually he selects a book and his father gives him the money to pay for it.

> **Thomas**: Kann ich das allein kaufen? *(Can I buy this by myself?)*
> **Father**: Ja, sicher. Hier ist das Geld. Bezahl den Mann da drüben. *(Yes, sure. Here's the money. Pay that man over there.)*
> **Thomas** (to shop assistant): I'll have this book.
> **Shop assistant**: Hm. (Takes book and money, wraps it and hands it back to Thomas.) Sag "Danke". *(Say "thank you".)*
> **Thomas** (astonished, turns and calls out to his father): Dieser Mann kann Deutsch! *(This man can speak German!)*

Fantini[176] reports similar reactions from his children when a language is used which is unexpected for a given context, for example, when his daughter Carla overhears two men speaking Spanish on a bus in Albuquerque:

> **Carla** (to father): ¡Esos hombres están hablando en español! *(Those men are speaking Spanish!)*

Frank even became, for a time, quite possessive about German, as evidenced by his reaction at age 4;3,26 when his father told him that everyone spoke German in Germany:

> **Father**: Da sprechen all die Leute Deutsch. *(All the people speak German there.)*
> **Frank** (somewhat indignantly): Bert, sie sind Nachäffer! Das ist unsere Sprache! *(Bert, they're copycats. That's our language!)*

However, despite his indignation that the Germans were copycats for speaking German, an interesting and amusing point of view, this was not accompanied by any negative feelings towards them, quite the opposite. It seems that he considered that, as fellow speakers of German, they must be nice, as can be seen in the continuation of the above conversation:

> **Father** (amused): Nachäffer? *(Copycats?)*
> **Frank**: Ja. *(Yes.)*
> **Father** (jokingly): Diese blöden Nachäffer! *(These stupid copycats!)*
> **Frank** (defensively): Sie sind nicht blöd, sie sind nett! *(They're not stupid, they're nice!)*

Father: Sie sind nett? Nette Nachäffer? *(They're nice? Nice copycats?)*
Frank: Ja. *(Yes.)*

Frank's view of German as a private family possession continued for some time. When he was aged 4;9,20 for instance, the following conversation took place:

Frank: Bert, warum mußt du in die Stadt gehen? *(Bert, why do you have to go to town?)*
Father: Um Bücher zu finden. Für die Studenten an der Hochschule. *(To find some books. For the students at the college.)*
Frank: Was sind Studenten? *(What are students?)*
Father: Leute, die an der Hochschule Dinge lernen, zum Beispiel, Deutsch. *(People, who learn things at the college, for example, German.)*
Frank (a bit annoyed): Oh sie sind Nachäffer! *(Oh, they're copycats!)*
Father (amused): Warum? *(Why?)*
Frank (noticing father's amusement and feigning rage): Deutsch gehört uns! Sie können es nicht haben! *(German belongs to us! They can't have it!)*

A few days later he is watching television with his father when a commercial for a chocolate drink comes on. A group of children express their pleasure about this drink by shouting "Hurra!" in unison. The usual Australian English expression is "Hooray!" and Frank (4;9,23) takes the expression used in the advertisement to be German "Hurra!"

Frank (surprised): Sie haben das in Deutsch gesagt! *(They said that in German!)*
Father: Was? *(What?)*
Frank: "Hurra". Die Blöden! Sie können unsere Sprache nicht haben! *("Hurra". The dummies! They can't have our language!)*

The father's accent and way of speaking German were obviously seen as being "proper" German. His German was the familiar language of the home. German accents which differed from his were found quaint or amusing. This applied particularly to female voices, simply because the children rarely heard the language used by girls or women. The father attempted to combat this feeling of strangeness about other German voices by purchasing and having made recordings of stories with a variety of voices and accents. This proved very successful, particularly as some of the stories were their favourites. Exposure to any German films which happened to be shown on television also helped. However, since most of the recordings and most films are in a reasonably neutral sort of German accent, very similar to that of their father, they still find other German accents strange and sometimes difficult to understand (see also pp. 224–226). On one occasion the children's grandfather picked up two German hitchhikers and invited them home for a drink and a snack. The two young men spoke to the children's parents in German, standard German but with a distinct Swabian accent. Both Thomas (6;2,7) and Frank (4;3,15) were obviously intrigued by their accents. At one point, Frank remarked to his mother, "Why do they talk funny German?" After the hitchhikers had resumed their journey, he made a similar comment to his father:

Frank: Warum haben diese Männer komisch gesprochen?
Father: Oh, sie kommen aus Süddeutschland. Da spricht man ein bißchen anders als wir. Die hatten einen süddeutschen Akzent. *(Oh, they come from south Germany. They speak a bit differently from us there. They had a South German accent.)*

Although exposing the children to a variety of German voices through recordings and on radio and television made them aware that their father's was not the only kind of German, it still retained its strong emotional ties. They can be seen in the following example when Thomas (6;1,23) joins his father who is listening to the DEUTSCHE WELLE *(Voice of Germany)* on his shortwave radio:

Announcer (with a fairly "neutral" accent) . . . jetzt zögerte sie, stockte sie . . . *(. . . now she hesitated, stopped . . .)*
Father: Kannst du ihn verstehen? *(Can you understand him?)*
Thomas: Ja, Bert. Er hat einen Akzent. *(Yes, Bert. He's got an accent.)*
Father: Einen Akzent? *(An accent?)*
Thomas: Ja. *(Yes.)*
Father: Spricht er anders als ich? *(Does he speak differently from me?)*
Thomas: Hm. Ich mag deine Stimme besser — das klingt fröhlicher. Er, er — seine Stimme ist ein bißchen streng. *(Hm. I like your voice better — it sounds more cheerful. He, he — his voice is a bit stern.)*

A similar comment came from Frank (4;9,30) while watching an episode of KONTAKTE, a BBC television course for beginners in German:

Frank: Sie sprechen gut Deutsch, Bert. *(They speak German well, Bert.)*
Father: Ja. *(Yes.)*
Frank: Aber du sprichst besser. *(But you speak better.)*
Father (surprised): Besser? *(Better?)*
Frank: Ja. Ich mag dein Deutsch. *(Yes. I like your German.)*

Not being a native speaker of German does have the psychological advantage that the father does not have the same emotional attachment to the language as do most native speakers. He can maintain a more detached attitude towards his children's acquisition of German. After all, he knows they are acquiring his own native language, English, at much the same rate as their monolingual peers. He is, therefore, perhaps more tolerant of aberrations in their German and of the fact that their ability in German may lag behind that of monolingual children in a German-speaking country. In addition, the fact that the children know that their father, like themselves, can function in a way which is indistinguishable from monolingual speakers of Australian English, would seem to be a definite advantage. In families with immigrant parents the children often reject the home language and try to assimilate as much as possible, because, to use Clyne's[177] words, "the parents, with their fixed values and speech habits, will always remain 'different' from the community."

The question of whether their father is a native speaker of German or not has been of little interest to the children. Speaking German to him is simply a fact of life. What to outsiders might appear to be an artificial situation, does not appear so from within the family itself. German is the language naturally used for playing or arguing with their father, seeking his advice, permission, consolation, telling him of their experiences, and so on. It is what Thomas aptly calls, in the following excerpt from a conversation, their *Vatersprache* (father tongue).

> **Thomas** (7;4,5) (speaking about a former colleague of the father): Pavel spricht sehr gut Deutsch. *(Pavel speaks very good German.)*
> **Father**: Ja, und auch sehr gut Tschechisch. Das ist seine Muttersprache. *(Yes, and also very good Czech. That's his mother tongue.)*
> **Thomas**: Ja, ich weiß. *(Yes, I know.)*
> **Father** (out of curiosity, since he does not think Thomas has heard the term "mother tongue" before): Was ist deine Muttersprache? *(What's your mother tongue?)*
> **Thomas** (spontaneously): Deutsch. *(German.)* (But then pauses, thoughtfully): Nein, Englisch ist meine Muttersprache. Deutsch ist meine Vatersprache. *(No, English is my mother tongue. German is my father tongue.)*

However, the children have shown some curiosity about the linguistic situation in the family. Just before his fourth birthday, Thomas began asking why his father was his only German-speaking relative. At age 4;11,24 Frank began wondering how his father came to speak German:

Frank: Bert, konntest du Deutsch sprechen, wenn du warst ein Junge?
(Bert, could you speak German when you were a boy?)
Father: Nur ein bißchen. Ich habe Deutsch erst in der Schule gelernt.
(Only a bit. I didn't learn German until I went to school.)
Frank: Was konntest du sagen? *(What could you say?)*

At the same age Thomas asked questions about his own bilingualism, e.g.:

Thomas (4;11,15): Not many people speak German in Australia, do they?
Mother: No, not many.
Thomas: Why do I speak German, Mum?
Mother: Well, so you can talk with your Dad, because he only speaks German to you.
Thomas (smiling): Yes.

Additional explanations to "so you can talk to your Dad" have been offered by the parents stressing the value of bilingualism in ways which appeal to the children, e.g.: "One day we might spend some time in Germany and if you didn't know German you wouldn't be able to understand or talk to anybody, watch television, etc." The children themselves have also independently mentioned aspects of their bilingualism which they perceive as advantageous, e.g. the fact that they have access to a much wider range of books, magazines, records, etc., than if they knew only one language.

Frank, whilst also recognizing the scarcity of German-speakers in Australia, did see in this a certain advantage:

Frank (5;1,8): Kann dein Boß Deutsch? *(Does your boss know German?)*
Father: Nein, leider. *(No, unfortunately.)*
Frank: Nicht viele Leute hier können Deutsch. *(Not many people here know German.)*
Father: Nein. *(No.)*
Frank: Das ist gut, Bert. *(That's good, Bert.)*
Father: Warum? *(Why?)*
Frank: Weil sie wissen unsere Geheimnisse nicht. *(Because they don't know our secrets.)*

Fantini's[178] son, Mario (8;1), saw similar advantages in using his Spanish in a predominantly English-speaking environment.

Other explanations given to the children are based less on reason and more on the emotional ties between them and their father, e.g.: "Ich spreche gern Deutsch mit dir/euch." (="I like speaking German to you.") Even a circular argument such as "Wenn ich mit dir nicht Deutsch spräche, dann würdest du doch niemanden haben, mit dem du Deutsch sprechen könntest." (=If I didn't speak German to you then you would have no-one to speak German to.") impressed Thomas at age 5;0,4. Whilst more sophisticated explanations can be given as the children get older, it is this type of explanation emphasizing the bonds of affection between parent and child which particularly pleases them in the pre-school period. Ronjat[179] stresses the importance of this affection in maintaining his son's French in what was at the time a predominantly German situation:

> "The position of German is thus very strong, but the position of French also remains very strong: It is the language of papa who knows lots of nice stories, who has taught him to pick out the good kinds of mushrooms, who knows how to fix broken toys, to glue back torn pages in picture books, etc. . . ."
> (Translated from the French)

And later, when Louis is exposed to much more French than German, Ronjat again remarks on the important role which mutual affection between child and parent plays in maintaining a language:

> "Since the 30th month everyone in constant contact with Louis, except his mother, has spoken French. Nevertheless, German maintains a very strong position. It never occurs to the child to abandon it and speak French to his mother, although he knows perfectly well that she understands and speaks this language very well. He continues to speak German out of affection for his mother for whom it is the preferred language . . ."
> (Translated from the French)

Thomas and Frank usually just take it for granted that German is spoken between them and their father although they all also know English. Their own opinion on the matter can be best summed up by quoting their (Thomas 5;9,29, Frank 3;11,6) identical replies to separate questions from a family friend as to why they spoke German to their father: "Because he speaks German to me", uttered in a tone of voice which suggested that the answer to the question was obvious.

Although the children hear their father speaking English every day to their mother and other people, and even ask him questions about English, e.g. to explain difficult dialogue in a television show, etc., he is so strongly identified in their minds as a speaker of German, as someone to whom they always speak German and from whom they always receive German in return, that they at times forget that he too knows English, e.g.:

(The kettle on the stove is boiling and steam is rushing out of the spout)
Frank (3;11,5): Kuck mal, Bert, Luft! *(Look, Bert, air!)*
Father: Ja, das ist Dampf. *(Yes, that's steam.)*
Frank: Ich sage Luft. *(I say air.)*
Father: Ich sage Dampf. Das heißt STEAM auf Englisch. *(I say DAMPF. That means "steam" in English.)*
Frank (looking somewhat puzzled): Wie weißt du das, Bert? Wie weißt du STEAM? *(How do you know that, Bert? How do you know "steam"?)*
Father (amused): Ich bin ja auch zweisprachig wie du und Ernie. Ich kann auch Deutsch und Englisch sprechen. *(Because I'm bilingual, too, like you and Ernie. I can speak German and English, too.)*

Even at an older age Thomas found it difficult to imagine his father in an English-speaking role. Thomas (5;10,4) had told his father that his physical education teacher had been away for some time and he wished he would soon return. His father jokingly suggested that he could fill in for the absent teacher:

Father: Ich könnte euer Sportlehrer sein. *(I could be your sports teacher.)*
Thomas (seriously): Aber du sprichst die falsche Sprache. *(But you speak the wrong language.)*
Father: Oh. Ich könnte doch alles in Englische übersetzen. *(Oh. I could translate everything into English, though.)*
Thomas: Oh, ja, Bert. *(Oh, yes, Bert.)* (said in a tone of voice indicating "I hadn't thought of that!")

Perhaps the initial reaction here is due to Thomas's realization that he would be in the class to be taken by the father if he became the sports teacher and that his father would thus naturally speak German to him and his classmates would be excluded.

Another example with Frank (4;9,21) shows that whilst he considered German the appropriate language for his father to use to him or, as in this case, for addressing himself in Frank's presence, he was aware that he did also use English. He also demonstrates his attachment to German as the only language to use to his father.

Father (singing): Hey Mr Tambourine Man, play a song for me —
Frank (amused): Du sprichst nicht Englisch! *(You don't speak English!)*
Father (a little taken aback): Oh. Welche Sprache spreche ich denn mit deiner Mutti? *(Oh. Which language do I speak to your mum then?)*
Frank: Englisch. *(English.)*
Father: Aber nicht mit dir? *(But not to you?)*

Frank: Nein. *(No.)*

Father: Was würdest du machen, wenn ich Englisch mit dir sprechen würde? *(What would you do if I spoke English to you?)*

Frank: Ich würde Deutsch zu dich sprechen. *(I'd speak German to you.)*

Mother (joining in father's laughter): You know the rules, don't you, Frank?

Frank (smiling): Yes.

No such objections are raised if the father's comments to himself are uttered in the presence of monolingual English speaking friends or relatives. But within the family unit it is obvious that the children prefer their father to address not only them but also himself in German, and, as a result, this is what he does.

Despite their occasionally seeming to forget that their father is also a speaker of English, both children (as has been seen elsewhere, e.g. on pages 143–144) have never shown any reluctance to seek his assistance with any difficulties they might have with English.

Once, Thomas (6;2,30) gave the following unsolicited view of his father's proficiency in the two languages, a view undoubtedly prejudiced in favour of German because it is the familiar, comfortable language used between him and his father:

Thomas: Ich glaube, dein Deutsch ist besser als dein Englisch. *(I think your German is better than your English.)*

Father (surprised): Oh, warum? *(Oh, why?)*

Thomas: Ah, ich weiß nicht. *(Ah, I don't know.)*

Father: Aber mein Englisch ist auch ziemlich gut, nicht? *(But my English is pretty good too, isn't it?)*

Thomas: Ja, Bert. Du sprichst wie Mutti. *(Yes, Bert. You speak like Mum.)*

Another interesting result of the children's speaking only German with their father is that, although they know that their father was born and raised in Tasmania, they sometimes find it difficult to reconcile this knowledge with the fact that he speaks German to them. This is probably due to the fact that most other fluent speakers of German with whom they have come in contact have been born outside Australia. For the children, the terms "German" and "German-speaking" seem to be synonymous and interchangeable. *Deutschland*, literally "German Land", is consequently the place of origin of German-speakers, e.g.:

Frank (4;7,14), Thomas (6;6,6) and their parents are at the railway station. A group of people go past speaking Vietnamese.

Thomas: Sie sprechen Chinesisch. *(They're speaking Chinese.)*
Father: Vietnamesisch, glaube ich. *(Vietnamese, I think.)*
Thomas: Was ist Vietnamesisch? *(What's Vietnamese?)*
Father: Die Sprache von Vietnam. Das ist ein Land südlich von China. *(The language of Vietnam. That's a country to the south of China.)*
Frank (to father): Du kommst aus Deutschland. *(You come from Germany.)*
Father (amused): Wer? *(Who?)*
Frank: Du. Bist du geboren in Deutschland? *(You. Were you born in Germany?)*
Father: Nein, in Tasmanien. *(No, in Tasmania.)*
Frank (looking somewhat perplexed): Ah!
Thomas (to Frank): Ah, er hat *(He —)* — but, Frankie, he lived there.
Father: Ja, ich habe in Deutschland gewohnt. *(Yes, I've lived in Germany.)*

This difficulty of separating the language German from the country Germany is also seen in the following example where Thomas (6;2,7) and his father are discussing an encounter with two hitchhikers from Germany:

Father: Johannes und Andreas kommen aus Süddeutschland. Sie haben einen anderen Akzent als ich. *(Johannes and Andreas come from South Germany. They've got a different accent from me.)*
Thomas: Wo kommst du her? *(Where do you come from?)*
Father: Oh, ich komme aus Australien. Ich bin ein Deutsch sprechender Australier. *(Oh, I come from Australia. I'm a German-speaking Australian.)*

And a bit later in the same conversation:

Father: Ihr habt also zwei echte Deutsche gesehen? *(So you saw two real Germans?)*
Thomas: Ja. Bist du ein echter Deutscher? *(Yes. Are you a real German?)*
Father: Nein, ich bin Australier. *(No, I'm an Australian.)*

On the other hand, even when the children do recognize that the father is not from Germany but from Tasmania, his speaking German clashes with what they know of Tasmania, e.g.:

Frank (5;1,11) is talking to his mother about the multilingual television station in Sydney.
Frank: When Daddy turns on the television they speak in other languages. Why do they do that?
Mother: They put the programmes on for people who come to Australia from other countries, where they speak other languages.

Frank: Daddy comes from another country. He speaks German.
Mother: Mmm –
Frank: He comes from Tasmania, but they speak English in Tasmania. He should speak English.
Mother: Yes, he does, but he speaks German to you and Thomas.
Frank: Yes.

The close association of the father with German in the children's minds becomes very evident when he has to be absent from home for any length of time. It has been observed that when they begin to miss him, as for example, when he was away for five days at a conference when Frank was 3;10 and Thomas 5;9, they tend to speak a considerable amount of German among themselves and in monologues, much more than would normally be the case. The lack of German in the home is a tangible sign of the father's absence, and the desire to see the father again and to speak "their" language, is given indirect expression through this increased use of German.

The father's use of only German to the children has had no adverse effects on the relationship between him and the children. In some ways it would even seem that this has enhanced the relationship. Because the father, representing virtually the children's only contact with German, feels directly responsible for ensuring the children's continued and unstressed progress in German, it has meant that he has perhaps given them more attention than would have been the case if he had spoken English to them.

Both children even have the desire to perpetuate the use of German in the family, e.g.:

Mother (to Frank, aged 5;2,2): When you grow up and have kids, what language will you speak to them?
Frank (after pondering the question for a few seconds): German.
Mother: Oh. What will your wife speak to them?
Frank: German. She'll have to learn it. They'll have to learn it. I'll teach them.
Mother: Who'll be their granddad?
Frank: Daddy. That's why I'll teach them.

German is obviously looked on very favourably and is considered an integral part of the children's lives.

7 Measuring proficiency in both languages

Introduction

Both children have been, and continue to be, exposed to much more English than German. Linguistic input in an average week would be at least 3:1 in favour of English. In view of this, it is logical to assume that the children's dominant language will be English and that they will display greater proficiency in that language. A number of tests showed this assumption to be basically true. But the results are still encouraging for anyone contemplating a similar experiment in bilingualism, as the gap between proficiency in English and German was found to be not great.

Receptive vocabulary

A person's receptive (or hearing) vocabulary is the number of words he or she *understands*. (All people have a larger receptive vocabulary than an active vocabulary, i.e. they know more words than they actually use.) The receptive vocabulary of both Frank and Thomas was measured using the Peabody Picture Vocabulary Test (PPVT) when they were aged 3;7 and 5;5 respectively; the test was re-administered exactly 22 months later, when Frank was 5;5 and Thomas 7;3. The two administrations of the test give a picture of the children's vocabulary development over almost two years, and also permit a comparison of their vocabulary at the same age, namely 5;5.

The English-language version of the PPVT, which was standardized on 4,012 subjects, aged from 2;3 to 18;5 in Nashville (U.S.A.), is commonly used to assess verbal intelligence and scholastic aptitude through the measurement of hearing vocabulary. The test, which can be quickly and easily administered, consists of a graduated series of plates, each with four pictures. The subject is required to indicate the picture on each plate which he believes best illustrates the meaning of the stimulus word presented orally by the examiner.

A German-language version of the PPVT was prepared by this writer, keeping in mind the dangers of test translation expressed by researchers such as Wiliam[181] and Peña & Bernal.[182] Wiliam sums up the problem clearly when he writes:

> ". . . an ad hoc translation (of tests) creates a testing situation in which the discrimination and difficulty values of the test items are not known; as standardization has not occurred in the ad hoc version, the validity of the items is uncertain . . . While it is quite possible for an item to retain a degree of validity in translation, it is a hazardous procedure to rely on the original statistical data as an indication of validity in a new situation."

Since the stimulus words in the English-language version become progressively more difficult, an attempt was made to preserve this increasing degree of difficulty in the German version produced. Simply translating the English stimulus words into German would, in some cases, produce items which, to use Nordberg's[183] terminology, would have greater lexical transparency in German, e.g. if *bronco* were rendered as *Wildpferd* (literally *wild horse*). An attempt was made to approximate the difficulty of the English items, and where the German translation would be much easier because of its lexical transparency or greater frequency, it was replaced by a less common or a more opaque item, e.g. *bronco* became *Hengst* (=stallion). Since the main aim of the test was a comparison of the children's receptive vocabulary in both their languages, such a procedure does not seem unreasonable.

In any case, even the use of the American English version of the PPVT to test Australian children could be seen as an example of what Peña & Bernal[182] call "the historical mispractice of test importation". Taylor, de Lacey & Nurcombe,[184] in their investigation of the use of PPVT for Australian children, write: "It was apparent that the order of difficulty of items does not progress regularly at some points in the sequence for Australian children." They mention, for example, the word *pledging*, which occurs at item 47, as being very difficult for an Australian child, mainly because it reflects a cultural difference: Australian school-children are simply not seen facing the flag, hand over heart, and pledging. On the other hand, a term such as *marsupial*, known, for obvious reasons, to even very young Australian children, occurs at item 144, i.e. in that section of the test normally considered only within the capabilities of adults. In addition, some of the stimulus words, whilst known to Australian children, are used in a different sense. For example, the word *shining* is known to most young Australian children, but only in the sense of giving out light or brightness. However, none of the four pictures on the plate for which *shining* is the stimulus word shows any object emitting brightness. The picture which is meant to depict this word shows a shoe resting on a last and being rubbed with a cloth. The usual Australian term for this activity is *cleaning* or *polishing*. Some other words, whilst common and easy for American children, e.g. *caboose* and *wiener*, are not used in Australian English. In fact, Taylor, de Lacey & Nurcombe[184] recommend the use of *guard's van* and *sausage* instead of *caboose* and *wiener* respectively, as well as *engine driver* in place of *engineer* when administering the test in Australia.

In some respects, therefore, the German version of the PPVT produced to test Thomas and Frank is as valid as the American English test. Even if a German-language version of the test, standardized in one of the German-speaking countries, were available, would it be any more valid for German-speaking Australians than the American English version for Australian English speakers? Peña & Bernal[182] note a similar problem with the testing of Spanish speakers in the U.S.A., pointing out the inadvisability and unreliability of using tests from other Spanish-speaking countries for this purpose.

However, despite their limitations, it is felt that in this case the tests have revealed much valuable information about the children's linguistic ability.

In the normal administration of the PPVT, the testee proceeds until he makes six errors in any eight consecutive presentations. At age 3;7 Frank was given Form A of the test in English and Form B in German. His raw score for English was 50, for German 46. At age 5;5 he was tested on the first 100 items of both the English and German versions of Forms A and B. (The PPVT Manual assumes that persons aged 17;6 and above would know the first 100 items.) Thomas was tested in the same way, first also at age 5;5, then at age 7;3. The results can be seen in Table 2.

TABLE 2

| Child and age | Number of items correct out of first 100 | | | |
| | English | | German | |
	Form A	Form B	Form A	Form B
Frank 5;5	66	70	70	74
Thomas 5;5	76	69	75	80
Thomas 7;3	80	79	82	92

Of 200 separate items, Frank (5;5) knew 144 in German, 135 in English. Thomas, at the same age, knew 155 items in German, 145 in English, and at age 7;3 he knew 174 items in German, 159 in English. The results may be biased slightly in favour of German because the German-language version of Form B seems to be slightly easier than the corresponding English version, despite efforts to avoid this. However, whilst this may be the case, the German version is easier in only a small number of items, not sufficient to account for the startling difference on Thomas's scores for that test at age 7;3 (German 92, English 82). The children's better performance in German than in English is interesting, in that it suggests that the 3:1 imbalance in favour of English in the linguistic input which the children receive is not as significant a factor in the acquisition of a receptive vocabulary as, as will be seen, in the acquisition of oral fluency and grammatical accuracy.

Swain[67] suggests that when both a bilingual's languages are examined, his total conceptual vocabulary may exceed that of a monolingual child. This would seem to be so in this case, since the vocabulary items not known by each boy were not exactly the same in each language, as can be seen in Table 3.

TABLE 3

	Forms A (100) + B (100) = 200 vocabulary items in each language								
Child and age	Items not known in both English & German			Items not known in English only			Items not known in German only		
	Form A	Form B	Total	Form A	Form B	Total	Form A	Form B	Total
Frank 5;5	20	17	37	14	12	26	11	9	20
Thomas 5;5	18	13	31	6	18	24	7	7	14
Thomas 7;3	11	7	18	9	13	22	7	1	8

In fact, of the total number of items missed on both Forms A and B of the PPVT in each language, only 44.6% (Frank, age 5;5), 44.9% (Thomas, age 5;5), and 27.5% (Thomas, age 7;3) were the same in English and German (such as *thoroughbred/Vollblut* which was missed by Frank and also Thomas at both his testings). In other words, whilst the remaining items missed on the test, comprising well over half of the total, were not known in *one* language (e.g. German *Wählscheibe* (=dial) or English *lubricating*, missed by both boys) they *were* known in the other. Thus, 163 of the 200 items were known by Frank in at least one of his languages, a much higher score than the 144 and 136 obtained for the monolingual German and English versions respectively. At the same age, 5;5, Thomas knew 169 items in at least one of his languages, also considerably superior to his scores of 155 for German and 145 for English. At age 7;3, 182 items were known to Thomas in either

English or German, compared to 174 on the German version and 159 on the English version.

Such results suggest the unfairness of assessing bilinguals for verbal intelligence as if they were simply two monolinguals. Since a bilingual's linguistic input is divided between two languages, it is most unlikely that the range of vocabulary heard or acquired will be identical in both languages. For example, in his test done at age 5;5, Thomas showed that he did not know the term *soldering* in English, but he responded instantly and accurately to the German equivalent, *löten*. The explanation for this is that his only experiences with soldering to that time had been with his father (and hence in German) and he had had no cause to talk about the subject in English. Similarly, he knew English *reel*, but failed to recognize German *Rolle*, the probable explanation being that the major part of his fishing experiences and conversations had been with his grandparents in English; the English term was thus a well established part of his vocabulary, whereas the German word had been rarely heard and could not be recalled.

A comparison of Thomas's performance at age 5;5 and then 7;3 shows an expected increase in knowledge of vocabulary in both languages. Words previously not known (e.g. English *archer*, German *errichten* (=erect) have been added to his receptive vocabulary. However, it is not only a question of gains: some words known in the first test have in the meantime been little heard and are as a result no longer recognized (e.g. English *erecting*, German *hissen* (=hoist). In fact, 32.5% (N=13) of the English items and 50.0% (N=15) of the German items missed by Thomas at age 7;3 were correctly identified by him at age 5;5. Whilst this may be partly due to the differences in guessing on the more difficult items at each testing, it does show that through disuse and lack of reinforcement items can be lost from a child's receptive vocabulary. For instance, in his test at age 5;5, Thomas easily identified the German *Profil*, but failed to recognize the corresponding English *tread* (i.e. on tyres). In the months preceding that test Thomas had been very interested in parts of cars and had acquired most of his car terminology in conversations and play with his father (in German). His knowledge of vocabulary in this area was consequently greater in German. When tested again at age 7;3, Thomas not only did not know *tread* but now also did not recognize *Profil*. This can be explained by the fact that soon after the first test his interest in car parts had waned and this vocabulary was seldom used in the twenty-two months until the second test.

The children were invited to make comments during the administering of the tests. These comments revealed that in two cases the children's bilingualism assisted them in correctly responding to the stimulus words.

Frank did not know English *walrus* but identified it from the German cognate *Walroß* which he knew well from a favourite story. Thomas (7;3) similarly successfully identified English *angling* with the comment: "That's like German *angeln*. Just as well I know the German word." (*Angling* is considered a less frequent, more technical word in English than *angeln* is in German.) Yet in other cases the existence of cognates did not help. Thomas (5;5) knew *Stadion* in German but could not connect it with English *stadium*; Frank (5;5), on the other hand knew *stadium* but not *Stadion*.

Since researchers such as Doyle *et al*[57] have found that bilingual children have a vocabulary lag in each of their languages, Thomas's and Frank's performances on the PPVT in English were assessed to see how they compared with monolingual American children of the same age. Using the Manual, raw scores were converted into mental age scores, percentiles, and standard score-type intelligence quotients. Full details are given in Table 4.

TABLE 4

	PPVT — Standardized English-language version							
Child and age	*Form A*				*Form B*			
	Raw score	*Percentile*	*Mental age*	*I.Q.*	*Raw score*	*Percentile*	*Mental age*	*I.Q.*
Frank 3;7	50	94	5;1	122	—	—	—	—
Frank 5;5	56	75	6;1	111	60	91	6;10	119
Thomas 5;5	60	93	6;10	118	63	95	7;5	125
Thomas 7;3	78	98	10;5	133	76	97	10;1	130

As can be seen, the percentile scores for both children at both ages are quite high. Percentile norms provide an index of brightness, as do I.Q.s, indicating how an individual compares with others of his own age. A percentile of 98 (as scored by Thomas at age 7;3), for instance, means that for every 100 children of the same age doing the test only 2 would score above him. Even the lowest percentile in the table, 75, scored by Frank (5;5) on Form A, indicates that his performance is better than 75% of children in that age category. Both children's English vocabulary, therefore, compares very favourably with that of their monolingual American peers. It could be argued that the children's scores on the PPVT might have been even higher if they also had been monolingual English speakers, but such a claim is impossible to prove or to refute. It is, however, possible that in a few cases, where the children knew German vocabulary items but not the English equivalents (e.g. both Thomas [5;5] and Frank [5;5] knew *Kunststück* but not *stunt*), they would have acquired the word from their father if he spoke

English to them (*Kunststück* being regularly used in circus games with the father). In any case, having a possibly slightly smaller vocabulary in English would seem to be a small price to pay for possessing, in addition, a similar vocabulary in German.

The results of the PPVT can also be considered in the way suggested by McLaughlin[185] in his book SECOND LANGUAGE ACQUISITION IN CHILD-HOOD, to see whether the children's bilingual experience has had any effect over time on their intelligence as measured by this particular test. The results suggest that the children's bilingualism has had no deleterious effect on their I.Q. over the period of twenty-two months; Frank's I.Q. has declined slightly in that time, whereas Thomas's has increased somewhat.

Estimating Fluency and Accuracy

A number of methods were employed to obtain a comparable measure of the children's fluency and "accuracy" in both languages, with "accuracy" taken to mean conformity to the grammatical norms of the adult standard language.

Storytelling

At age 5;7,1, Thomas was taped telling the same three stories both in English and German. Two of the stories, LITTLE RED RIDING HOOD and JACK AND THE BEANSTALK were told first in German, then in English, while the third, THE THREE PIGS, was told first in English. Since he had never heard JACK AND THE BEANSTALK in German, it was assumed that his performance in German for this story would not be as fluent as for the other two. The number of words (tokens), excluding repeats (e.g. "I, I, I did it" would be counted as three words, not five) and filled pauses (e.g. ah, um, and the like) was calculated for each version, as was the time taken to utter them, the assumption being that in the language in which a speaker is more fluent he will utter more words per minute. Since he will also presumably produce fewer repeats and filled pauses, and make fewer grammatical errors, with every 100 words of speech in the language in which he is more proficient, these were also calculated.

Results of the analysis are given in Table 5. As expected, Thomas's German version of JACK AND THE BEANSTALK was told at a slower rate and contained more repeats with every 100 words than the other German stories. Yet, unexpectedly, it contained the least errors per 100 words.

The rather low number of words to tell THE THREE PIGS in German can be explained by the fact that it was the sixth story told and Thomas, understandably, was beginning to tire; the German version is a summary of the story.

Averaging the results of the three stories, we find that he produced 95.9 (Standard Deviation 4.63) words per minute in English, 69.3 (SD 4.33) in German. He made 2.1 (SD 0.41) errors per 100 words in English, compared with 4.5 (SD 0.91) in German. With every 100 words he made 10.7 (SD 3.48) filled pauses in English and 21.6 (SD 3.70) in German. In only one aspect, namely repeats, did he perform better in German, having 10.9 (SD 2.04) with every 100 words in English, but only 7.1 (SD 2.16) in German.

The overall impression is that Thomas's English is more fluent and accurate than his German. The fact that German, unlike English, has a rather complex case and gender system, accounts for most (64.7 per cent) of his German errors, and the majority of these are attributable to the fact that he assigns masculine gender to most neuter nouns.

TABLE 5

Story and language	Errors per 100 words	Words per minute	Filled pauses with 100 words	Repeats with 100 words	Length in words	Time (min:sec)
Little Red Riding Hood						
English	2.1	100.0	6.7	9.2	195	1:57
German	5.5	68.5	25.8	5.0	225	3:17
Jack and the Beanstalk						
English	2.9	89.4	15.2	13.8	277	3:06
German	3.3	64.5	22.2	10.1	257	3:59
The Three Pigs						
English	1.6	98.2	10.3	9.8	185	1:53
German	4.7	75.0	16.8	6.3	95	1:16

At age 7;5 Thomas was again recorded telling a story first in English and then, twelve days later, in German. He had already heard the story, OOTAHS GLÜCKSTAG[155] *(Ootah's Lucky Day)* a number of times in German, but not in the two months preceding his being taped telling it. He had never heard the story in English and had never before been asked to tell it himself in either language. For both his German and English narration he was permitted to use the pictures in the book (with the text covered) as a stimulus, the distraction of which accounts for the slower than normal rate of delivery. (Parts of his narration in both languages are given in the section on quotational switching in storytelling, pp. 106ff; another part is included after the immediately following remarks on Frank's storytelling.)

The results of Thomas's telling of OOTAHS GLÜCKSTAG are given in Table 6.

TABLE 6

Story and language	Errors per 100 words	Words per minute	Filled pauses with 100 words	Repeats with 100 words	Length in words	Time (min:sec)
Ootah's Lucky Day						
English	1.1	67.5	1.7	3.7	351	5:12
German	4.5	62.8	0.6	3.7	513	8:10

Again his German is shown to be less accurate than his English, despite his having some familiarity with the story in German. However, in only a few instances does his narration reproduce the original text word for word; the story is basically re-told in his own words. Once more the majority of his errors in German, in fact this time a high 82.6%, are errors in case or gender. In the twenty-two months since his storytelling detailed in Table 5, Thomas's speech has improved noticeably in fluency in both languages, the number of filled pauses and repeats having decreased quite dramatically.

At age 5;5, Frank was also taped telling stories, although this proved organizationally more difficult than with Thomas. As discussed elsewhere with regard to quotational switching in storytelling (pp. 106ff.), Frank could not be persuaded to re-tell a story in a language in which he had not heard it and with which he did not associate it.

However, he did tell in both languages one story he had heard in English and German, namely THE THREE PIGS. Even so, his German narration was based on a German version of the story, whilst his English narration was based on a much longer English version containing more incidents, which accounts in part for the considerable difference in length of Frank's two stories.

One story which he told only in German (*Ootahs Glückstag*)[155] and one which he told only in English (*The Story of Little Black Sambo*)[186] were also analysed. The results of the analysis are given in Table 7 on page 168.

Errors of case and gender also accounted for a significant proportion of Frank's errors in German, namely 36.4% in THE THREE PIGS and 42.9% in OOTAH'S LUCKY DAY.

Since it is both boys' German which deviates most from the adult standard language, their English being very close to the adult standard, it is interesting to examine a segment of their German produced during the

TABLE 7

Story and language	Errors per 100 words	Words per minute	Filled pauses with 100 words	Repeats with 100 words	Length in words	Time (min:sec)
The Three Pigs						
English	0.3	114	1.4	2.8	359	3:09
German	8.8	85	0.0	5.6	125	1:28
Ootah's Lucky Day						
German	8.9	65	0.3	3.2	315	4:51
Little Black Sambo						
English	1.1	91.5	0.0	0.7	276	3:01

above storytelling. An idea of the quality of both Thomas's and Frank's German can be gained from the following excerpt containing one incident from OOTAH'S LUCKY DAY. The original text of the story is also given for comparison, as is Thomas's somewhat briefer account in English:

Frank (5;5) German	*Thomas (7;5) Ger.*	*Thomas (7;5) Eng.*	*Original text*
Ootah seht einen grauen Flecken. *(Ootah sees a grey speck.)*	Ootah sieht ein schwarzer Fleck. *(Ootah sees a black speck.)*	Soon he sees a little black dot.	Dann blickt Ootah über das gefrorene Meer. Weit hinten sieht er einen schwarzen Fleck. . Der Fleck bewegt sich nicht. *(Then Ootah looks across the frozen sea. In the distance he sees a black speck. The speck does not move.)*
,,Vielleicht ist das ein Seehund!" *("Perhaps it's a seal!")*	,,Vielleicht ist das ein, ein Eis—, ein Seehund," sagt er. ,,Seehundfleisch schmeckt gut." *("Perhaps it's a, a polar—, a seal," he says. "Seal meat tastes good.")*	"Maybe it might be a seal. Seal meat is very nice."	,,Vielleicht ist es ein Seehund," sagt Ootah. ,,Seehund- fleisch schmeckt gut. Seehundtran gibt ein gutes Feuer. O bitte, laß es einen Seehund sein!" *("Perhaps it's a seal," says Ootah. "Seal meat tastes good. Seal oil makes a good fire. Oh please, let it be a seal!")*

Frank (5;5) German	Thomas (7;5) Ger.	Thomas (7;5) Eng.	Original text
Er kommt NEAR das. ,,Nein! Das ist ein Walroß. Walroßtran ist sehr gut. Walroß- fleisch ist sehr gut." *(He comes near to it. "No! That's a walrus. Walrus oil is very good. Walrus meat is very good.")*	Der Fleck wird größer und größer. ,,Das ist ein Walroß," sagt er. *(The speck gets bigger and bigger. "That's a walrus," he says.)*		Ootah fährt mit seinem Schlitten auf das Eis. Der Fleck wird größer und größer. ,,Ein Walroß! Es ist ein Walroß!" denkt Ootah. ,,Ein Walroß ist noch größer als ein Seehund." *(Ootah drives his sled on to the ice. The speck gets bigger and bigger. "A walrus! It's a walrus!" thinks Ootah. "A walrus is even bigger than a seal.")*
Das Walroß gleitet zurück in Eis. Ootah war —, Ootah wartet sehr still. *(The walrus slides back into ice. Ootah wai —, Ootah waits very quietly.)*	Das Walroß darf ihn nicht sehen und nicht hören. Er war —, er wartet bis er raus das Eis kommt, aus das — der Tümpel kommt. Er, er schneidet ein Loch in das Eis und steckt die Schnur von seiner Harpune rein, und, und gießt Wasser über das, damit wenn der Walroß getötet ist, kann er nicht rausbrechen. *(The walrus mustn't see or hear him. He wai —, he waits till he comes out of the ice, comes out of the, the pool. He, he cuts a hole in the ice and puts the cord of his harpoon in it, and, and pours water over it, so that when the walrus is killed, he can't break out.)*		Ootah weiß, was er tun muß. Er bohrt ein tiefes, enges Loch in das Eis. Er steckt das Ende seiner Harpunen- leine in das Loch und gießt Wasser darüber. ,,So," sagt er. ,,Das Wasser wird frieren. Wenn ich meine Harpune werfe, wird die Leine festsitzen. Das Walroß kann nicht fliehen." Ootah hockt sich hin und wartet. Ootah sitzt still, ganz still. Das Walroß darf ihn nicht sehen. Das Walroß darf ihn nicht hören. Ootah wartet und wartet . . . *(Ootah knows what he has to do. He bores a deep narrow hole in the ice. He puts the end of his harpoon line in the hole and pours water over it. "There," he says. "The water will freeze. When I throw my harpoon, the line will stick fast. The*

Frank (5;5) German	*Thomas (7;5) Ger.*	*Thomas (7;5) Eng.*	*Original text*
			walrus won't be able to get away." Ootah crouches down and waits. Ootah sits quietly, very quietly. The walrus must not see him. The walrus must not hear him. Ootah waits and waits . . .)
Plötzlich hört er ein Platschen. Das walru—, das Walroß kommt raus das Eis. ,,Jetzt!'' sagt Ootah. Er schmeißt sein Harpune, und das geht in das Walroß. *(Suddenly he hears a splash. The walro —, the walrus comes out of the ice. "Now!" says Ootah. He throws his harpoon and it goes into the walrus.)*	Plötzlich kommt er aus das Wasser, und er — Ootah wartet bis der richtige Moment — und dann mit aller Kraft, ah, zielt er auf der, ah, auf der Walroß, und das Walroß kommt immer weiter aus das Wasser. Dann, dann, ah, zielt er mit seiner Harpune, und, und, dann wartet er bis der richtige Moment. Mit aller Kraft schmeißt er seine Harpune sehr weit, und sie trifft das Walroß. Ootah sagt: ,,Ich habe ein Walroß getötet!'' *(Suddenly he comes out of the water, and he — Ootah waits until the right moment — and then with all his strength, ah, he aims at the, ah, at the walrus, and the walrus comes further out of the water. Then, then, ah, he aims with his harpoon, and, and, and then he waits until the right moment. With all his strength he throws his harpoon very far and it hits the walrus. Ootah says, "I've killed a walrus!")*	Then he killed the walrus and . . .	Plötzlich hört er ein Platschen. Er sieht eine schwarze Nase aus dem Loch hervorkommen. Ein runzliger Kopf folgt. Ootah packt seine Harpune fester. Er hält den Atem an. Er muß genau den richtigen Augenblick abwarten. Das Walroß kommt immer weiter aus dem Wasser heraus. ,,Jetzt!'' denkt Ootah. Mit aller Kraft wirft er die Harpune. Die Harpune trifft das Walroß. Das Walroß stürzt auf das Eis. Ootah starrt das große Tier an. ,,Ich habe es geschafft!'' flüstert er. ,,Ich habe ein Walroß getötet!'' *(Suddenly he hears a splash. He sees a black nose come out of the hole. A wrinkly head follows. Ootah holds his harpoon more tightly. He holds his breath. He must wait for precisely the right moment. The walrus comes further and further out of the water. "Now!" thinks Ootah. With all his strength he throws the harpoon.*

Frank (5;5) German	Thomas (7;5) Ger.	Thomas (7;5) Eng.	Original text
			The harpoon hits the walrus. The walrus falls onto the ice. Ootah gazes at the huge animal. "I did it!" he whispers. "I killed a walrus.")

The German of both children is delivered confidently and fluently and, despite its containing more errors than would usually be found in the speech of monolingual German-speaking children, is quite clear and comprehensible. In view of the particular circumstances under which Thomas and Frank have acquired their German, this would seem to be a significant and worthwhile achievement.

Free speech

For the purpose of comparison, a five minute sample of the children's speech taped at the same times as the storytelling in each language, was analysed. Results are given in Table 8. The speech samples were representative of their normal speech in either language.

TABLE 8

Child and age Language	Thomas 5;7 German	English	Thomas 7;5 German	English	Frank 5;5 German	English
Words per minute	80.2	85.3	124.9	122.7	96.3	152.9
Repeats with every 100 words	3.3	4.9	3.0	5.8	2.6	4.8
Filled pauses with every 100 words	15.7	21.0	4.3	3.6	0.9	1.0
Errors per 100 words	4.1	0.7	4.3	0.0	8.8	0.5

It can be seen that in Thomas's free speech at both age 5;7 and 7;5, the differences between his two languages are not great. The only difference really noticeable to a listener is the larger number of grammatical errors made in his German, although these would rarely detract from its intelligibility to a monolingual speaker of German.

In Frank's free speech, as in his storytelling, his English is delivered at a more rapid rate than his German. This may in part be attributable to his having less confidence in his German and needing to concentrate more on formulating his sentences in that language than in English. It may also be partly due to the different nature of conversations he has in both languages. When speaking English, particularly with playmates, there is often a need to say one's piece quickly so that one can finish before someone interrupts.

(This accounts for the very high 152.9 words per minute in the free speech sample, for instance; Frank, his brother and a friend were trying to outdo each other in recalling incidents in a television show they had seen.) By contrast, when speaking German with his father, this pressure is normally absent, and he can speak at a more relaxed pace. Even so, 96.3 words per minute, his rate of delivery in German, is not exactly slow and is faster than Thomas's speech in either language at a similar age.

A look at the children's accuracy over time

To obtain a clearer diachronic picture of the frequency and type of errors made by the children, an analysis was made of taped material covering for Thomas the period from age 3;10 to 8;0 and for Frank the period from age 3;0 to 6;0. Ages 3;10 and 3;0 were chosen as the starting points because from then on over 95% of words directed by Thomas and Frank respectively at their father were in German (see chapter 6). Each speech sample contained approximately 400 words and was considered to be representative of the children's speech at that particular point in time. The results are given in Figure 1.

The average number of errors in Thomas's German for the 50 month period was 4.7 per 100 words (Standard Deviation 1.0), compared with 0.7 per 100 words (SD 0.8) in his English. Frank's German from age 3;0–6;0 contained an average of 8.3 errors per 100 words (SD 1.0), whereas his English contained only 1.5 errors per 100 words (SD 0.8). In other words, both children make about five to six times as many errors in German as they do in English.

As can be seen in Figure 1, Thomas's German is consistently more accurate than Frank's. A partial explanation for this difference may be their different positions in the family and the different circumstances arising from this. The age difference of 22 months between them, for instance, means that at the time Thomas was beginning to speak, he could virtually have the undivided attention of his father, that is, without, as was the case with Frank, having to compete for speaking time with an already quite voluble brother. Thomas thus had much more opportunity to practise speaking German in his first two years of speech. However, whilst Frank at the same age had less opportunity to *speak* German, he may have had more opportunities to *hear* the language, since he heard not only the German spoken to him by his father (as in Thomas's case), but could also listen to conversations between his father and Thomas. This is borne out by both children's ability to *understand* German — there has been little perceptible difference between the two at similar ages (e.g. see Table 2 on p. 161 for the results of tests of their receptive vocabulary at age 5;5).

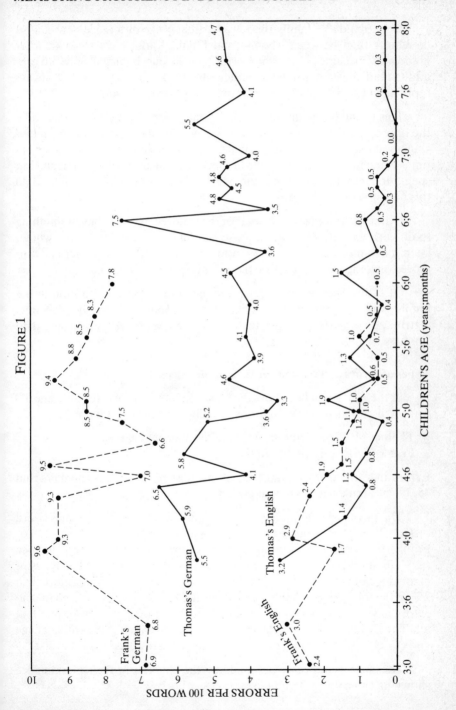

FIGURE 1

In Leopold's[187] family there was a greater age difference between his daughters than between Thomas and Frank. Karla, born six years after Hildegard, became, unlike her sister, a receiving bilingual only, able to understand most of what her father said to her in German, but always replying in English; her spoken German was extremely limited.

This is one of the disadvantages of one parent representing practically the only source of one of a child's languages. Depending on family circumstances, it may be possible to combat this to some extent by arranging certain times when the younger child can be alone with the particular parent and can speak unhampered by sibling competition. The father has been able to do this occasionally with Frank.

Differing attitudes on the part of the children may also have something to do with their differing accuracy in German. Thomas has, on the whole, been much more amenable to occasional correction by this father and also more concerned with the correctness of his speech than Frank.

Of future interest, with regard to age differences and position in the family, will be what level of bilingualism is obtained by the boys's sister, Katrina, five years younger than Frank and seven years younger than Thomas.

Types of errors and reasons for their occurrence

In the *English* of both boys the most common type of error until age 6;0 was the use of incorrect verb forms, usually analogical past tenses, e.g.:

Thomas (4;2,16): Peter *throwed* the clay pigeon real high.
Frank (4;4,28): I *speaked* to them.

Errors in verb forms account for an average of 40.7% of Thomas's and 35.3% of Frank's errors in that period.

The next easily definable type of error in English is, for Thomas, word order, although this makes up an average of only 4.9% of all errors. For Frank, the second most common type of error is semantic transference (explained on page 180), comprising 13.7% of his errors. Other types of errors for both children are so varied that no one type constitutes more than 2% of the total errors. In the period from age 5;10 to 7;6, it was found that no errors in verb forms or word order occurred in Thomas's English speech at all. The children's English deviates little from the adult standard language and closely resembles that of their monolingual age peers.

The main types of errors made by the children in their German are shown in Table 9.

TABLE 9

	Types of errors in German				
	Gender/ Case	Verb form	Word order	Semantic transference	Lexical transference
Frank 3;10–6;0	37.8%(SD 9.1)	14.1%(SD 7.0)	13.5%(SD7.9)	9.2%(SD5.1)	7.1%(SD6.4)
Thomas 3;10–6;0	52.8%(SD14.8)	12.8%(SD10.3)	4.8%(SD5.1)	11.6%(SD7.4)	6.8%(SD7.9)
Thomas 6;0–8;0	56.5%(SD 8.2)	5.5%(SD 5.0)	5.0%(SD5.0)	10.0%(SD6.1)	1.5%(SD1.9)

These different types of errors will be explained and discussed below.

Most of the errors made in English and many of those made in German are the type made by monolingual children in either language as they progress towards mastery of the adult form, e.g.:

Thomas (3;9,21): What else Grandma said? (i.e. What else did Grandma say?)

Thomas (3;10,7): Was diese Männer machen? *(What these men do?)* (i.e. What are these men doing?)
(This utterance was not an echo-question, in which case Thomas's word order would be correct, but simply an initial enquiry, where normal German would require *"Was machen diese Männer?"*)

Other types of errors seem to arise specifically because the children have two languages, the grammatical systems of which influence each other to a certain degree, in other words, because of what Weinreich[24] calls "interference" and what Clyne[25] prefers to refer to by the more neutral term "transference".

As will be shown in the following discussion, it is not always possible to decide whether an error in one language is due to the influence of another language. Nevertheless, it does seem clear that many errors made by Thomas and Frank can be attributed to this influence.

Syntactic transference

Syntactic transference is defined by Clyne[188] as "the taking over by one language of a sentence pattern or system of inflections of the other language".

(a) Case and gender

As was seen in Table 9 above, the majority of errors made by Thomas and Frank in German were errors of case and/or gender. In fact, one half of

Thomas's errors in German are of this type. The gap between the children's accuracy in English and German would be reduced considerably if German did not have three genders and a complicated case system.

The following sketch, though a simplification of the situation, will give an idea of how complex the German system is in comparison with English: German has 6 words for English *the*, and the decision as to which is required in a particular instance is made on the basis of whether the following noun is *masculine, feminine, neuter* or *plural* (and gender, as a rule, follows no logical system, e.g. *Löffel* [=spoon] is masculine, *Gabel* [=fork] is feminine, *Messer* [=knife] is neuter), and in which of four cases (nominative, accusative, genitive and dative) the noun is. The six words for *the* are: *der* (masculine nominative singular, feminine dative singular, feminine genitive singular, genitive plural), *die* (feminine nominative/accusative singular, nominative/accusative plural), *das* (neuter nominative/accusative singular), *den* (masculine accusative singular, dative plural), *dem* (masculine/neuter dative singular), *des* (masculine/neuter genitive singular).

Thus in each of the following four simple sentences English has "*the* man", whereas German requires four different words for *the*:

The man is old.	*Der* Mann ist alt.
I know *the* man.	Ich kenne *den* Mann.
I help *the* man.	Ich helfe *dem* Mann.
Despite *the* man.	¡Trotz *des* Mannes.

Monolingual German-speaking children obviously require much more time to master such a system than English-speaking children to acquire the very simple English system. It is possible, however, that Thomas's and Frank's difficulties with this aspect of German are partly an attempt to "rationalize" the German system, to make it more like English. After all, use of the wrong word for *the* rarely interferes with comprehension in German.

In Thomas's case, until age 6;0 he assigned masculine gender to most neuter nouns (but usually correctly marked feminine, masculine and plural), and ignored most of the case distinctions. Frank "simplified" the system even further, generally using *das* as singular *the* (for all genders and cases) and *die* for plural *the*. Some success has been achieved since Thomas's sixth birthday in making him aware of neuter nouns (e.g. through play, such as quizzes, and through short writing exercises), so that by age 8;0 he knows approximately the hundred most common neuter nouns, and, more often than not, he uses them correctly in his speech. His awareness and proficiency in the use of the various cases has also been improved in that period. Similar methods were beginning to make some impression on Frank as he approached his sixth birthday.

(b) Word order

The word-order of German and English differs in many respects, so that it is likely that some influence of the one or the other will be evident in bilinguals' speech. (This is confirmed by Clyne.[25])

The main ways in which German word-order differs from that of English are as follows:

(i)   In a German statement sentence the verb occupies second position. This means that if the first word is not the subject, the subject then follows the verb, e.g.:

   Frank (3;11,13): Und manchmal *sprechen wir* mit Jack. (Literally: And sometimes *speak we* to Jack.

(ii)   Certain German conjunctions (such as *weil* [because], *wenn* [when, if], *damit* [so that], etc.) require the verb to be placed in the final position in a clause, e.g.:

   Thomas (4;1,14) (with camera): Man drückt da drauf, wenn man das aufmachen *will*. (Literally: You press on this when you that open *want to*.)

(iii) Certain German verbs (e.g. the so-called modal verbs such as *müssen* [must, have to], *können* [can, be able to], and *werden* [will] used to form the future tense) require a following infinitive to occupy the final position in the clause, e.g.:

   Frank (2;11,10): Kannst du das *lesen*? (Literally: Can you that *read*?)

(iv)   German past participles come not after the auxiliary verb as in English, but at the end of the clause, e.g.:

   Thomas (4;1,13): Eine Biene hat meinen Fuß *gestochen*! (Literally: A bee has my foot *stung*!)

(v)   Relative pronouns (*who, which, that*) cause the verb to occupy the final position in a clause, e.g.:

   Thomas (4;3,23): Ein Dolmetscher hilft Leute, *die* nur eine Sprache *sprechen*. (Literally: An interpreter helps people *who* only one language *speak*.)

(vi) German has verbs which have a separable prefix which occupies the
      final position in the clause, e.g. *aufwachen* (=wake up):

> **Frank** (5;5,22): Er wacht sehr früh *auf*. (Literally: He wakes very
> early *up*.)

(vii) The normal order of adverbs or adverbial expressions in a German
      sentence is time-manner-place, whereas in English adverbs of place
      usually take precedence, e.g.:

> **Thomas** (7;6,12): Wir fahren morgen nach Sydney. (Literally: We
> go tomorrow to Sydney, cf. normal English: We're going to
> Sydney tomorrow.)

Of course, various combinations of the factors mentioned in (i) – (vii)
may also occur. For example, the following utterance combines the rules of
(ii), (iii) and (iv):

> **Thomas** (4;7,21): Ich habe Frankie gesagt, er muß das hier halten, damit
> das warm bleibt. (Literally: I have Frankie told, he must this here
> hold, so that this warm stays.)

As can be seen, the potential for the word order of one language to influence
that of the other in a bilingual's speech is quite large. In the speech of both
Thomas and Frank, the transference of word order patterns is predominantly in one direction, namely from English to German. However, as can be
seen in Table 9 on page 175, errors in German word order make up only a
very small proportion of the errors the children make.

Occasional influences of German word order on the children's English
are also observed, and these can be attributed *exclusively* to types (vi) and
(vii) outlined above, e.g.:

> **Thomas** (5;5,2): Mum, I had my school jumper all day on.

> **Frank** (5;9,18): Shane said he gets early to school.

The children have not mastered word order as well in German as in English,
and most deviations from normal German word order seem to be word order
patterns transferred from English. If we compare the speech of both children from the age of 5;0, we find that there are considerable differences
between their mastery of German word order.

Thomas's one real, persistent word order mistake occurs in type (ii)
above, but only in clauses beginning with *weil* (=because); instead of putting
the verb at the end of the clause as required, he gives the clauses the same
word order as English *because* clauses, e.g.:

Thomas (6;11,9): Du mußt die Säcke Gold tragen, weil sie sind zu schwer. *(You have to carry the bags of gold because they're too heavy.)* (The verb *sind* [=are] should be in the final position in the sentence.)

Interestingly, Thomas went through a period of time (ca. 4;2–5;0) when he did consistently produce such *weil*-sentences with correct word order, although from age 5;0 he has rarely uttered one with correct word order. But if he *writes* a *weil*-sentence, it almost invariably has correct word order. He can also correct, without difficulty, one of his spoken *weil*-sentences if requested to do so.

Frank's German word order is somewhat more deviant, but even so, mistakes in sentence types (i), (iii), (iv) and (vi) mentioned above are rare. Most of his errors occur in sentence type (ii) where his German sentences often have the word order of their English counterparts, almost invariably so if they are *weil*-sentences, e.g.:

Father (reluctant to go out on a long walk): Du wirst müde werden. *(You'll get tired.)*
Frank (5;3,11): Nein, weil es *ist* nicht sehr weit. *(No, because it's not very far.)* (*Ist* [=is] should be last in the sentence.)

With other conjunctions, use may fluctuate within a single conversation:

Frank (4;9,30): Wenn ich mit dieser Finger *drücke*, . . . *(If I with this finger press*, i.e. correct German word order.)

And a few minutes later:

Frank: Wenn Shane *kommt* rüber. *(When Shane comes over.)* (*Kommt* [=comes] should be at the end of the clause.)

(c) Plurals

One area where errors would be expected to be quite frequent in the children's German is in forming the plural of nouns, yet in this respect their German is surprisingly accurate. In English, forming the plural is relatively simple, it being in most cases phonologically conditioned, that is, the final sound in a noun determines whether the plural is pronounced /z/, /s/ (both spelt -s) (e.g. dog→dogs, cat→cats) or /əz/ (spelt -es) (e.g. bush→bushes). There are not many exceptions: sheep→sheep; goose→geese, plus a few others. In contrast, the formation of the plural in German is quite complex and is not phonologically conditioned. There are, depending on the criteria for classification, about a dozen different ways of making nouns plural, e.g.:

1. +e: Hund→Hunde (dog[s]);   2. +¨e: Hut→Hüte (hat[s]);
3. +er: Rind→Rinder (cow[s]);   4. +¨er: Loch→Löcher (hole[s]);
5. +en: Uhr→Uhren (clock[s]);   6. +n: Eichel→Eicheln (acorn[s]);
7. +—: Zimmer→Zimmer (room[s]);   8. +¨: Vogel→Vögel (bird[s]);
9. +ien: Reptil→Reptilien (reptile[s]); 10. +s: Pulli→Pullis (jumper[s]).

Thomas and Frank did make errors on their way to mastering German plurals, but, in view of the complexity of the German system, the number of errors was surprisingly low — in most of the speech samples analysed they simply do not occur. Most of the errors which are made are due to the addition of an -n to the plural forms 1–4 and 7, 8 given above, e.g.:

> **Frank** (5;0,3): Sie haben keine Kleidern (instead of Kleider). *(They have no clothes.)*

But this is most probably because the children do sometimes hear an -n added to these plural endings, but *only* in the dative case, e.g. in diesen Kleidern (in these clothes), and are still uncertain as to when the -n should be added and when not. Such errors are thus more errors of case than of plural formation. Influence from the English plural ending -s has occurred, e.g.:

> **Thomas** (3;10,7): Brauchen Straßenbahns (instead of Straßenbahnen) ein Gleis? *(Do trams need a track?)*

But such occurrences have been negligible.

Semantic transference

Clyne[25] introduced this term to refer to the transference of the sense, but not the word-form, of a word in one language to a *cognate* (a word in one language related in origin and meaning to one in the other), *partial equivalent*, or *(near)-homophone* (a word sounding [nearly] the same in another language). He found three types of semantic transference in the speech of his informants, and these were also present in the speech of Thomas and Frank:

(i) the literal translation of an idiom or compound (also called a "calque" or a "loan translation"), e.g.:

> **Frank** (4;9,2): The peppermint is *all*. (From German *alle* which, besides meaning "all", also means "all gone", "finished".)

> **Thomas** (3;11,1) (showing his mother a picture in a book): Look, Mum. Two bears, a moose and — and a *washbear*. ("Washbear" is a literal translation of the German word *Waschbär* meaning "racoon".)

(ii) the transference of the meaning of a word in one language to a word in another which is *sometimes* an equivalent (also called a "loan meaning" or a "semantic extension"), e.g.:

> **Frank** (4;10,0) (telling his mother that he and his father have bought air tickets for the summer holidays): Mum, we got the *cards*.
> **Mother** (not understanding): What cards?
> **Frank**: The *cards* so we could go to Grandma's. (The meaning of English "card" has been "extended" to include "ticket"; the German word *Karte* means "card", "ticket" or even "map", depending on context.)

(iii) the transference of the meaning of a word in one language to a word form in the other language which sounds the same or similar but which is never an equivalent. Only a few instances of this type have occurred, e.g.:

> **Thomas** (4;4,9): I like this bread *while* it's very nice. (From German *weil*, which means "because", the sense intended in this sentence.)

> **Thomas** (5;4,20): Oh! Ich kann nicht sehen! Die Sonne ist sehr *breit*. *(Oh! I can't see! The sun's very BRIGHT.)* (The German word *breit*, whilst very similar in sound to English "bright", means "broad", "wide". The German sentence would require *grell* or *hell* to convey this meaning.)

On rare occasions the semantic transference may be made not by the speaker but by the listener, i.e. by his decoding a word incorrectly because he thinks of a similar sounding word in the other language:

> **Mother** (reading *Puss in Boots* to Frank): "Good day, your Majesty, my master, the Marquis of Carrabas sent me with this *gift*."
> **Frank** (4;0,16) (highly amused): Why did he send that? Why did he send poison?
> **Mother** (also amused): Not poison. *Gift* means poison in German, but in English gift is another word for present.

In both of the children's languages, examples of semantic transfers are to be found, although they are far less common in English. (Tapes show, for example, that from age 3;10–6;0, Thomas made an average of 1 semantic transfer per 1,000 words of English, and 7 per 1,000 words of German; for the same age range, Frank averaged 2 semantic transfers per 1,000 words of English, and 9 per 1,000 words of German.)

Most of the semantic transfers which occur in the children's English do not attract the attention of monolinguals because, whilst they may sound quaint, they are easily understandable and resemble deviations from the adult norm heard from monolingual children, e.g.:

Frank (3;11,11) (playing dentists): *Make* your mouth *open*. (cf. German: "*Mach* deinen Mund *auf*." and Standard English "Open your mouth.")

Thomas (5;0,6): He *goes me* on *the* nerves! (cf. German "Er *geht mir* auf *die* Nerven!" and Standard English "He gets on my nerves!")

Very few of the semantic transfers occurring in their English have been misunderstood by monolinguals, e.g.:

Thomas (4;10,2): Daddy didn't know *what for* feet Big Bird had. (The listener interpreted "what for" as "why", whereas it was a literal translation of German *was für*, meaning "what sort of".)

Many of the semantic transfers in the children's German sound odd, but are readily intelligible to monolinguals, e.g.:

Thomas (5;6,3) (worried that he will be late for school): Bert, ich kriege Ärger mit Frau Harris, WENN ICH SPÄT BIN. *(Bert, I'll get into trouble with Mrs Harris IF I'M LATE.)* (The usual German expression here would be WENN ICH ZU SPÄT KOMME [literally: IF I COME TOO LATE], although a form close to the English [and Thomas's] const-ruction is gaining acceptance, as can be seen in this example taken from the children's magazine SAFRAN, 8/1979, p. 14: "OFT IST ER ZU SPÄT. Dann sagen wir ihm aber die Meinung." [HE'S OFTEN LATE. We really give him a piece of our mind then.])

But in their German there are more semantic transfers which would probably cause comprehension difficulties for a monolingual speaker, e.g.:

Thomas (4;9,11) (talking about a girl he knows): Sie ist auf der Telefon. *(She's on the telephone.)* (Thomas has used a word-for-word rendi-tion of the English expression "She's on the telephone", i.e. "She's a telephone subscriber". The sentence in German should be "Sie hat Telefon". [Literally: She has telephone.] Thomas's expression could conjure up an image of someone being physically on top of a telephone, or be mistaken for "*am* Telefon", i.e. "[speaking] on the telephone".)

There are a number of possible reasons for the occurrence of semantic transfers in the children's two languages.

Firstly, they may occur because of a vocabulary gap in one language. For example, Thomas, at age 3;10,24, used *Geleefisch*, a literal translation of *jellyfish*, the correct *Qualle* being not yet known. Or the word may be known but not come readily to mind, e.g. Frank's (5;3,11) use of *Sternfisch*, a literal translation of English *starfish*, the correct German *Seestern* (literally SEA STAR) having been used frequently in conversations the previous day.

Secondly, the type of semantic transfer described in category (ii) on page 181 is difficult to avoid completely, since it is quite rare that one language has a word which has a single equivalent covering exactly the same semantic range in another. Often one word in one language may have several meanings, each of which requires a different word in the other language. If we take as an example the German word *böse*, we find it can mean "bad" in the sense of "naughty" (as of a child) or of causing distress (e.g. bad news, a bad dream), "evil", "very sore" or "inflamed" (part of body), as well as "angry" or "annoyed", to give but a simplified explanation of its meanings; there are also a number of other German words, such as *schlimm, schlecht*, etc., which overlap with some of these meanings of *böse* and which also cannot be adequately translated by one English word. Two examples from Thomas's speech illustrate how this can lead to the use of semantic transfers:

> Thomas (4;2,29) and his father are pretending to be hunters and, to Thomas's amusement, his father repeatedly misses his target.
>
> **Thomas**: Warum bist du ein BÖSER Schütze? *(Why are you a bad shot?)* (Here, Thomas's expression would mean "a wicked marksman", that is "bad" in a moral sense. "Bad" in the sense of "poor", that is "lacking the necessary qualities or skills", would have to be SCHLECHT [the word Thomas would normally use in this sense].)
>
> **Frank** (3;11,7): Thomas, I ate your big chocolate up.
>
> **Thomas** (5;9,30) (runs to check, discovers that this is true, and expresses more surprise than annoyance): Frank, you're a very ANGRY boy. (He means "naughty", one of the meanings of German BÖSE, another being "angry", the word used here.)

There is also considerable motivation for the children at times to resort to the use of semantic transfers, particularly in their German. Firstly, they are a means of avoiding lexical transfers which are discouraged by the father. Secondly, the chances of success between two languages such as English and German are quite good, e.g. at age 5;0 Thomas first heard *Teppichschlange (Morelia argus)* in German and "rock kangaroo" (*Petragale*) in English and simply translated them literally as "carpet snake" and *Felsenkänguruh*, which, in this case, happened to be the correct terms in the other language. The father, too, has on occasion resorted with some success to loan translations for relatively new concepts still absent from dictionaries, translating, for example, "playgroup" as *Spielgruppe* and "adventure playground" as *Abenteuerspielplatz*, both of which he later found used in German magazines.

The unique flora and fauna of Australia present a particular vocabulary problem which is conducive to loan translation. Only half a dozen of the best-known animals have common German names, some using, as does English, a form taken from one of the Aboriginal Australian languages, e.g. *Dingo, Känguruh, Koala,* others a specially created German word, e.g. *Schnabeltier* (literally "beak animal") for platypus (*Ornithorhynchus anatinus*).

But once one gets away from these well-known terms, the situation is more difficult, as can be seen in the following incident. Thomas (5;1,30), playing outside near the wood-heap at his grandparents' holiday home, had been warned by his grandfather to watch out for jackjumpers. (Jackjumpers [*Myrmecia pulosa*], also called jumping jacks and well-known to Australians, are quite ferocious ants, about 13 mm long and capable of inflicting a very painful sting. They are aggressive and will attack anything that disturbs them, sometimes jumping 150 or 200 mm to make their attack, hence their common name in Australian English. Since, with their larger relatives, the bull ants [*Myrmecia forficata*, etc.], they belong to a distinct subfamily of ants, the Myrmeciinae, which is confined entirely to Australia, no common name exists in German.)

> **Thomas**: Bert, ich habe ein paar — ah, ein paar Ameisen gesehen. *(Bert, I saw a few — ah, a few ants.)*
> **Father**: So? Wo? *(Did you? Where?)*
> **Thomas**: Draußen, wo Opa Holz hackt. Man muß aufpassen, weil sie beißen. *(Outside where Granddad's chopping wood. You have to be careful because they bite.)* (Then, thoughtfully): Wie heißt, ,,jackjumper'' auf deutsch? *(What's "jackjumper" called in German?)*
> **Father** (stalling for time, as he does not know): Ah —
> **Thomas** (spontaneously suggesting a literal translation of jackjumper): Johannspringer?
> **Father** (amused): Johannspringer? Das klingt gut. *(JOHANNSPRINGER? That sounds good.)*
> **Thomas**: Ja, Johannspringer. *(Yes, JOHANNSPRINGER.)*

From that time on, this loan translation *Johannspringer* became the family's German word for this fierce little ant. Another term formed in the same way and also suggested by Thomas was *Peitschenschlange* (literally "whip snake") to refer to a small snake (*Drysdalia coronoides*), known commonly in Tasmania as a whip snake.

This type of loan translation is an alternative to using the English word and is a procedure often followed by writers in German-language publications when referring to Australian fauna. Villwod, the translator of Bergamini's THE LAND AND WILDLIFE OF AUSTRALIA[189] into German, in which it appeared as AUSTRALIEN. FLORA UND FAUNA,[190] for example, translates tiger snake (*Notechis ater*) literally as *Tigerschlange*. Similarly, Rukschio translated MAGPIE ISLAND, the title of a popular children's book by Australian author Colin Thiele, into German as DIE INSEL DES FLÖTEN-VOGELS[191] (*The Island of the Flute Bird*). The bird referred to, *Gymnorhina tibicen*, is known generally to Australia as a magpie, although it is quite distinct from the European magpie (*Pica pica*). But in some parts of the country the Australian magpie is known, because of its singing ability, as a "flute bird", a literal translation of which the German translator has cleverly used rather than *Elster* (=*magpie*), which readers outside Australia would associate with the European magpie, a quite different bird.

In this study, the father, when referring to Australian wildlife, normally uses a German term, preferably one which seems to have gained some acceptance in German writings, e.g. *Hühnergans* (literally "hen goose") for Cape Barren goose (*Ceropsis novaehollandiae*) or *Beutelteufel* (literally "pouched devil") for Tasmanian devil (*Sarcophilus harrisii*). This seems an advisable procedure as it gives the children a vocabulary which will enable them to understand German publications and broadcasts about Australian animals and to converse about them with monolingual German speakers. Since the children know the English equivalents anyway, communication is not hampered with Australian German-English bilinguals, many of whom refer to Australian wildlife by the English names, e.g. *der Platypus*. And if the few family loan translations such as *Johannspringer* for "jackjumper" are not immediately understood, they can then supply the English term.

Of course, finding an acceptable German term for certain Australian animals, etc., has at times involved lengthy, albeit interesting, searches of German books and articles referring to Australia, since English-German dictionaries deal only with those Australian animals which are reasonably well-known to Europeans. When such searching proves fruitless, and the particular word has no readily translatable parts to enable the creation of a loan translation (such as *Plattkopf* for the Australian fish "flathead" [*Platycephalus fuscus*]), the English term is used out of necessity, e.g. another Australian fish, the "trevally" [trə'væli] (*Caranx georgianus*), is called *Trevally* [trə'vali] in the family's German.

Another source of semantic transfers of the loan translation type are proper nouns. Shortly before his fourth birthday, Thomas showed a strong desire for there to be a separate word for everything in his two languages. He began translating English proper nouns into German and even insisting that his father supply him with an equivalent if he could not think of it himself. If this could not be done, he contented himself with giving a German pronunciation to the English word, e.g. Hobart, pronounced [hʌuba:t] in Australian English, became [ho:bart]. This desire is understandable. After all, he already knew, for example, that London was [lʌndən] in English but [lɔndɔn] in German, and that Köln was Cologne in English. Thomas gave the Melbourne suburb Pinewood the name *Tannenholz*, a literal translation, and referred in German to his kindergarten teacher as Frau Niedrig (*Mrs Low*). (Actually her surname was Chinese, Loh!)

Whilst at that stage such translations were made and accepted to satisfy Thomas's strong feeling that this should be done, they have carried on in the family as a kind of linguistic game from which the children (and their parents) gain considerable amusement. Initially the name is usually translated consciously, but the translated form then quickly becomes part of the family's German. Thus when Thomas (6;5) first started at a new school he referred smilingly, in conversation with his father, to the deputy-principal as Frau Zauberstab (*Mrs [Magic] Wand*), by which name she has been referred to in German ever since. (Her name was actually Whan [wɒn], which Thomas had heard as Wand.) Sometimes a name may be translated apparently quite unconsciously without any thought of creating a humorous effect, e.g.

> **Thomas** (6;9,6): Bert, ein Schulinspektor kommt bald zu unserer Schule. Er heißt Herr Krähe. *(Bert, a school inspector is coming to our school soon. His name's Mr Crow.)* (The man's name was Crowe.)

Clyne,[192] in his study of Australian German-English bilinguals, refers to the translation of proper nouns as "hypercorrectness", and reports that 5% of his informants do this in an attempt to keep their German free of English lexical transfers. He cites words such as *Collinsstraße*, instead of Collins Street, as examples of hypercorrectness. However, every language does this to a certain extent, and many examples can be found in German and English publications meant for a monolingual readership. For example, in the German version of *Magpie Island* mentioned above, the Eyre Peninsula is referred to as *"die Halbinsel Eyre"*, and the well-known German zoologist Bernhard Grzimek, in his book MIT GRZIMEK DURCH AUSTRALIEN[193] (*Around Australia with Grzimek*), uses a German translation for Kangaroo Island, an island situated off the South Australian coast:

> ,,*Die Känguruhinsel* ist 144 Kilometer lang und durchschnittlich 40 Kilometer breit." *(KANGAROO ISLAND is 144 kilometres long and has an average width of 40 kilometres.)*

Some loan translations of proper nouns have a long history, e.g. most English-speakers when speaking English refer to the Black Forest rather than the Schwarzwald. However, this type of translation does not extend to the translation of people's surnames, although first names may be translated.

In the case of the children in this study there seems little harm in the use of loan translations for proper nouns, even of people's names. If not understood, they can give the name in the original language.

It has been seen that there is a good chance of what is in fact a semantic transfer turning out to be the correct word or expression in the other language. It is usually only when such direct translations fail that they attract attention, as can be seen in the following examples:

Thomas (6;8,9): Ist ein Rabe so schwarz wie INDIANERTINTE? *(Is a raven as black as Indian ink?)* (Thomas has put INDIANER [*American*] *Indian*] together with TINTE [*ink*] to translate Indian ink, which, however, is known in German as TUSCHE.)

Frank (4;5,26): Mum, I saw a spider and *she* was only a tiny one.

Thomas (6;6,21): Mum, in my dream I saw this snake and *she* was curled around the table, and *she* got up and . . . (In normal English, the pronoun *it*, or more colloquially *he*, is used to refer to most animals. The children's use of the feminine pronoun *she* is, however, not a blow struck for women's liberation, as some monolingual listeners may have thought, but a semantic transfer from German where a number of common animals are grammatically feminine and require the pronoun *she*, e.g. *Spinne* (=spider), *Schlange* (=snake), *Ameise* (=ant), *Fliege* (=fly), *Biene* (=bee), *Wespe* (=wasp), *Maus* (=mouse), etc.)

In a small number of cases, although the children know the correct word, they continue to use a semantic transfer by preference, considering it a better way of expressing the concept in question, e.g.:

Thomas (6;11,12): I use a knife to eat *mirror eggs*.
Mother: Yeah — mirror eggs? What are they called? Fried eggs.
Thomas: But I call them mirror eggs because they've got an orange mirror in the middle.

He persisted with "mirror eggs", a direct translation of *Spiegeleier*, because he considered it more descriptive than "fried eggs" which refers to the process by which they were cooked rather than to their appearance. (Interestingly, the German word *Spiegeleier* is itself an eighteenth century loan translation from the French *oeufs au miroir*.) Again this is harmless enough. Monolinguals find the few semantic transfers used consciously in this way quaint and, if they do not understand them, the children know and can provide the normally used term.

The actual number of semantic transfers employed by Thomas and Frank is difficult to assess accurately. Most of the successful semantic transfers in their German are detectable because it is possible to monitor their linguistic input quite closely. With regard to their English, however, there is such a variety of input that it is often impossible to judge with certainty whether some words and phrases are semantic transfers from German or are due to the influence of other types of English heard by the children, as in the following example:

Thomas (4;9,13) (at airport): Mum! The plane's *lifting off!*

In the children's family, and generally in Australian English, if "lift off" is used, it is used in reference to craft such as rockets which leave the ground vertically, "take off" being used for aeroplanes. Thomas's utterance could thus be regarded as semantic transference from the German "Das Flugzeug *hebt ab*". However, "lift off" is used in aviation language, particularly in American English, and the expression is beginning to appear in Australian English, e.g.:

> ". . . the plane suffered an electrical fault as it was about to *lift off*." (*The Herald*, 28.5.1979, p. 1)

It cannot, therefore, be discounted that Thomas had already heard the expression at some stage.

A word of caution is thus perhaps appropriate here with regard to determining what is a semantic transfer from one language to another, particularly in children's speech. Some constructions which seem to be due to the influence of the other language may in fact also occur in the speech of monolingual children before they acquire the adult norm. Consider two examples from Thomas's speech:

Thomas (5;9,29): Jim, I've seen the man who changes into the Incredible Hulk.
Jim (a family friend): Oh, where did you see him?
Thomas: *In* T.V.

Mother: How do you know how to make chocolate? Did you see it somewhere?
Thomas (5;5,4): Yes, *at* television.

In both cases English requires "*on* T.V./television". But can it be said that the first example ("in T.V.") is a case of semantic transference from German *im Fernsehen*, whereas the second example, "at television", is merely a deviation from the norm, an example of the correct usage not yet having been established? However, if Thomas's other language were French, a semantic transfer from "*à* la télévision", could be suspected for "at television" and "in television" regarded as a mere deviation from the adult norm.

Semantic transfers, particularly in the speech of young children and especially with regard to prepositions, can perhaps only be identified with any degree of certainty if the particular expression is used frequently over a period of time. Grimm[194] shows, for instance, in experiments with 115 monolingual German preschoolers aged 2;7 to 5;11 and 22 first-graders, that

17.9% of all utterances containing locative prepositions were irregular in the sense of incorrect word choice. For example, the children aged 2;7 to 3;6 produced such constructions as *"in* Straße laufen" (=run into street — German requires *"auf* die Straße laufen", literally "run on to the street"), *"im* Stuhl sein" (=to be in the chair — German requires *"auf* dem Stuhl", i.e. "on the chair"). A child aged 5;6 even said "geben *zu* dir" (=give *to* you — where German does not use a preposition at all), cf. Thomas (4;1,2): Wer hat das *zu* dir gegeben? (=Who gave that *to* you?). If these particular constructions had been produced by German-English bilingual children, there is a strong likelihood that they would have been classified as semantic transfers from English.

Similarly, Horgan[195] gives examples of passives produced by 5–13 year-old monolingual speakers of English which contain the prepositions *of* and *from*, instead of *by* to denote the agent, e.g.: They got shot *from* Japanese. If the sentences had been produced by an English-German bilingual, the deviant prepositional usage would probably have been attributed to interference from German *von*, the preposition used to denote the author or doer of a deed in German passives, but which is also used in other constructions where English would require *from* or *of*.

Semantic transference, particularly in the form of loan translation, is one way in which German, English and other languages deal with new concepts originating in another language. Carstensen[196] states, for example, that both English *brain washing* and German *Gehirnwäsche* are literal translations of a term first used in Chinese, namely *hsi-nao* (literally "wash brain"). Carstensen documents many examples of semantic transfers from English which are now used and accepted in the German-speaking countries. A problem with attempting to avoid semantic transfers is that one can be too vigilant, rejecting, for example, words and expressions which seem to be or in fact are direct translations from Engilsh, but which are or are becoming acceptable usage. One example from a German children's book will illustrate this. Clyne,[197] in 1967 and 1981, lists the following among his examples of semantic transference:

Student: Das neue Flugzeug geht . . . einfach in die Luft. *(The new aeroplane simply goes up in the air.)*

He explains that the German expression *"in die Luft gehen"* means not "to go up in the air" (i.e. "take off") but "to blow up", "explode". Dictionaries support this interpretation. However, consider the following extract from DAS WUNDERBARE BETTMOBIL *(The Wonderful Bedmobile)* by Achim Bröger and Gisela Kalow,[198] published in 1975:

,,Herr Hinzel schmunzelte nur, warf den Propeller an und GING mit dem Bett IN DIE LUFT. Über den Hausdächern flog er spazieren." *(Mr Hinzel just smiled, swung the propeller and WENT UP IN THE AIR on the bed. He went for a joyride over the roofs of the houses.)*

Here the expression *"in die Luft gehen"* obviously does not mean "explode", but is used in the same way as English "go up in the air".

The father in this study has also not been entirely immune from interpreting acceptable German utterances as semantic transfers from English. For example, at age 5;10,5, Thomas said, while pointing at a tape recorder: "Das ist an!" (=That's on!), which the father took to be (and which *may* well have been) a literal translation of the English expression. However, the expression *is* possible in German, as the father later discovered in a German publication:

Monika (a teacher): Das Bügeleisen ist an.[199] *(The iron is on.)*

However, there is no denying that some vigilance is required by parents to detect semantic transfers in their own and their children's speech, particularly those which would lead to misunderstandings with monolingual speakers of the language (e.g. using *breit* in German in the sense of "bright", when it means "wide"). This has remained the goal throughout this study.

Of the various semantic transfers which have occurred in the speech of Thomas and Frank, many have been short-lived, either because they represent a momentary lapse, the correct form already being well-known, or because the children have then heard the correct term and adopted it. However, some semantic transfers do continue to recur in their speech and prove difficult to budge. In English, the three most persistent are the use of *from* to include the meaning of *of* (as with German *von*), the use of *side* also in the sense of *page* (of a book, as with German *Seite*), and the expression "Good that . . ." from German *"Gut, daß . . .",* as in "Good that I noticed it" (meaning "[It's] a good thing [that] I noticed it"). In the children's German, there are, as has been seen, many more instances of semantic transference, the most persistent being undoubtedly the following: *auf*+ vehicle, modelled on English *on*+vehicle (e.g. *on* the bus) where German requires *in* (=in) or *mit* (=with) (e.g. *mit* dem Bus); the use of a preposition +adverb of place, e.g. *in da* (from English "in there") where German requires *(da) d(a)(r)*+preposition (e.g. *d(a)rin* or *da drin*) as in older English *therein*; the use of *mich* or *mir* (=me) instead of *ich* (=I) in cases where English now prefers the object pronoun *me*, e.g. Who did it? *Me.*; difficulties with expressing *when* in German. English *when* can be translated in three ways: *wann* (used interrogatively and conjunctionally in the sense "at what time"), *als* (used to refer to a single occurrence or state in the past), and *wenn* (used to refer to the present and future and, if used in the past tense, to indicate a repeated occurrence, similar to English "whenever"). Thomas has always used *wann* correctly, as has Frank from about age 4;6, but both have consistently used *wenn* for all other situations, including those where, as in the following exmple, *als* is required:

> **Thomas** (5;1,21): Bert, hast du auch Schlangen gesehen, WENN du ein Junge warst? *(Bert, did you see snakes, too, WHEN you were a boy?)*

This failure to distinguish between *als* and *wenn* is most probably due to the influence of the similar sounding English *when*, although this might not be the full story. Firstly, it is often difficult for a child to deduce that *wenn* used in the past tense does not refer to a single action but to one that is repeated. In the following excerpt from the children's book ASTRID LINDGREN ERZÄHLT[200] *(Stories by Astrid Lindgren)* we find, for example, first *als* used to refer to a single happening and then in the very next sentence *wenn* employed to indicate that a particular action occurred more than once:

> ,,ALS sie aus der Schule kamen, begleitete Gunnar Peter und Petra ein Stück, denn sie hatten denselben Weg. Peter und Petra hielten sich fest an den Händen, und sie sahen sich ganz vorsichtig um, WENN sie über die Straße gehen mußten." *(WHEN [i.e. on this single occasion] they got out of school Gunnar accompanied Peter and Petra for a bit since they went the same way. Peter and Petra held each other's hands very tightly, and they looked very carefully to the left and right WHEN [i.e. each time] they had to cross the road.)*

Secondly, the use of *wenn* and *als* in German children's books, with which Thomas and Frank have contact every day, does not conform to normal accepted usage, since, in stories told entirely in the *present* tense, *als* is often employed to denote a single activity, as in the following example from the popular story JAKOB IM WALD *(Jacob in the Forest)* by Ilse Christensen:[201]

> ,,Es ist schon spät, ALS Jakob ins Bett geht." *(It's already late WHEN Jacob goes to bed.)*

In a normal German conversation *wenn* would be used here, not *als*. Considering the fact that children pick up expressions from such books and indeed get to know favourite stories practically by heart, it would not be surprising if the distinction between *wenn* and *als* became confused or that the two words came to be regarded by a child as synonymous and interchangeable. That it is *wenn* and not *als* which is then predominantly used by

Frank and Thomas *is* probably attributable to its similarity to English "when". The rule for correct use is, after all, quite complex, particularly since the rule applying in normal conversational German differs from that encountered in storybooks. And for a child living in a predominantly non-German-speaking environment storybooks represent a much larger percentage of his exposure to German than would be the case with a child in a German-speaking country. Nevertheless, progress is gradually being made. At age 7;7, Thomas's awareness of when *als* or *wenn* would be appropriate was developing. Asked to decide which word should be inserted in ten sentences, he was able to make a correct decision in seven; failure to recognize that *wenn* was required to refer to repeated occurrences in the past accounted for the errors. At age 5;9 Frank could not yet discriminate between *wenn* and *als*.

Both children show some awareness that semantic transfers are not always successful and often either utter them a little hesitantly while glancing at a parent for confirmation, or, as in the following example, explain in words they are sure of:

Thomas (6;0,15) has just been read a chapter of an exciting adventure story by his father and is comparing it with a more sedate story being read to him by his mother, a story his mother has called "a bit tame after Daddy's". Thomas knows that German *zahm* is used like English *tame* to refer to animals which are not wild, but (justifiably) shows doubts about whether it can also be used in the sense of "dull".
Thomas: Bert, Muttis Geschichte ist ein bißchen ZAHM — ah, ist nicht so spannend. *(Bert, Mum's story is a bit TAME — ah, isn't as exciting.)*

If a semantic transfer is not possible because the particular term is not divisible into easily translatable parts, recourse may be had to what Hancock[202] calls *incoining*, that is, creating a new descriptive term from words (or parts of words) already existing in the language, e.g.:

Thomas (5;11,17) (watching children hurdling, a word he knows only in English): Das ist SPRINGLAUFEN, Bert. *(That's JUMP-RUNNING, Bert.)*

(Incoining is one of the means used by many languages to create new terminology when confronted with new phenomena, e.g. for "alcohol" the speakers of the Aboriginal Australian language Guugu Yimidhirr combined two existing words, *buurraay* [=water] and *gaga* [=poison] to incoin the term *buurraay gaga*, literally "poison water".)

Sometimes this procedure is followed even when a literal translation could easily be made of a word known in one language only, but it is suspected that the resultant loan translation would not be correct, e.g.:

> **Thomas** (5;10,5) (to his father who has come to break up a fraternal fight in the bath-tub): Bert, Frankie hat mich in der Hals getreten — da, in meine, ah, voice — ah, SPRECHDOSE. *(Bert, Frankie kicked me in the neck — there, in my, ah, SPEAKING-BOX.)*

"Voicebox" is the English model, and Thomas's word *Sprechdose* is what Weinreich[203] calls a loan rendition, one element being translated literally (*Dose*=box), the other freely (*Sprech-*=speak[ing]).

Lexical transference

In the speech samples of Thomas and Frank lexical transfers have been counted as errors. Lexical transference is Clyne's[204] term for the transference in form and meaning of a word from one language to another, e.g.:

> **Frank** (4;9,14) (watching television): Mum, I saw the Opera House in a WERBESPOT. *(commercial)*

Speakers of all languages at times use words from other languages in this way, usually to fill a perceived or actual vocabulary gap. What begins as an impromptu use of a foreign word may then be accepted and adopted by other speakers and become part of the language as a whole as what is known as a *loanword* (its "foreignness" usually being removed in the process by "integrating" it, that is, by making it sound and function as if it were a native word of the language adopting it). For example, when the British mariner and explorer, James Cook, landed in June 1770 at the mouth of the Endeavour River on the north-eastern coast of Australia, he and his companions saw for the first time a strange grey animal which had a long tail, resembled a greyhound, but which jumped instead of running.[205] The Aboriginal inhabitants of the area (present-day Cooktown), who speak Guugu Yimidhirr, one of many Aboriginal Australian languages, referred to the animal as /gaŋurru/, which was recorded by Cook as "kangaroo" or "kanguru".[206] Thus the Guugu Yimidhirr word became the English word for this animal, "kangaroo". Subsequently, this word was adopted from English by most non-Australian languages, e.g. German *Känguruh*, French *kangourou*, Indonesian *kangguru*, Afrikaans *kangoeroe*, etc.

A lexical transfer, as the term is used for the purpose of this study, differs from such a loanword in that it is not generally accepted as part of the other language: a person speaking English who uses the Guugu Yimidhirr word "kangaroo" is using a loanword, but if he uses the Guugu Yimidhirr word *dyaarbaa* (=snake) in his English, he is then using a lexical transfer, since *dyaarbaa* is not recognized as being part of English.

Lexical transfers are not frequent in the children's speech, mainly because they are not encouraged. Speech samples of both Thomas and Frank from age 3;10 to ages 8;0 and 6;0 respectively contain an average of less than one lexical transfer per 200 words in both languages. (For further details see Table 9 on page 175.) Most occur but a few times before disappearing. They occur under the following circumstances:

(a) Because of a *vocabulary gap*. The child may have acquired a word for a particular concept in only one language, or have acquired a word in both languages but at the moment of speaking can recall only one and be forced to use it when speaking the other language. This is done consciously, the child usually indicating that he is using a lexical transfer by pausing slightly before uttering the word or by giving the word special emphasis, thus marking it off as an "intruder". This use of verbal quotation marks is also often a sign that linguistic assistance is being sought, e.g.:

Thomas (5;4,23) (showing his mother his sore tongue): What's on my tongue?
Mother: Show me. Is it a pimple?
Thomas: It might be a GESCHWÜR *(ulcer)*. (He hesitated slightly before the word GESCHWÜR and gave a slightly embarrassed grin as he said it.)
Mother: Oh, you mean an ulcer, do you?
Thomas: Yeah, that's the word.

Linguistic assistance may also be explicitly requested, e.g.:

Frank (3;11,11) (playing in sandpit, to father): Ich habe mein CELLAR nicht fertig. Was ist CELLAR in Deutsch? *(I haven't finished my "cellar". What's "cellar" in German?)*
Father: Keller. *(Cellar.)*
Frank: Mein Keller ist nicht fertig. *(My cellar isn't finished.)*

Sometimes assistance may be sought with identifying a suspected lexical transfer, e.g.:

Frank (4;6,9) (pointing at food being prepared by his mother for a party): Is that for Daddy's work people?
Mother: Yes.
Frank: I don't think they'll eat all of that. Then they'll PLATZ. (Pauses) Is that English?
Mother: No, it's German. You say "burst" in English.
Frank: Then they'll burst!

Occasionally an attempt is made to "disguise" a lexical transfer by integrating it phonologically and/or grammatically, e.g.:

Father (to Frank and Thomas playing cowboys): Habt ihr Pferde? *(Have you got horses?)*

Thomas: Ja. Draußen auf die — auf die RANGE. *(Yes. Out there on the — on the range.)* (The word *Range* was pronounced [Re:ntʃ], that is, as if it were a German word, and not [rʌɪndʒ] as in Australian English.)

Father: Auf der Prärie . . . *(On the prairie . . .)*

Prior to this Thomas had become acquainted with most of the vocabulary to do with cowboys, etc., but had met the word "range" only in English. His adapting the word phonologically to German is logical and in his opinion probably had a reasonable chance of being acceptable considering the number of German words in this word field which differ only slightly in pronunciation from their English counterparts, e.g. *Cowboy, Ranch, Lasso, Mokassin, Wigwam, Kanu.*

The children often make a definite effort, however, to avoid having to use a lexical transfer. Sometimes one is used somewhat reluctantly and then an explanatory comment added, e.g.:

Thomas (4;0,7) (at beach): That's — ah — TANG *(seaweed)*, Mum — that's plants that grow in the water.

A lexical transfer may be used and then immediately self-corrected, e.g.:

Frank (3;11,8) (watching television, to father): Warum wollen sie das Frau SHOOTEN [ʃu:tən] — (2 second pause) — schießen? *(Why do they want to SHOOT [English] — (2 second pause) — shoot [German] the woman?)*

One device employed by the children to avoid lexical transfers is the use of circumlocution, as can be seen in the following examples:

Thomas (5;3,4) (telling his mother about a great uncle who was blinded in one eye as a young man): Do you know when Tommy came out of hospital he had a VER-, — ah, ah, ah, a piece of cloth over his eye?

Mother: Oh, you mean a bandage?

Thomas: Yes.

(Thomas obviously has a mental block regarding the English word "bandage" and begins to use the German word *Verband*, but recognizes its inappropriateness and escapes from his dilemma by paraphrasing.)

Mimic gestures may even be resorted to in order to explain or avoid a lexical transfer, e.g.:

Frank (4;9,20) (playing cops and robbers with his father): Mum, I hit Daddy BEWUSSTLOS *(unconscious)* — ah, ah, that's — (he whirls around, drops to the floor and closes his eyes. Then he says): But you're not dead.

(b) A word for a particular concept is acquired in only one language, but the child assumes that it is also the word in the other language, i.e. he is seemingly unaware that he is using a lexical transfer. This applies particularly if the word has a pronunciation which fits easily into the other language. This type of lexical transfer is more prevalent in the early years of speech, as seen in chapter 6, but also occurs spasmodically in later years. It is also the type of lexical transfer most likely to occur in speech to monolinguals, since the child is completely unaware that it belongs to only one of his languages, e.g.:

Thomas (4;4,2) (to mother): Frank is two ABER I'm four. (Thomas used ABER [=but] in both languages for about a month at this age, apparently oblivious of the fact that it was a German word only.)

However, such lexical transfers have caused few problems in the case of Thomas and Frank, since they are so few in number and it is rarely long before the children become aware of the situation, perhaps through a listener's failure to understand or by having it pointed out by their parents.

An interesting aspect of this type of lexical transfer from German has been that not only do Thomas and Frank not realize initially that they are not also English words, but occasionally monolingual English-speaking playmates also take them to be English and use them, e.g.:

Playmate (age 6) (holding a stick upright in his hand): I've got a FACKEL [fakəl] so I can see.

A *Fackel* is a torch, a burning piece of wood used as a light. However, in Australian English "torch" is also used to mean a small battery-powered electric lamp (American English "flashlight", German *Stablampe* or *Taschenlampe*). Thomas and Frank consistently used "torch" to refer only to the electric lamp, but for the quite different object, namely the burning torch, used the German *Fackel*, the word they had first heard to describe this object and which was adopted by their friend. The children only slowly accepted that English "torch" could have both senses.

(c) A lexical transfer thus may be used for what the child considers to be greater precision, that is, to make a distinction in one language which is normally not made in the other, as in the use of *Fackel* above. In fact, this can be a useful way of ensuring that a listener (at least a bilingual listener) understands which sense of a word is intended. This can be seen in the following example where Thomas needs to distinguish between two meanings of the word "chips". In Australian English, "chips" is used to designate two different foodstuffs: (i) French fried potatoes (known in German as *Fritten* or by the French name *Pommes frites*), and (ii) thin, crisp potato wafers bought in packets and eaten cold (known in British English as "potato crisps" and in German by the English loanword *Chips*).

Mother (asking about an outing) . . . And what did you have for dinner?
Thomas (4;7,3): Chips. (And then, as if to prevent any misunderstanding, adds): FRITTEN *(French fries).*

(d) Clyne[207] gives as one of the main causes of the use of lexical transfers in the German of German-speaking immigrants in Australia the fact that they are confronted in their new country with many concepts which they did not know or which did not exist in their homeland (e.g. "brick veneer home"), or which do not correspond exactly to what they understood by the nearest German equivalent (e.g. the Australian "drover", "rounding up" sheep on horseback, is seen as different from the German "shepherd" [*Schafhirt* or *Schäfer*] "tending" sheep on foot).

However, for Thomas and Frank the situation is different. They have acquired their German in an Australian context with input also from books and films from German-speaking countries. Asked to describe the same picture used by Clyne[208] showing a typical Australian scene with a drover on horseback, a type of scene they had not previously described in German, they responded as follows:

Thomas (5;10,24): Ich kann ein Pferd und einen Schäfer sehen — auf der Pferd — und er paßt auf seine Schafe auf . . . *(I can see a horse and a shepherd — on the horse — and he's looking after his sheep.)*

Frank (5;7,22): Der Bauer bringt all seine Schafe rein . . . *(The farmer is bringing all his sheep in . . .)*

Asked to describe a picture from a German magazine showing a typical European countryside with a shepherd on foot and holding a crook, both boys used the same terms, *Schäfer* (=shepherd) and *Bauer* (=farmer), to describe the man as they had used to refer to the Australian drover. A *Schäfer* is simply seen as a man who works with sheep, however he may be dressed or in whatever setting he may be.

The children's attitude to English loanwords used in German

A result of the children's being encouraged not to use, if possible, any English words when speaking German is their often adverse reaction, particularly on the part of Thomas, to what they consider to be English words in German books, films, etc. Haugen[209] calls this phenomenon "negative interference" which occurs "when bilinguals avoid acceptable native terms because they sound too much like certain foreign terms". In this case these are words which have been taken into German from English and which are now more or less accepted as part of that language, e.g. *okay, Teenager, Computer*, etc. Carstensen[210] and others have shown that since the Second World War the influence of English on German has been, and continues to be, great, giving rise to a large number of such loanwords.

In the case of Thomas and Frank, these loanwords prove to be a problem only when they refer to a concept for which the children have first acquired a "native" German word, as can be seen in the following example:

Thomas (4;10,1) and his father are reading about an airport in the KINDERDUDEN,[211] a children's illustrated dictionary.

Father (reading): "Was hast du denn da eigentlich in der Hand?" fragt der Vater . . . *("What's that you've got in your hand?" asks his father . . .)* "Na, mein TICKET natürlich! . . ." antwortet Peter. *("Why, my TICKET of course! . . ." Peter replies.)*

Thomas (looking incredulously at his father): Du hast "Ticket" gesagt! *(You said "ticket"!)*

The English word "ticket" is now frequently used in German, pronounced practically the same as in English, but only to refer to an *air* ticket, for which concept Thomas had only ever heard *Flugkarte*. Other words of English origin used on the same page, such as *Cockpit*, did not provoke the same reaction since they were the only words he knew for these concepts in German.

Two years later, at age 6;11,9, Thomas's attitude to such words had not changed:

Father (reading Thomas an adventure story set in Africa): . . . und MOSKITOnetze werden wir bestimmt brauchen. Auf — *(. . . and we'll certainly need mosquito [MOSKITO-] nets. On —)*

Thomas (interrupting): Sag MÜCKENnetze, Bert. *(Say mosquito [MÜCKEN] nets, Bert.)*

In German the word *Moskito* frequently replaces *Mücke* when referring to mosquitoes in tropical countries. Since *Mücke* is the only word used in German in the family, Thomas sees *Moskito* here as an unnecessary use of

English (although it and English "mosquito", unbeknown to him, really come from the Spanish word for "little fly"). Yet on the very next page of the German story Thomas did not object to the use of *Corned beef*, again for the simple reason that this is what it is called in German, too, and he thus knew no other word.

An amusing sidelight of this attitude occurred once when the children recognized a German word of English origin only as a German word. They had learnt the normal Australian English word for a female flight attendant, namely "air hostess", and had acquired the German equivalent, *Stewardeß*, from their father:

> Thomas (4;11,0) and Frank (3;0,8) are watching an American television programme.
> **Voice on TV**: My daughter's a stewardess with Pan Am . . .
> **Thomas** (surprised): Sie hat das auf deutsch gesagt! *(She said that in German!)*

As already briefly mentioned, the children do not object to a word being used in German simply because it sounds and means much the same as an English word. After all, because of the fairly close relationship between these two Germanic languages, there are many familiar words which fall into this category, e.g. house/*Haus*, arm/*Arm*, ox/*Ochs*, beer/*Bier*, to name but a few. This fact is recognized by the children, e.g.:

> **Thomas** (6;2,0) (talking to his paternal grandfather): Did you know, beer is a funny word because you use it in English and German.
> **Grandfather**: Yeah, English and German.

Even so, the children do seem to have a desire to keep the two languages as separate as possible, so that if there are two German words for a concept, one of which resembles the English, they show a definite preference for the one least like English, irrespective of the order of acquisition. For example, there are two words for "grapefruit" in German, *Grapefruit* and *Pampelmuse*, the first of which was the word used by the father and the children in their German. However, when at age 7;6 Thomas discovered that there was also the word *Pampelmuse*, he commented, "Ich wußte nicht, daß es ein deutsches Wort gibt." *(I didn't know there was a German word.)* He was obviously happy to make this discovery and began to use *Pampelmuse* in his speech.

The children's avoidance of what they regard as English words in favour of "native" German words causes no communication problems. After all, they can understand such words when they hear them and are able to make themselves easily understood with their "more German" equivalents.

Phonological transference

Phonological transference is Clyne's[212] term to describe the transference of a phoneme or an allophone (or absence thereof) from one language to another. Put more simply, this means that a sound in one language is identified with and pronounced like the closest available sound in another language, e.g. a speaker of German, a language which does not have the /θ/ sound as in *"think"*, may identify this sound with German /t/ or /s/ and pronounce "think" as *"tink"* or *"sink"*. In other words, phonological transference is what is perceptible in a person's speech as a foreign accent. Depending on the type and number of such sound transfers, as well as on the tolerance of listeners, communication with native speakers of the language may be hampered to varying degrees.

This type of problem is usually confined to persons who have become bilingual after the age of about 12. Children who acquire a language before this age, usually do so with no or very few traces of a foreign accent. In 1959 Penfield & Roberts[213] argued, as did Lenneberg[214] in 1967, that there is a physiological reason for this: the brain of the child has a plasticity which is lost after puberty; the brain of an adult is rigid and set. In 1969, Scovel,[215] after considering the available evidence, also concluded that it is the nature of the human brain which is involved here:

> ". . . the onset of cerebral dominance, which seems to occur around the age of twelve, inhibits the ability of a person to master the sound patterns of a second language without an impinging foreign accent."

This may not, however, be the reason, since it has been argued in the meantime, first in 1973 by Krashen[216] and then again in 1978 by Schnitzer,[217] that cerebral lateralization is complete well before puberty, perhaps around age 5, or even earlier. Schnitzer feels that the critical period of language development may be related to other maturational factors. Only future research will reveal the answer, but whatever it is, all researchers acknowledge that most people lose, after puberty, the capacity to acquire completely the sound system of another language. It should therefore follow that infant and child bilinguals will have much less difficulty than adults in acquiring a native or native-like accent in both their languages.

In the case of Thomas and Frank there is, and has been, little phonological transference between their two languages. Most deviations from adult pronunciation in either language have been developmental rather than attributable to the influence of the other language, e.g. the difficulty with the consonant cluster /sk/, as in *skin*, which both boys pronounced as /s/ until they were almost 6 years of age, a difficulty shared with many of their peers. (Some others are mentioned below.) In both children's German, however, the /l/ sound after vowels tends to be velarized to some degree, resembling the "dark" *l* occurring after vowels in most forms of English. Consequently, the German word *bellt* (=barks) sounds very like Australian English *belt* [bɛɫt], whereas most varieties of German require a "light" *l* after a vowel (the same sound which English has *before* a vowel, for example, as in "lake").

Frank has also shown a tendency not to phonologically integrate some English words which have been taken over into and now also belong to German, that is, he gives such words their English pronunciation. For example, for quite some time he pronounced the word *Baby*, which in German is pronounced [be:bi] as [bʌɪbi], with a definite Australian English diphthong. Some of these pronunciations persist for some time in his speech, even after his attention has been drawn to them.

The influence of the German sound system on the children's English has been minimal. From age 5;0 to 5;6 Thomas substituted the German voiceless *velar* fricative /x/ (the same as the *ch* in Scottish "loch") for the English voiceless *dental* fricative /θ/ (the *th* sound in "cloth") after the vowels *a* and *o*. So instead of saying [ba:θ] for "bath", he said [ba:x] (very similar to the German word *Bach* [=creek] which is pronounced [bax]).

It should be noted here that just as children can understand what is said to them before they are able to produce similar utterances independently, they can also often clearly perceive, in hearing, differences between sounds which they do not yet make in their speech. To take one example: when Thomas was aged 4;5 it was noticed that he seldom distinguished between /t/, /k/ and /tʃ/ when they occurred before a vowel in the initial position in a word, so that *talk*, *cork* and *chalk* were all pronounced by him as [kɔ:k] (the normal pronunciation of Australian English *cork*). A simple translation experiment, in which these words were interspersed among other words for translation, verified, however, that he clearly discriminated correctly between the words when listening:

Father: Wie sagt man TALK [tɔ:k] auf deutsch? *(How do you say "talk" in German?)*
Thomas: Sprechen. *(Talk.)* . . .
Father: Wie sagt man CORK [kɔ:k]? *(How do you say "cork"?)*
Thomas: Ah, Korken. *(Ah, cork.)* . . .
Father: Und wie sagt man CHALK [tʃɔ:k]? *(And how do you say "chalk"?)*
Thomas: Kreide. *(Chalk.)*

Adults should thus avoid imitating children's deviant pronunciation. Both Thomas and Frank, as well as other children mentioned in the literature (e.g. by Priestly),[218] have reacted to such imitations with considerable annoyance and frustration and have, understandably, been reluctant to continue with the conversation.

Whilst children are often unaware that their own pronunciation deviates from the adult norm, they can sometimes detect that their pronunciation is not what it should be (although they may not be able to correct the defect). This can be seen in the following amusing incident which occurred at a stage when Thomas pronounced /s/ very much like /ʃ/ (the *sh* of shoe):

Thomas (3;7,26) (sitting on the branch of a tree while his mother watches): I sitting (pronounced [ʃɪtɪŋ]) in tree. (Then, realizing what he has actually said, as opposed to what he intended to say, he laughs and switches to German to explain his amusement to his mother): I sage kacken, Mum! *(I'm saying "shitting", Mum!)*

A possible danger to establishing bilingualism is for parents to be too critical of children's pronunciation in either language, particularly in the early stages. A child's failure to fulfill parental expectations regarding pronunciation may be attributed to the child's bilingualism and could be seen as a reason for discontinuing his or her bilingual upbringing. Research into children's language indicates that, whatever the language, certain sounds are mastered more easily and at an earlier age than others. Menyuk,[219] for instance, lists w, h, m, n, b, f, p, d, k, g, l, y as consonants generally mastered by four years of age, whilst t, z, v, s, ʃ (*shi*p), ʒ (mea*s*ure), tʃ (*ch*op), r, dʒ (*j*ob), ŋ (si*ng*), θ (*th*ink) and ð (*th*at) are given as sounds which are generally mastered *after* four years of age. The literature on child language (e.g. Priestly)[218] contains many examples of the kinds of sound substitutions made by children before they master the correct sounds, e.g. /f/ for /θ/ (*f*ink for *th*ink), *t* for *k* (or vice versa) (*t*um for *c*ome), *w* for *r* (*w*ed for *r*ed), etc. It is important that parents be aware that this is not abnormal and that most children will have mastered all the sounds of their language(s) by the age of six or shortly afterwards. In most cases, therefore, there is no need to become concerned about defects in young children's pronunciation or any reason to blame them on the children's bilingualism. The majority of the deviations in pronunciation will not be a result of bilingualism but will be the sort heard in the speech of monolingual children. Unfortunately, some parents seem to expect from bilingual children a level of phonological development ahead of that of many monolingual children of the same age. In a recent article, Søndergaard,[220] for example, gives as one of the reasons he and his wife did not continue with raising their son bilingually in Danish and Finnish in Denmark the fact that "especially phonetically, the language development was remarkably late." However, if we look at the examples Søndergaard gives of this "late development" for his son at age 2;8 *(sic)* (e.g. *l* for *r, d* for *g, t* for *k*), it is clear that they are not really indicative of any significant retardation in the child's phonological development. To take one example, the child's substitution of *t* for *k* (e.g. *toni* for *Conny*) is by no means unusual even in young monolingual children's speech, and is called by Priestly[218] the "tum phenomenon" (from "tum" instead of "come"). Beck[221] reports on a monolingual English-speaking child who said *t* for *k* until he was nearly five. In this study, Thomas and Frank, both said a sound resembling *k* for both *k* and *t* in both English and German until just after they turned five. So probably the best advice for parents is to be patient and tolerant of children's efforts to master the sound system of the adult language. As in most things, some children, be they monolingual or bilingual, will simply reach this mastery more quickly than others.

To sum up, then: Thomas's and Frank's English is, at the time of writing, practically indistinguishable from that of their monolingual Australian English speaking peers in Sydney. The few differences detectable are not due to the influence of German but to the Tasmanian English heard within the family, which differs in some small details from mainland Australian English, e.g. Thomas and Frank say [ɪəɫ] for *eel* and [puəɫ] for *pool*, whereas their playmates say [əɪəɫ] and [pəʊɫ]. The children's German contains, as has been seen, a few deviations from normal German pronunciation. However, these do not interfere with comprehension and would no doubt rapidly disappear if the children were placed in an all German environment.

Communicative competence

To communicate effectively with speakers of a particular language, one needs not only to know the language but also to know how to function in the language in a culturally appropriate way. If one simply transfers the social conventions of one language into another, communication breakdown (to use Clyne's[226] terminology) may take place, that is, what one says may have a different effect on the listener than was intended, e.g. a German-English bilingual of the writer's acquaintance leaves many a monolingual English-speaker a little bewildered by simply answering "Thank you" to their query "How are you?"; in German, "Danke" is a sufficient polite reply to the same question, whereas English requires an introductory "good" or "well". In some cases the result may not just be communication breakdown but communication conflict, e.g. when what is intended as a polite remark is interpreted as rudeness. In a case known to this writer, a German-speaking Australian teenager visiting Germany asked a middle-aged man at the counter in a post-office: "Hast du die neuen Briefmarken?" *("Do you have the new stamps?")* To her surprise and embarrassment, she was severely reprimanded for her impudence. The reason for this reaction (which is not evident from the innocuous English translation) is that for the English pronoun "you", German has an informal pronoun *du* and a formal pronoun *Sie*. School-age children in German-speaking countries address most adults who are not relatives with the formal *Sie* and until well into their teens receive the informal *du* back. To use *du* when *Sie* is called for is considered cheeky or insulting. But this unfortunate girl, accustomed as she was to speaking German at home in Australia only with her parents and family friends (and thus only using *du*), had forgotten that her question should have begun not with "Hast *du* . . ." but with "Haben *Sie* . . ."

This could also be a problem for Thomas and Frank, at least initially, if they visited Germany. Although they are familiar with and use normal politeness routines, etc., in German (which in some cases differ from those in Australian English, e.g. they say "Guten Appetit" before beginning a meal), they, too, rarely hear the formal *Sie*, except in stories and films, and have never needed to use it themselves in Australia. Firstly, the formal *Sie* is obviously not needed when speaking to their father. Secondly, partly because of the children's age and partly because of the situation in Australia, *Sie* is not essential in communication with other German speakers living there; German-English bilinguals tend to use the informal *du* much more freely in Australia than in the German-speaking countries (perhaps as a mark of solidarity between fellow German-speakers and perhaps also because English, the dominant language of the society in which they live, has only one word, "you", for both formal and informal use). However, from their stories, Thomas and Frank do know what *Sie* is and roughly how it is used, a knowledge which could probably be easily activated if in a German-speaking country to prevent giving offence to adults.

It is difficult to separate a language from the culture(s) of the people who speak it. German books, magazines, films, etc., cannot but contain elements of German culture. Through these and discussions with their parents, Thomas and Frank have become aware of differences in way of life, customs, beliefs, food, etc., in Australia and the German-speaking countries (just as they have become aware of the differences between Australia and the other English-speaking countries from their reading, etc.), an awareness which would be needed to complement their linguistic knowledge in communication with people in those countries.

Conclusions about the children's accuracy

In 1978 Politzer[222] tested the reactions of 146 teenage native speakers of German to 60 test items, all of which contained an error of some sort. Using their responses, he drew up a list of what they considered to be the worst types of errors. These are, arranged in order from the most serious to the least serious error, as follows: 1. wrong vocabulary; 2. incorrect verb forms; 3. incorrect word order; 4. gender confusion; 5. faulty pronunciation; 6. wrong case. The three most serious categories of errors, as well as the fifth, do not feature significantly in errors made by Thomas or Frank.

A parallel can be drawn between the linguistic situation and performance of Thomas and Frank *vis-à-vis* Standard German and that of native German children who speak a German dialect at home. In 1975 Reitmajer[223] tested the speech and writing of 30 grade 4 children (approximate age 10 years) who at home spoke predominantly Bavarian dialect, a dialect differing in many ways from Standard German, the language of the school. These children made 11.8 errors per 100 words in speech and 16.3 errors per 100 words in writing. Of these errors, 61.9% in speech and 41.3% in writing were due to transference of features from the dialect to the standard language, e.g. lexical transfers from the dialect, such as *Schär* for Standard German *Maulwurf* (=mole). Reitmajer also analysed the speech of two other groups of children who were just about to start school (aged approximately 7 years). One group, which spoke both Standard German and the Bavarian dialect at home, made 8 errors per 100 words, whereas the group which spoke only dialect at home made 25 errors per 100 words. Since, according to a 1966 survey[224] 78% of the Bavarian population speaks dialect at home, mastering of the standard language is a not insignificant problem for Bavarian schoolchildren, or for that matter for speakers of other dialects. Reitmajer's criteria for assessing errors in Standard German were somewhat stricter than those used to judge Thomas's and Frank's speech, e.g. such widespread acceptable colloquial usage as the use of *raus* (=out) for *heraus* or *hinaus* was counted as an error. Even so, there is some similarity between the accuracy in Standard German of Thomas and Frank and the bidialectal German children, a similarity which perhaps allows the two boys' level of achievement to be seen in a more favourable light. In the case of Thomas and Frank it is another language, English, which affects their acquisition of German, whereas in the case of the German children it is their dialect which affects their mastery of Standard German.

Measuring degree of bilingualism

A bilingual is rarely equally proficient in every respect in his or her two languages: one language is dominant. A bilingual usually performs better in one language than the other, although he or she is not necessarily more proficient in *one* particular language in all situations. For example, someone who is bilingual in German and English could have been trained as a mechanic in English and in this occupation deal predominantly with English-speaking customers. As a result, his ability to discuss the functioning of a car engine in English might be superior to his ability to do the same in German. Yet, in some other contexts, his proficiency in German could be superior, for example, if he has a hobby which is associated primarily with the use of German.

The linguistic dominance of Thomas and Frank was tested using the contextualized measure of degree of bilingualism employed by Edelman[225] to tap children's bilingual proficiency in several domains. Children are asked to name in 45 seconds, first in one language, then in the other, as many things as possible that can be found in the domains of family, school, church and neighbourhood, the assumption being that they will produce more words in the language in which they are more proficient, or dominant. A ratio of language dominance is then calculated for each domain, using the formula:

$$\left(\frac{\text{Number of English words} - \text{Number of German words}}{\text{Larger of the above two}} + 1 \right) \div 2$$

Results are given on a scale from 0 to 1, with 0.50 indicating "balance" between the two languages (i.e. that the same score was obtained in both languages, e.g. 16 words in German, 16 words in English). A result of zero would indicate *no* responses at all in English, while 1 would indicate that *all* responses were in English (i.e. none in German).

The results obtained for Thomas when he was first tested at age 5;6 were: home domain 0.58, school domain 0.50. The neighbourhood domain was split up into several specific settings: fruit shop (0.50), supermarket (0.54), and zoo (0.63). The church domain was not relevant, so was omitted. As can be seen, English is slightly more dominant, except in the case of school and the fruit-shop where it is in balance with German. The school result was unexpected since the test was conducted when Thomas had spent one term in a monolingual Australian school. A possible explanation may be that his father frequently discussed school with him and attempted to keep his German school vocabulary on a par with his English.

Thomas was given the same test again two years later at age 7;6, with the following results: home domain 0.58, school domain 0.67, and in the three neighbourhood settings 0.64 for fruit shop, 0.58 for supermarket, and 0.47 for zoo. All results indicate dominance in English, except the 0.47 for zoo, where there is a slight dominance in German. The English dominance in the school domain is particularly noticeable and is no doubt attributable to his at this stage having attended monolingual Australian schools for 2¼ years. School has thus become closely associated with English. There is a similar increase in dominance in German from age 5;6 to age 7;6 with regard to the zoo setting, for which, however, there is no apparent explanation.

Such word-naming tests can only be regarded as rough indicators of a child's language dominance. For the home domain, for example, Thomas was initially asked to mention in 45 seconds as many things as possible associated with the word *home* (or, in German *Haus*). He named 19 items in English, 16 in German, which, computed as described above, gives a score of 0.58, indicating slight dominance in English. Edelman, however, got the children he tested to react to the word *kitchen* as representative of the home domain. Yet in Thomas's case, when individual rooms were taken for the stimulus word, the results varied depending on which part of the house it was. For *kitchen*, for example, the result was 0.43, indicating dominance in German, whereas for *bedroom* it was 0.66, indicating dominance in English.

The results can also vary on a subsequent retesting a short time later. Even if monolinguals were tested on a particular domain one day and then retested a week later it is very unlikely that they would obtain exactly the same score on both occasions. It is, therefore, perhaps only considerable differences in performance between the two languages which can be considered significant.

Frank was tested at age 4;0, but because of concentration problems, due probably to his age and unfamiliarity with such a task, was given only two domains: home, for which he scored 0.44, indicating a slight dominance in German, and kindergarten, for which he scored 0.50, showing "balance".

Frank was re-tested at age 5;7. This time he scored 0.55 for both the home domain and the school domain, showing a slight dominance in English. For the neighbourhood domain he performed slightly better in German than in English, scoring 0.47.

The language dominance of the parents was also tested, with the following results:

Domain	Score	
	Mother	*Father*
Home	0.75	0.42
Work	0.70	0.46
Neighbourhood	0.60	0.56

The results for the mother, indicating a reasonably clear dominance in English, particularly in the domains of home and work, were as expected. Whilst she constantly hears German, she has few oportunities to speak it.

The results for the father were somewhat surprising, since they indicate dominance in German in the domains of home and work. The father had been convinced that English was his dominant language and that he would perform better in it on all the word naming tasks. In view of the unexpectedness of the results, the father was retested twice, but with no significant change in the results: in the home and work domains he still came out ahead in German. He was then tested with regard to various other settings, with the following results:

Domain	Father's score
Zoo	0.43
Tools	0.45
Church	0.48
Supermarket	0.48
Fruitshop	0.50
Car	0.52
Hospital	0.54

As can be seen, for tools, church, zoo and supermarket he scored slightly better in German, for fruitshop he scored the same in both languages, and for cars and hospital he performed slightly better in English. These results are interesting, since the father feels that English is his better language and he is more confident in using it, particularly at higher levels. However, the results are consistent with the nature of this particular task and the uses to which he puts his two languages. Such a word naming task is something which he rarely has to do in English, whereas, as a teacher of German, he is frequently required to produce quickly lists of related vocabulary items for the benefit of students.

8 Biliteracy

A problem facing parents who wish to raise their children bilingually is the question of when, or if, they should be introduced to reading and writing in the language not taught in the normal school system. Many bilingual children growing up in a community where no provision is made in the school system for one of their languages may speak that language well but be unable to read or write it.

Smolicz & Harris,[227] for example, in their 1977 study of language use and maintenance among Australian students of various ethnic backgrounds, discovered that:

> "The ethnic children's use of their native tongue in reading and writing was even more restricted than their ethnic speech patterns (. . .) Two thirds or more of the students . . . admitted they had very little or no competency in reading and writing their ethnic language."

Of 70 children of Polish-Polish parents only 7% regularly wrote letters in Polish and only 1% regularly read books in Polish. Yet 83% of these same children spoke either only Polish or Polish and English to their parents, while *all* of them spoke Polish or Polish and English to their grandparents. Illiteracy in one of a bilingual's languages represents a considerable loss to the individual and to the community as a whole. Literacy in the home language greatly extends its use and makes possible its reinforcement and enrichment.

In their *Handbook of Bilingual Education*, published in 1971, Saville & Troike[228] recommend that a bilingual child should begin reading in his or her dominant language and that the transfer to a second language should not be made until initial reading skills have been well established, usually during grade two at school. There is considerable evidence to support this recommendation (e.g. in Rosier & Farella's[244] 1976 report on their research with Navajo-English bilingual children).

But what can be done if, as is often the case, schools make no provision for such children? Again the home would appear to be a possible answer. Some writers (e.g. Lado,[229] Christian[230]) consider it advisable that minority children become literate in their home language *before* entering school, which means, in most cases, that some sort of home literacy programme be attempted by the parents. Research indicates that even very young children can learn to read, and many parents have already successfully taught their young children to read, using, for example, the system suggested by Doman[231] in his readily available book *Teach Your Baby To Read*. One parent, Christian,[230] for instance, reports that he taught his two children to read in their home language, Spanish; later when they began school they quickly learned to read English as well.

Sharp,[232] in his book *Language in Bilingual Communities*, also advises that children begin reading in their dominant language in order to avoid mental confusion. However, he does add that those children who have what he calls "genuine bilingual proficiency" should not be held back by this consideration.

Past[88] shows that a functionally bilingual child has little difficulty in learning to read two languages simultaneously. He found that there was practically no confusion caused by learning to read two languages at the same time, far less, in fact, than there was in learning to speak the two. Past's findings are supported by observations of Thomas and Frank in this study. Thomas first became interested in the alphabet at age 4;0, mainly through watching the television programme *Sesame Street*, and began asking about German equivalents of the letters. At age 5;3 he started school and began learning to read formally (in English). At the same time his father introduced him to reading in German. The fact that different letters may represent different sounds in each language rarely troubled him. Indeed, this knowledge stood him in good stead as he progressed with English reading and encountered such words as *city* where *c* was no longer pronounced as in *cat*, etc. There has been no perceptible adverse effect on his English reading. He reads well for his age and has consistently been among the best readers in his class at school. In his school report which he received at the end of grade one (age 7;1), his teacher wrote the following comments:

> "Thomas's reading comprehension is excellent . . . In spelling his general word knowledge is very good . . . He has a very good general knowledge and an excellent vocabulary."

His exposure to English reading is considerably greater than that to German, the latter being confined to half a dozen sentences which he reads to his father each evening. Nevertheless, it seems that the skill of reading, practised constantly in English at school, transfers readily to his other language, since his ability to read German is roughly equal to his reading ability in English. German does also have an advantage over English in that its writing system has a more regular correspondence between letters and sounds. This advantage is shared with some other languages such as Finnish, Pitjantjatjara and Spanish. Gaarder[233] reports that, because of this, children in Spanish-speaking countries master reading and writing much more quickly than their counterparts in English-speaking countries. Thomas has at times indicated his awareness of the logic of German spelling compared with English spelling. On one occasion, for example, he (6;6,23) was showing his father how he could read an English book, but stumbled over a number of words, such as *busy, mystery*, which could not be sounded out. After a few of these he gave a little groan and exclaimed, "Oh, englisches Lesen ist nicht so leicht wie Deutsch!" (*Oh, English reading isn't as easy as German!*)

Thomas began writing occasional simple words in German and English before commencing school. Since starting school, his German writing has been continued at home, in small daily doses. He has a writing exercise book, prepared by his father, in which almost each day he writes several sentences — initially this usually involved answering questions and/or selecting and writing out the correct sentence to describe a picture. Other exercises included simple crossword puzzles and short dictations. As his proficiency developed, more complicated exercises have been able to be interspersed with those just mentioned, for example, exercises which practise grammatical features with which he has difficulty (gender, case, etc.), and free writing exercises (e.g. writing four sentences about an outing, or an interesting film). A facsimile of a page from his exercise book which was done when Thomas was aged 7;5 is shown in Figure 2; it is shown in its uncorrected form and an English translation has been added for readers' benefit.

It has been found that by making the writing tasks reasonably relevant and interesting or amusing and by restricting them in length so that he can complete them in 5–10 minutes, his interest has been sustained and he has made steady progress. He is able to write German which orthographically is nearly as accurate as his English, although the gap between the two would probably be wider if English had a more consistent spelling system. Very few spelling errors he makes in either language could be attributed to interference between the two languages. It seems that his simultaneous introduction to the two writing systems has made him aware of the differences right from

FIGURE 2

<u>SAMPLE PAGE FROM THOMAS'S WRITING EXERCISE BOOK</u> (AGE 7;5)
(ANSWERS NOT CORRECTED. ENGLISH TRANSLATION ADDED.)

<u>Füll die Lücken:</u> (FILL THE GAPS:)

Am Freitag sind Bert und ich *mit* d*e m* Zug *nach* Sydney
ge*fahren*. Dort haben wir uns viele deutsche *Büche*
ange*kuckt*. Zum Mittagessen haben wir *Fisch und Fritten* gegessen.

(ON FRIDAY BERT AND I <u>WENT</u> <u>ON</u> <u>THE</u> TRAIN <u>TO</u> SYDNEY. THERE WE <u>LOOKED</u>
AT LOTS OF GERMAN <u>BOOKS</u>. <u>FOR</u> DINNER WE <u>HAD</u> <u>FISH AND CHIPS</u>.)

In welcher Sprache ist das schöne Buch, das Du Dir gekauft hast?
Englisch (IN WHAT LANGUAGE IS THE NICE BOOK THAT YOU BOUGHT
              YOURSELF? <u>ENGLISH</u>.)
Wovon handelt das Buch?   *von Riesen und Trolle*
(WHAT'S THE BOOK ABOUT?   <u>ABOUT GIANTS AND TROLLS</u>.)

<u>Schreib etwas in die Sprechblasen</u> (WRITE SOMETHING IN THE BALLOONS)

au ich mag diese blöder Hund nicht

; ha ha ich will diese Junge beißen!

(BOY: OW I DON'T LIKE
      THIS STUPID DOG
DOG: HAHA I WANT TO
      BITE THIS BOY!)

<u>Schreib einen Satz, der das Bild beschreibt.</u>
(WRITE A SENTENCE DESCRIBING THE PICTURE.)

Diese Junge ist von ein Hund gebisen worden.
(THIS BOY HAS BEEN BITTEN BY A DOG.)

Was würdest Du machen, wenn ein Hund Dich angreifen würde?
(WHAT WOULD YOU DO IF A DOG ATTACKED YOU?)

Ich würde ein stock nemen und ihn schlagen.
(I WOULD TAKE A STICK AND HIT HIM.)

<u>Beantworte die folgenden Fragen:</u>
(ANSWER THE FOLLOWING QUESTIONS:)

1. Was ist das Gegenteil von <u>billig</u>?   *teuer*
   (WHAT IS THE OPPOSITE OF CHEAP?)   (DEAR)

2. Was ist ein Synonym für <u>feucht</u>?   *naß*
   (WHAT IS A SYNONYM OF <u>DAMP</u>?)   (WET)

3. Was ist ein Dingo?   *eine Art wildhund*
   (WHAT IS A DINGO?)   (A KIND OF WILD DOG)

the start and helped him to keep the two separate. The writing tasks have also proved to be a useful way of making him more conscious of grammatical defects in his spoken German, e.g. the constant use of "Was *ist* passiert?" in his work book has helped oust 'Was *hat* passiert?" from his speech. (The question means "What has happened?", but in German one must say "What *is* happened?") Other exercises have increased his awareness of gender and case, the main source of errors in his German (see pp. 174ff.), and this awareness is gradually influencing his spoken German.

Thomas's written German is mainly used to write notes or letters to his father. Most of his own creative writing (stories, etc.) is done in English, no doubt because this sort of activity is largely associated with school and English. When he does write something for himself in German, it has usually been directly inspired by a German story or film.

An example of his creative writing in both English and German is given in Figure 3. These two original stories were written, without assistance, within a few days of each other when he was aged 7;9. The two pieces are reproduced with their original spelling and line length retained. The German story is 67 words long, the English one 96 words. In the English story the only error is the mis-spelling of "police" as "poilce" (although the punctuation of the first sentence could also be questioned, as could the use of just END instead of THE END, this probably being due to the influence of German where THE *is* omitted). In the German story there is one clear grammatical error (*gespint* [spinned] instead of *gesponnen* [spun]), two possible grammatical errors ("in ein [instead of "ein*en*"] Raum", and "dein [instead of "dein*en*"] Kopf", although these could be attempted spellings of what may be pronounced "ein'n" and "dein'n"), and several spelling mistakes (*Keiser* for *Kaiser*, *besikt* for *besiegt*, *säke* for *Säcke*), and failure to write nouns consistently with capital letters as is required in German, e.g. *gold* for *Gold*; this type of error may be attributable to the influence of English where usually only proper nouns require capital letters, although German schoolchildren have difficulty with this aspect of German spelling too. Despite the errors, the German story is easily readable.

A word about correction is appropriate here. The amount of correction of Thomas's written work was at the beginning of writing minimal. Emphasis was placed not so much on correct spelling or grammar as on intelligibility, i.e. what could not be readily understood (e.g. *Pozli* for *Polizei* [=police]) was corrected. It was felt that it was more important that he gain confidence in writing the language first. Gradually the amount of correction has increased, but never to the extent that it might discourage him from wanting to write German, and he has always been amply praised for the good work he

FIGURE 3

Thomas's creative writing (age 7;6)

GERMAN

Wu-en-ti und die Räuber

Wu-en-ti konnte aus Stroh
Gold spinnen. Der Keiser hat
ihn in ein raum gesteckt und
hat gesagt ,,Spinne dieses stroh
zu gold oder ich nehme dein
Kopf". Wu-en-ti hat das stroh zu
Gold gespint. Dann sind viele
Räuber gekommen und er hat sie
besikt. Der Keiser hat ihm 50
säke mit Gold gegeben. Und ihn
frei gelassen. Wu-en-ti ist nach
hause gegangen. Ende

(English translation:

Wu-en-ti and the robbers

*Wu-en-ti could spin gold from straw.
The emperor put him in a room and
said, "Spin this straw to gold or I'll
have your head." Wu-en-ti spun the
straw into gold. Then many robbers
came and he defeated them. The
emperor gave him 50 sacks of gold.
And set him free. Wu-en-ti went
home. THE END)*

ENGLISH

The nightmare

Jeff was in town doing some shopping
for his mother, it was school
holidays. After the shopping he went
to the bank. Eight men with guns
were there. They were holding up the
bank. One man in the bank called
the poilce. Seven poilce cars pulled
up outside of the bank. 14 poilcmen
got out and put the robbers in the
poilce cars and drove off. That night
Jeff had a nightmare about robbers
trying to kill him. The next
morning Jeff told his mother about
what he had seen the day before.
END

produces. Parents are best guided by their children's reactions with regard to the amount of correction which is advisable, and these reactions may vary from day to day due to tiredness, etc. If correction is undertaken in moderation and sympathetically, the children's interest will most probably be maintained and their writing will gradually move towards the adult norms of spelling.

That Thomas appreciated the feedback he received was shown one day when the father realized that he was being a bit over-zealous in correcting a writing exercise:

Father (contritely): Es geht dir wohl auf die Nerven, wenn ich dein Schreiben dauernd korrigiere? *(I suppose it gets on your nerves if I'm correcting your writing all the time?)*

Thomas (7;6,26): Nein, Bert — ich will lernen, richtig zu schreiben. *(No, Bert — I want to learn to write properly.)* (Smiling sheepishly): Aber manchmal mache ich blöde Fehler. *(But sometimes I make silly mistakes.)*

Much of what has been said above about Thomas's learning to read and write also applies to Frank. At age 5;4, when he started school, he was introduced to reading and writing by his father at home. This did not hinder in any way his acquisition of the same skills in English at school, the two writing systems being kept remarkably separate.

One problem faced by parents wishing to bring up their children literate in a language which is not the dominant language of the community and which is not used in the school system, is procuring suitable printed material to carry out this teaching themselves. In the present study, it was found to be cheaper and more relevant for the father to prepare short writing exercises in German himself than to try to use or adapt materials produced specifically for German schools. This procedure also enables the child to have some say in what sort of exercises should be included. For example, Thomas, at age 7;2,24, at a time when the pop group KISS was very popular with school-children, asked whether he could draw the pop group and write something about them. He drew two pictures and wrote the following (original spelling retained), taking the opportunity to have a good-natured shot at his parents for teasing him about his interest in the singers:

> "ich mag die Musik von Kiss. mein Vater sagt sie sind zu laut und blöd. Meine Mutter mag sie auch nicht. Die Sänger Heißen Gene Simmons, Eric Carr, Paul Stanley, Ace Frehley. KISS ist gut!"
> *(I like the music of Kiss. My father says they are too loud and silly. My mother doesn't like them either. The singers' names are Gene Simmons, Eric Carr, Paul Stanley, Ace Frehley. KISS is good!)*

The preparation of the writing exercises does, of course, require time, about fifteen minutes a day in this case. But, in view of the results which can be achieved, this is time well spent.

In the initial stages of the children's reading it was again found to be simpler to use home-made reading materials. These contained plenty of pictures of interest to the particular child, either cut from magazines or hand-drawn, and had simple captions describing the pictures. Humorous and incongruous pictures were very popular, e.g.:

Die Maus frißt ein Auto
(The mouse is eating a car)

Often the children would volunteer to draw a picture and suggest a caption for their father to write in (as was the case with the above drawing by Frank). From these home-made readers the children graduated to reading simple German storybooks which had much less text than pictures. From these they can then move on to more complicated books.

Storybooks may not be easy to obtain in languages other than the dominant language of the community. Most Australian libraries do now have available some material in languages other than English, or can procure it for borrowers through interloan, although whether this proves adequate or satisfactory for a particular family depends largely on what language is required and where the library is located.

Fortunately, however, it is possible to buy reasonably cheap paperback children's books, either through a foreign language bookshop or by establishing contact with a bookshop or publisher in the country where the language is spoken (or by arranging for friends or relatives in the country to post suitable material); the occasional arrival of a parcel of books, comics or magazines from abroad can do a lot to maintain or renew interest and enthusiasm. Such books are a worthwhile investment and do not strain the purse-strings too much. In the case of Thomas and Frank, the father's expenditure on German books over a year would amount to about the equivalent of the price of two or three loaves of bread per week. Moreover, the books get well used. They are used initially as storybooks which are read aloud by their father, usually first to Thomas, and then, as he reaches that particular level of linguistic sophistication, also to Frank (though some books are suitable for reading to both at the same time). Both boys cope well with books a few years in advance of the age recommended by publishers on the covers of their books, e.g. when Frank was aged 6;3 and Thomas 8;2, they were read DER LETZTE HÄUPTLING DER APACHEN (*The Last Chief of the Apaches*), an exciting adventure novel by Thomas Jeier,[234] recommended for children from ten years of age, which they both understood easily and which they enjoyed very much. Later, the books are used by the children as reading books. For encouraging them to read independently in German, German comic books have proved to be very useful — and popular.

The efforts to make the two boys literate in German as well as in English have helped them to realize that German is a living language which extends far beyond their own immediate family and which can be, and is, used for all the functions which English is. Moreover, there is the realization that knowing German can be a definite advantage, since many attractive and interesting stories are just not available in English.

9 How the children view bilingualism

The children's attitudes to their two languages

In view of the analysis of the children's English and German described on pp. 172ff. and elsewhere, it is interesting to examine the children's own attitude to their bilingualism to see whether they show a preference for one or the other language, and whether they consider themselves more competent in one than the other.

It is true, as has been seen in chapter 6, that both children independently went through an approximately 5-month period (Thomas 3;5 to 3;10 and Frank 2;7 to 3;0) during which they showed some reluctance to speak German to their father. This reluctance was particularly noticeable when the children were extremely tired or upset; as in the following example:

Thomas (3;9,25), who is feeling tired and irritable, is building a toy railway.
Father: Das ist ein schönes Gleis. Und wieviele Tunnel [tʊnəl] hast du? *(That's a nice track. And how many tunnels have you got?)*
Thomas (obviously agitated): Ah, ah, ah *tunnels!* [tʌnəɫz] I want to talk English!
Father (appeasingly): Okay, wenn du willst. *(All right, if you want to.)*
Thomas then explains in English.

It does not seem that this reluctance to speak German was the result of the children's finding German more difficult than English, but rather an attempt by them to rationalize their linguistic situation, a situation in which they were expected to communicate in English with everyone except one person, their father, who, they knew, could in any case both understand and speak English too. After all, if pressed, they could express themselves perfectly adequately in German.

Once this temporary resistance to German was overcome in a relatively short time, the children have been quite willing to speak the language to their father. In situations where they have a choice of which language they may use (usually when addressing both parents simultaneously — see pp. 50–52 for the strategies involved here), they do seem to have a preference for English, their more widely used language. This is particularly noticeable when the children have just come from an intensive all-English situation, such as school, when there seems to be a desire not to break the continuity of the day spent in English, some effort being involved in changing over to German. Even when there is no language choice involved, for instance when the father alone is to be addressed, there may at times be some reluctance to reformulate in German events experienced entirely in English. This can be seen in the following example, where Thomas (4;7,3), arriving home tired after an exciting day visiting friends with his mother and brother, finds it difficult to get his German flowing freely and, rather than resort to English, seeks help from his mother:

Thomas (to father): Sie haben einen kleinen roten, ah, einen kleinen roten — *(They've got a little red, ah, a little red —)* (to mother): Tell Daddy, ah, they had a little red slide you could get down to the sand on.
Mother: Yes.

However, again, whilst this preference for English exists in these circumstances and may indicate a sub-conscious feeling that it is easier to operate in English, the children can function fluently and intelligibly in German in the very same circumstances if they have to. The above conversation, for example, continues as follows:

Father: Was haben sie? *(What have they got?)*
Thomas: Eine rote Rutschbahn, und man kann rutschen gehen — runter zu der Sand. *(A red slide and you can go sliding — down to the sand.)*

Even so, it is interesting that when, after a day speaking only English at school, the children have to speak German, it takes them a while to distance themselves from this English influence, this being reflected in the quality of their German. Einar Haugen,[83] born in the U.S.A. of Norwegian immigrant parents, recalls similar problems during his childhood.

"My earliest recollections are from the problems I encountered in keeping apart the Norwegian I spoke at home with my parents and the English I spoke on the street with my playmates . . . Thanks to my parents' adamant insistence on my speaking their native language at home, the threshold of the home became the cue to my code switch . . . I know that in coming in from a lively

time among my playmates I committed many a violation of
Norwegian idiom . . .

The parents' subjective observations about the quality of the children's
German after a period of intensive contact with only English were tested by
means of a series of tape-recordings made of the children's speech before
and after such situations. These recordings confirm the subjective impres-
sions to a large extent. For example, when Thomas was aged 5;10,5 his
speech was taped at home before school and then again immediately after
school when his father met him at the school gate and took him home.
Although his speed of delivery was roughly the same on both occasions,
namely 88.9 words per minute before and 89.9 words per minute after
school, his fluency was much better before school, his speech containing
only 9.4 filled pauses and 3.5 repeats with every 100 words compared with
15.0 and 4.5 respectively after school. His German was also not as accurate
after school, containing 5.5 errors per 100 words, as compared with 4.0 per
100 words before school.

It could be argued that the performance after school might simply not
be as good because of the child's natural tiredness after spending 6½ hours
in the classroom and playground. However, examinations of the children's
English before and after school reveal no significant differences in performance. Despite the fact that both children do not speak German as accurately
as they do English, they seldom seem aware of, or troubled by this. They
appear as confident about their ability to speak German as they do to speak
English, a confidence which is not without justification, since they can, after
all, communicate easily and effectively in German. Moreover this confidence is bolstered by their parents' frequent encouragement and their and
others' recognition of their ability to express themselves in German.

Even at age 3;5, an age when he was not particularly willing to speak
German, Thomas obviously did not regard the language as difficult. On
being told by an uncle that he could not understand a German storybook
Thomas had handed to him, Thomas looked a bit non-plussed and then
earnestly made a comment which would hardly convince learners of either
language:

Thomas: But, Graeme, German's just like English, just a bit different.

At age 5;0,9, Thomas, when asked by his father why he preferred to speak
English to himself, replied: "Englisch ist leichter — nicht so schwer wie
Deutsch." (*English is easier — not as difficult as German.*) However, it is
difficult to judge whether this was his actual opinion or whether it was a
justification thought up on the spur of the moment to explain something he

probably had not before considered. For, only ten days later, he expressed a different opinion. His father was telling Thomas that he was trying to obtain a cassette in German of SESAME STREET, one of the children's favourite television programmes at that time:

Thomas (to father): Das würde sehr gut sein. *(That would be very good.)*
Mother: Why's that, Tom?
Thomas: Because I'm very interested in German and I can understand it
    better.

However, here his response may have been motivated by his enthusiasm at the prospect of obtaining the German cassette and by a desire to please his father who was going to the trouble of obtaining it for him.

On another occasion, both Thomas (5;9,29) and Frank (3;11,6) were being questioned by a family friend about their bilingualism:

Friend: Do you talk to Daddy *all* the time in German?
Thomas: Yes.
Frank: Hm.
Friend: Isn't that hard work?
Thomas: No.
Friend: Is it just as easy as English?
Thomas: Yes.
Frank: Yes.

The same type of confident assessment of his own ability was also apparent when Thomas was 6;3,2. His father, playing the role of a reporter for the DEUTSCHE WELLE *(The Voice of Germany)* doing a report on Australia, questioned him among other things about his bilingualism:

"Reporter": Welche Sprache kannst du am besten sprechen? *(Which
    language can you speak best?)*
Thomas (without hesitation and in a matter-of-fact tone of voice):
    Englisch und Deutsch. *(English and German.)*
"Reporter": Beide? *(Both?)*
Thomas: Ja. *(Yes.)*

This confidence extended to his perceived ability to read the two languages (see also chapter 8). At age 6;7,5, for instance, when he was making good progress in reading in both languages, he considered that he could read both equally well:

Father (casually): Welche Sprache kannst du am besten lesen? *(Which
    language can you read best?)*
Thomas: Ah, beide. *(Ah, both.)*

This self-assessment corresponded more or less with reality. The fact that he was receiving much more practice in English reading at school was compensated for to a large extent by the much closer correspondence between German spelling and sounds. Indeed, the comparative complexity of the English spelling system, which makes previously unseen words much more difficult for a beginner to decipher than German words seen for the first time (cf. English *brought* [brɔːt], *though* [ðʌʊ] with German *brachte* [braxtə], *doch* [dɔx]), was recognized by Thomas, the following spontaneous remark typical of his view of the matter:

> **Thomas** (7;2,26): Ich mag Deutsch besser als Englisch, Bert, weil, weil —
> ich kann nicht sehr gut in Englisch lesen. *(I like German better than
> English, Bert, because, because — I can't read very well in English.)*

This self-judgement was not really true, since his English reading at that time, was, due both to the many hours of practice at school and his enthusiasm for reading, on a par with, if not slightly better than, his reading in German. It is a judgement, therefore, based not on his actual reading performance but perhaps on the realization that much more effort and practice is required to read English.

Frank has to date made very little comment on his ability in both languages, answering any questions on the subject with a non-committal, "I don't know". However, on one occasion, when he was able to count better in German than in English and he was looking ahead to the following year when he would start school, he made the following comments which suggest that he had few doubts about his ability to function satisfactorily in German:

> **Frank** (4;9,20): Bert, ich kann nicht so gut in Englisch zählen. Du mußt
> eine deutsche Schule für mich funden *(sic)*. Dann kann ich in
> Deutsch lernen. *(Bert, I can't count as well in English. You'll have to
> find a German school for me. Then I can learn in German.)*

Lest an impression be conveyed of total confidence on the part of the children in their ability in German, it should be pointed out that on occasions doubts have been expressed. When this does happen, the parents consider it important that the children receive assurance and encouragement. Whilst some of the mistakes in the children's speech might be lamented, the children should not be deterred from using the language to communicate because of any doubts about their ability to speak it accurately. This does not mean that grammatical accuracy must be discarded as a goal, but it should never take precedence over having the children using the language spontaneously and naturally for everyday communication. In the following example, Thomas (6;1,25) has obviously been worrying about the correct form of various utterances and has asked his father several questions about them. Then, after some thought, he asks:

> **Thomas**: Bert, spreche ich sehr gut Deutsch? *(Bert, do I speak very good German?)*
> **Father**: Ja. Warum fragst du denn? *(Yes. Why do you ask?)*
> **Thomas**: Weil, weil, ich habe ein paar kleine Fehler gemacht. *(Because, because, I made a few little mistakes.)*
> **Father**: Ein paar kleine Fehler? Das macht doch nichts. Wir machen ja alle Fehler. *(A few little mistakes? That doesn't matter. We all make mistakes.)*
> **Thomas**: Oh. Gibt es niemand in die Welt, das keine Fehler macht? *(Oh. Isn't there anybody in the world who doesn't make mistakes?)*
> **Father**: Nein, niemand. Ich mache auch manchmal Fehler, wenn ich Deutsche spreche, und auch wenn ich Englisch spreche. *(No, nobody. I make mistakes too sometimes when I'm speaking German, and also when I'm speaking English.)*

Thomas's reading, and even more so writing exercises he does in German for his father, have brought home to him that some features of his speech do not conform to the grammar of Standard German (see chapter 8 for further details on biliteracy). This does not, as a rule, seem to worry him, probably because he is already used to it, but on a much lesser scale, from English language work at school. However, at times he obviously does ponder the matter. In the following example it is about half an hour after Thomas (7;2,29) has completed almost faultlessly a quite difficult writing exercise for his father for which he has received some well-deserved praise. He suddenly broaches the subject of his German with his mother:

> **Thomas**: Mum, do *you* think my German's good?
> **Mother**: Yes, very good, Thomas.
> **Thomas**: Is your German good, Mum?
> **Mother**: Oh, pretty good. I make different sorts of mistakes to you.
> **Father**: Was hältst *du* von deinem Deutsch, Ernie? *(What do you think of your German, Ernie?)*
> **Thomas**: Gut. *(Good.)*
> **Mother**: Do you think you speak it well, Thomas?
> **Thomas**: Yes, Mum.
> **Mother**: So do I, really well.

Doubts about their ability to comprehend spoken German have arisen from time to time when the children have been confronted with an unfamiliar variety of German, particularly if spoken rapidly and/or indistinctly. This is no doubt attributable to their having really only one source of German input, and an adult one at that (see pp. 146ff.). On one occasion, for example, the children watched a German film, DIE VORSTADTKROKODILE (*The Suburban Crocodiles*) (based on the novel of the same name by Max von der Grün) on the Sydney multilingual television station, Channel 0/28. The picture and sound quality was marred by poor reception and this did not facilitate comprehension, but what really startled both Thomas (6;11,19) and Frank (5;0,27) was the very rapid speech of the child characters which they followed with great difficulty. On the other hand, adults in the film, whose diction was clearer and slower, were understood relatively easily. Thomas, who was visibly a little upset by his inability to understand all that the children in the film said, was apparently not deterred by the experience, as evidenced by the following excerpt from a conversation with friends the following day, even allowing for a certain amount of peer one-upmanship:

Frank: Shane, did you see that crocodile film?
Shane (uncertain): Yes.
Thomas: Did you have to read that English writing (i.e. sub-titles)? I didn't have to because it was in German and it was real easy for me. It was called "Die Vorstadtkrokodile".

Different accents of German also cause the children some constern-ation, again simply because they have little contact with anything but the type of "standard" North German accent normally used on German radio and television, in commercially available recorded stories, and by their father. In English, however, they are used to hearing a wide variety of both native and non-native accents of English, both in everyday life and in radio and television programmes. When faced with a pronounced South German accent, for example, particularly if used in rapid speech, the children are often baffled. While watching a film ANSCHI UND MICHAEL, which was set in Bavaria, Thomas (7;6,1) made the following somewhat exasperated comment:

Thomas: Bert, ich kann diesen blöden Jungen Michael nicht verstehen. Er spricht so schnell und komisch. Aber ich kann seine Mutter verstehen, und seine Freundin auch. Und die Eltern von seiner Freundin. Warum spricht Michael anders? (*Bert, I can't understand this stupid boy Michael. He speaks so fast and funny. But I can understand his mother, and his girl-friend, too. And his girl-friend's parents. Why does Michael speak differently?*)

The boy Michael referred to, a toolmaking apprentice, spoke rapidly with a distinct Bavarian accent, occasionally even switching into Bavarian dialect, whilst the other characters mentioned spoke more distinctly and with an accent closer to Standard German. Even a short utterance, produced rapidly and with an unfamiliar pronunciation and intonation, might not be understood, e.g. *Die hoaßt nit Claudia!* instead of standard *Die heißt nicht Claudia!* (Her name's not Claudia!). In this case, the father attempted to dispel Thomas's concern by drawing parallels with similar instances in English-language films when the children have had initial comprehension difficulties with various accents and dialects (e.g. Yorkshire English in the B.B.C. television serial "The Secret Garden": "Thou mon talk like that to Master Colin. Thou'll make him laugh and there's nowt as good for ill folk as laughin' is."; compare Australian English: "You should talk like that to Master Colin. You'll make him laugh and there's nothing as good for sick people as laughing is."), and by explaining that some practice and perseverance were needed before different kinds of German and English could be understood easily. This explanation was accepted readily enough, with Thomas recalling accent variations he had encountered previously in English and then going on to enjoy the film, aided by his father when the Bavarian German proved too much for him. Nevertheless, the experience did make an impression on him, as evidenced by his remarks towards the end of the film:

Thomas: Bert, gibt es ein Norddeutschland-Deutsch? *(Bert, is there a North Germany German?)*
Father: Ja, Ernie. *(Yes, Ernie.)*
Thomas: Ist das wie unser Deutsch? *(Is that like our German?)*
Father: Ja. *(Yes.)*
Thomas: Werden wir nach Norddeutschland gehen, wenn wir nach Deutschland gehen? *(Will we go to North Germany when we go to Germany?)*
Father (realizing the significance of the question and laughing): Ich glaube ja. Warum denn? *(I think so. Why?)*
Thomas (smiling): Damit wir die Leute verstehen können! *(So that we can understand the people!)*

Fortunately, the majority of German films the children have seen have been in more or less Standard German and, despite the fact that the dialogue in many of them, being aimed primarily at an adult audience (e.g. Werner Herzog's film AGUIRRE, DER ZORN GOTTES [*Aguirre, the Wrath of God*]), has been quite complex, they have understood them well, almost as well as adult English films. These successes have done much to strengthen their confidence in their competence in German.

The children have been encouraged at home to regard their bilingualism as something positive and advantageous, and their behaviour reflects this attitude. They not only have confidence but also pride in their ability to speak German in addition to English. There is, after all, a certain amount of prestige attached to a skill which is outside the scope of most of their friends and acquaintances.

The children and language and languages

It is most probable that a child's bilingualism will arouse his or her interest not only in his or her own two languages (e.g. why and when, where and to whom each is to be used), but also in other languages, who speaks them and where, and so on. This has been the case with both Thomas and Frank.

At age 3;6, after some contact with people other than his father who spoke German, Thomas began to show great curiosity about exactly who could and who could not speak the language. This curiosity continued unabated for several months. It seemed from his interminable questions that each individual person had to be classified as knowing German or not, e.g.:

Father: Der Techniker an der Universität hat mein Radio repariert. *(The technician at the university fixed my wireless.)*
Thomas (3;8,3): Hast du Deutsch gesprochen? *(Did you speak German?)*
Father: Nein, Englisch. *(No, English.)*
Thomas: Kann der Techniker kein Deutsch? *(Doesn't the technician know any German?)*

When Thomas was aged 3;7, his father showed him a Malay primary school reading book and, for fun, read him some of it in Malay. His initial reaction was one of amazement, which quickly turned to curiosity. He wanted to know how to say various things in Malay and quickly learnt a number of greetings and other words which he delighted in using, e.g.:

Thomas (3;8,1): Apa kabar? *(How are you?)*
Father: Baik, terima kasih. *(Well, thank you.)*
Thomas: Saya suka kau. *(I like you.)*

The realization that there were other languages besides German and English led him to ask about them and to request to be taught how to say various things in them. This obviously fascinated him, and his confidence after mastering a few words was boundless, as evidenced by the following amusing/embarrassing incident when his father was enrolling him in a German-language kindergarten (see also p. 241):

Teacher (to Thomas): Sprichst du zu Hause Deutsch? *(Do you speak German at home?)*

Thomas (3;8,0): Ja, und Englisch und (Fran)zösisch und Malaiisch. *(Yes, and English and French and Malay.)*

Teacher (taken aback, addressing the father with concern): Glauben Sie nicht, daß das ein bißchen zuviel ist? *(Don't you think that's a bit too much?)*

In another incident, he (5;0,2) was praised at his English-language kindergarten for singing the Christmas song "Jingle Bells" so fluently and with so much expression in Spanish. The whole song was, however, unbeknown to his teachers, in his own *invented* Spanish!

At age 4;6 Thomas invented an imaginary friend to whom he gave the name Kinnetkopf and who spoke an imaginary language called Gedisch. If Kinnetkopf wanted to communicate with other members of the family, or they with him, Thomas had to act as interpreter, since only he and Kinnetkopf spoke Gedisch.

Thomas's realization that quite a bit of Dutch and Afrikaans, read to him from magazines for fun, was intelligible to someone knowing German and English (e.g. Afrikaans *perd*=German *Pferd* [horse], Afrikaans *siek*= English *sick*, thus "My perd is siek"="My horse is sick"), started him on a new track of enquiry: which languages are similar, related, and why? For example:

Thomas (5;1,0): Mum, is ESTNISCH *(Estonian)* related to Hungarian?
Mother: Oh, I don't know, Thomas. You'll have to ask Daddy about that.
Thomas (somewhat accusingly): Aren't you interested in languages?
Mother (amused): Yes, I'm interested, I just don't know.

In games, Thomas frequently requested that his father speak other languages to him, particularly languages such as Dutch, much of which he could understand if spoken slowly and clearly and if vocabulary was used which was similar to the German or English words, as in the following game where Thomas is a doctor, the father a Dutch patient:

Father (groaning): Ooh! Goeden middag, dokter. *(DUTCH: Ooh! Good afternoon, doctor.)*
Thomas (6;0,4): Guten Tag. Was ist los? *(GERMAN: Good day. What's the matter?)*
Father: Ooh! Ik ben ziek. *(DUTCH: Ooh! I'm sick.)*
Thomas (listens with his stethoscope and then reaches for his scalpel): Ja, du bist sehr krank. *(GERMAN: Yes, you're very sick.)*
Father (in mock fear): Was is dat? Een mes? Wat doet u met het mes? *(DUTCH: What's that? A knife? What are you going to do with the knife?)*

Thomas: Ich muß operieren . . . *(GERMAN: I have to operate . . .)*

Not long after he began to read and write (see chapter 8), Thomas became aware that some languages did not use the same writing system as English and German. Consequently Chinese, Japanese, Arabic, Hindi, etc., became objects of fascination. Since then he has often amused himself by imitating these scripts and then reading out, in pseudo-Arabic etc., what he has written, e.g.:

Father (teasing): Was ist dieses Gekritzel? *(What's this scribble?)*
Thomas (6;3,22): Das ist arabisches Schreiben! Man muß nur Linien und
    Punkte machen. Ich kann das lesen: gremetaretascho dublich — ah,
    ich sage das jetzt in Deutsch: Lieber Vetter, ich hoffe, daß du dieses
    Jahr schwimmen lernst . . . *(That's Arabic writing! You only have*
    to make lines and dots. I can read it: Gremetaretascho dublich — ah,
    I'll say that in German now: Dear cousin, I hope you learn to swim
    this year . . .)

Frank has also shown interest in other languages, although a less intense interest than Thomas. He, too, has learnt phrases from various languages which he uses at times, usually only within the family to create some special effect. One interesting exception to this occurred when he was aged 3;10,3. Some time before, he had learnt the Chinese expression "Ni hao ma?" *(How are you?)* from an English story called *Moy Moy*.[235] On this occasion he was in a building waiting with his parents for the lift to reach their floor. When the lift did eventually arrive, it was packed with people. The first person Frank saw was a Chinese woman, and to his parents' great surprise he immediately and quite spontaneously exclaimed, "Ni hao ma?" Before the startled woman could respond in any way to indicate whether she had understood Frank's version of the Chinese greeting, the doors snapped shut and the lift moved on.

The advent of an Australian multilingual television station (see pp. 234–237), as well as contact with various bilingual children who speak languages other than English at home has maintained Thomas's and Frank's interest in other languages. For example, Thomas's best friend in grade one at school was a girl called Helen who spoke Greek at home, and for that same year Frank and Thomas had as next-door neighbours children who spoke Dutch to their parents.

The fact that both parents are interested in languages as well and have been willing to discuss them with the children has no doubt also contributed to their continuing interest.

Bilingualism and an interest in other languages have given the children an appreciation of the fact that no particular language is superior to any other. One incident can clearly illustrate this awareness. The father was reading to Thomas (7;11,9) from a German translation of an adventure novel by the Russian author Juri Korinetz,[236] called DORT, WEIT HINTER DEM FLUß (*There, Far Beyond the River*).

The particular chapter being read was called DIE FORELLENSPRACHE (*The Trout Language*), and in it the central character, a young boy called Mischa who speaks only Russian, is told by his uncle that trout have their own language which is a perfectly adequate means of communication; the boy reacts as follows:

> **Mischa**: Es gibt doch nur eine wirklich reiche Sprache, nur eine wahre und eine freie! Unsere russische Sprache! Alle anderen Sprachen sind schlechter und ärger, überhaupt blödsinnig! *(But there's only one really rich language, only one true and free language! Our Russian language! All other languages are worse and inferior, altogether stupid!)*

At this point Thomas interjected in disbelief.

> **Thomas**: Nein — das ist nicht wahr, Bert. Es gibt viele andere Sprachen, die das haben: Englisch, Spanisch, Polnisch, Portugiesisch, und Tschechisch und Dänisch, und, ah — alle! *(No, that's not true, Bert. There are lots of other languages which have that* [i.e. these qualities]: *English, Spanish, Polish, Portuguese, and Czech and Danish, and, ah — all of them!)*

This, in fact, turned out to be exactly the point of this particular chapter, as the uncle then proceeds, by comparing Russian and Uzbek (a Turkic language of central Asia), to convincingly cure his nephew of his linguistic chauvinism. The uncle's final remarks met with Thomas's obvious approval:

> **Uncle**: Alle Sprachen sind groß und jede Sprache ist groß auf ihre Art . . . *(All languages are great and every language is great in its own way.)*
> **Thomas**: Ja. *(Yes.)*

Not until Thomas was aged 7;10,19 did he begin to ponder the actual mechanisms of bilingualism. He then speculated on how the two languages might be kept separate in the brain, and came up with his own original explanation. His speculation was prompted by what he perceived as his mother's use of an English /r/ instead of a rolled /r/ when reading out a

German word. He attempted to explain how the two sounds of the two languages could be kept separate:

> **Thomas** (quite earnestly): It's easy, Mum. I'll explain it to you. Ah, in your brain there's two visions (=divisions) — one's for German and one's for English, and you use one 'vision when you want to speak German and the other one if you want to speak English. So you wouldn't say "*r*abbit" (pronouncing it with a rolled r) in English and you wouldn't say "rows" (pronounced with an English r and diphthong), you'd say *raus* (=out). You have to use the right 'vision.
>
> **Mother** (amused): That's all right for you, but what about your poor old mum?

His explanation, despite its simplicity, is not *so* very different from some of the theories put forward by linguists and psychologists to explain how a bilingual keeps his languages separate (see pp. 21–22).

10 Other aids to the development of bilingualism

So far in this study various ways used by the family to foster bilingualism in the home have been mentioned, some in detail, some in passing, e.g. co-operation between the parents to provide vocabulary for new experiences for the children by allowing them to hear it from their mother in English and from their father in German.

In this section a number of aids are discussed which parents can utilize to develop their children's bilingualism.

Books

The value of books and storytelling in language maintenance has already been touched on in the sections on biliteracy (pp. 210ff.) and storytelling by the parents (pp. 89ff.), but a few additional points are worth mentioning here. From an early age, both children have had stories read aloud to them daily in German by their father, and in English by their mother. This has had a definite beneficial effect on both children's German and English vocabulary. Any vocabulary acquired from material read to them is more easily detectable in their German, since, apart from their father, their only other regular source of German is stories (including recorded stories — see p. 233). Such vocabulary extension has occurred, with both children actively using words and expressions heard in stories but perhaps not even used by their parents, e.g.:

Thomas (5;10,13): Oh, jetzt *besinne* ich mich. *(Oh, now I remember.)* (The father's expression would be "Jetzt *erinnere* ich mich.")

It is not only the children's vocabulary which benefits. Stories have also exposed the children to and in some cases made them aware of different

232

styles and levels of formality in German speech, differences which would be absent from the informal German spoken with their father (see pp. 204ff.).

Books are also useful for acquainting the children with the poetic uses of language, particularly in German, since this is something they are becoming more and more familiar with in English at school. This has encouraged them to experiment with such forms of language themselves. For example, at age 6;2,30 Thomas was reading aloud short rhymes from a German children's magazine, SAFRAN (12/1972, p. 32), such as the following:

> Der Wal, der Wal
> rutscht auf dem Bauch ins Tal.
> *(The whale, the whale,*
> *slides on his belly into the vale.)*

He found these rhymes amusing and then spontaneously produced one of his own:

> Der Bert, der Bert
> Er sprang auf ein Pferd.
> *(Bert, Bert, of course*
> *He jumped on a horse.)*

Although by no means a poetic masterpiece, it does rhyme and shows his awareness of the literary past tense *sprang* for "jumped" which has been acquired only from stories; in his own speech he would say *ist gesprungen* for "jumped", as in fact do most German-speakers in everyday conversation.

Records and cassettes

Records and cassettes of songs and stories are a useful aid for fostering a minority language. They help children who may be used to hearing a language in one particular variety from a small number of speakers, to become acquainted with different accents and varieties of the languages. They have proved beneficial for this purpose in the case of Thomas and Frank (see pp. 150ff.).

At the first playing of new recordings the father listens with the children and explains any difficulties they may have with the vocabulary or accent used. Stories which are especially interesting or exciting are requested frequently and, just as in the case of written stories, words and expressions heard on the recordings make their way into the children's speech.

If commercial recordings are not easily available or are too expensive, parents can easily make their own, for example by reading or simply telling favourite stories onto tape. Relatives, friends or acquaintances who speak the language, if possible with a variety of accents, speaking speeds, etc., can be asked to assist in the making of such tapes. With practice and a bit of ingenuity with sound effects and the like, quite professional-sounding recordings can be produced. A number of such recordings have been made for Thomas and Frank and have proven popular. They are not seen by the father, or the children, as normally being a substitute for actually reading and telling stories to the children in person, but rather as a supplement to this, or for use when the father has to be absent for some reason.

Video cassettes would also be very useful, especially if there were no regular opportunity to see films in the minority language on television or at a cinema. However, the financial outlay, which is at present considerable, may well prove prohibitive for many parents.

Using tapes, whether audio or video, can also be a useful means of maintaining close contact with relatives and friends in the country where the language is spoken. For young children particularly they are much more meaningful than letters, since for a short time it is as if the person speaking were actually there in person. (Telephone calls between countries can also fulfil this function, with the added advantage of enabling a two-way conversation.)

A parent who has to be absent from home for a period of time can also use tape recordings to good effect, sending them in addition to letters, postcards or making telephone calls to the children. When Thomas was aged 3;6,4 and Frank 1;7,2, for instance, their father went overseas for a month. He took a small cassette recorder with him and each week while he was away he sent home one or two cassettes on which he talked to the children about his trip. In addition, he left at home stories read on to tape which were played to the children at bedtime. This occurred at a time when Thomas was somewhat reluctant to speak German: two weeks before the father's departure Thomas was speaking only 59% German to him. As a temporary language maintenance measure the tapes proved helpful: two weeks after the father's return the amount of German Thomas was speaking to him had increased to 69% (see p. 142).

Radio and television

Until fairly recently, Australians who wished to be informed or entertained via the electronic media in a language other than English had to rely on overseas shortwave broadcasts. However, due to fluctuating reception conditions, and because virtually no shortwave broadcaster caters in any way for children, these transmissions have been of limited use in language maintenance as far as children are concerned.

These shortwave broadcasts can, however, be very helpful for parents. The father in this study has found a good quality shortwave receiver to be an invaluable aid in maintaining and extending his own German. Despite the vagaries of atmospheric conditions, German-language transmissions can usually be picked up in Australia reasonably clearly from a variety of stations, the main ones being the Deutsche Welle (Federal Republic of Germany), Radio Berlin International (German Democratic Republic), Swiss Radio International, and Radio Austria. Other shortwave stations, such as Radio Japan, Radio Sweden and the B.B.C., to name but a few, also broadcast German-language programmes which, although intended for listeners in Europe, can be received in Australia from time to time. But wherever one happens to live and whatever country one wishes to pick up, to ensure that the best quality shortwave reception is obtained with one's radio it is advisable to erect some sort of outdoor aerial, however simple, e.g. a length of wire attached to the branch of a nearby tree.

In Australia itself, radio and television transmissions in languages other than English were severely limited by law until the end of 1973; they could not exceed 2.5% of a station's total broadcast time and had to be accompanied by an English translation. However, since then there has been a growing awareness and recognition of the multilingual nature of Australian society. After experiments with broadcasting in non-English languages from 1975, the government established the Special Broadcasting Service (S.B.S.) in 1978. Its two radio stations in Sydney and Melbourne now broadcast in over forty languages. The S.B.S. is also linked to some public broadcasting stations in other towns throughout Australia. That this has been a boon for immigrants is probably illustrated no more spectacularly than by the case of a Turkish-speaking lorry driver reported in *The Sydney Morning Herald* (7.6.1982):

> "Driving down Parramatta Road in his vehicle, the Turk suddenly happened upon 2EA (Sydney's multilingual radio station), while tuning his truck radio. Halting the lorry, he leaped to the roadway dancing and singing with joy. 'That's my language, that's my music!', he rejoiced as a huge traffic jam built up."

In 1979 and 1980 experimental television programmes in languages other than English were broadcast for three hours per week. Since late 1980 the S.B.S. has been operating a multilingual television station, Channel 0/28, in both Sydney and Melbourne. It transmits daily for approximately five hours in many languages, including some news and documentary pro-grammes in English. All programmes not in English are provided with English subtitles.

Few of the S.B.S. radio programmes in languages other than English cater very much for young children. (Of the seven hours of German broad-cast each week in Sydney, for example, only a quarter of an hour is for children.) However, Channel 0/28 does devote a reasonable amount of its time to children's programmes. These have proved very useful in fostering the linguistic and cultural awareness of Thomas and Frank. The programmes which are in German are (as already mentioned on pp. 225ff.) valuable for exposing them to different varieties of German, especially the German of children, and making them aware that in other parts of the world German is just as English is in Australia, i.e. at school, with playmates, etc.

When watching German films, Thomas, as his reading ability im-proved, began to compare the English subtitles, if they were not flashed on the screen too rapidly, with the German sound-track. For example, at age 7;8,8 he was watching a scene in the German children's series "Timm Thaler", in which a flying instructor deliberately stalled the plane's engine to give his pupil emergency landing practice:

Pupil: Was ist los? *(What's wrong?)*
Instructor: Oh, der Motor ist ausgefallen. *(Oh, the engine's packed it in.)*
Pupil: Sind Sie verrückt?! *(Are' you crazy?!)*
Thomas: Er sagt: ,,Sind Sie verrückt?", und da steht: *(He says, "Are you crazy?", and it says there* [i.e. in the sub-titles] "Are you joking?" (Obviously surprised at the English version, although in the context it is not really inappropriate.)

Of course, when children can read well, the subtitles can prove distracting. A narrow strip of paper stuck along the bottom of the television screen solves this problem.

The children's programmes on Channel 0/28 in languages other than German have also proved to be valuable. Firstly, since the programmes are for children in Australia and since children are encouraged to write to the station, their letters being mentioned in a mailbag session, Frank and Thomas have gained an increased appreciation of the fact that there are many other Australian children like themselves who at home speak a lang-uage other than English, a realization which can only help maintain their positive attitude to their own bilingual situation. Secondly, their father uses such films to provide the children with additional exposure to German by translating the English subtitles into German for them. This works very well, although it can be somewhat exhausting for the father if a film contains very rapid dialogue. In addition, if the children become engrossed in the programme, they may forget that it is the father who is providing the soundtrack and ask him questions about, or make comments to him about the action or plot. Nevertheless, they obviously enjoy watching children's programmes from a variety of countries and are appreciative of the father's simultaneous translations into German — and fortunately sympathetic when he falls behind very rapid subtitles!

Only one fifth of the children's weekly television watching (total 7–9 hours) is on the multilingual channel. The rest is in English. However, it has been found that even English-language programmes can be utilized to foster German if they are viewed with the children. A difficult plot and/or difficult vocabulary can be explained by the father in German. Whilst such explanations were required more when the children were younger, as they get older they can still be encouraged to discuss what has happened or might happen in a programme. Such explanations and discussions have proved to be an effective way not only of helping to keep the children's German vocabulary apace of their English vocabulary, but also of improving their English vocabulary, e.g. when the word "monotremes" occurred in a nature programme, it was not only explained:

Father: Das sind australische Tiere, die Säugetiere sind, die aber auch Eier legen — wie das Schnabeltier und der Ameisenigel. *(They're Australian animals which are mammals but which also lay eggs — like the platypus and the echidna.)*

but the German term was also given:

Father: Auf deutsch heißen "monotremes" Kloakentiere. *(In German "monotremes" are called KLOAKENTIERE.)*

Some English-language programmes have also been useful for conferring esteem on bilingualism; some of the principal characters have been bilingual and this has been portrayed as an ability which is a definite advantage and to be admired.

Another possibility with regard to radio and television, at least as far as certain languages are concerned, is programmes specially prepared and broadcast for people studying these languages as foreign languages. Various programmes of this type are broadcast in Australia for students of German, e.g. the B.B.C. series KONTAKTE, and some of these have proved usable with Thomas and Frank. From age 4;7 to 5;0, for example, Frank looked forward to watching KONTAKTE (which is entirely in German) each Friday on television just as much as he did to watching *Playschool* (in English). The language used in KONTAKTE is simple and clear, much of the dialogue is humorous, and a good view is given of life in present-day Germany. Radio plays produced by the B.B.C. for Higher School Certificate students have also been used with the children after about age 6. The language in these is more complex than in KONTAKTE, but has presented few difficulties to the children, and, most importantly, the stories have proved popular because they are interesting and exciting.

Games

Games played with the children are a very useful and enjoyable means of reinforcing and extending their language, particularly in German. From a very early age the children quickly acquired the German vocabulary needed to play particular games with their father, e.g. it is much more effective to say *"Hüh!"* (giddy-up) to a horse (=the father) who obviously seems to understand no English. These games may be invented by the children or be based on a story they have heard (in either language), a television programme, a game played at school, etc. The playing with the father of a game already played frequently with playmates in English offers an ideal opportunity to create a vocabulary of similar sophistication in German. A simple game of *Räuber und Gendarm* (cops and robbers), for instance imparts a wide range of German vocabulary connected with crime and law enforcement, e.g. "Untersuch die Waffe auf Fingerabdrücke." (*Examine the weapon for fingerprints.*) The frequent repetition of such phrases quickly establishes them as part of the children's active vocabulary and helps restore the balance between English and German. In addition, such games offer an opportunity to iron out some grammatical problems relatively unobtrusively.

Even reading and writing can be incorporated painlessly into games, e.g. with a treasure hunt at the beach in which the treasure can only be found by following a series of clues written with a stick in the sand.

The most important thing, of course, about games is that they are an enjoyable and reasonably effortless way of increasing and consolidating the children's range of language.

Outings

In families where only one parent speaks the minority language to the children, it can prove very useful for that parent occasionally to arrange some sort of interesting outing alone with the children, an outing on which the language can be used exclusively. The father in this study has found that outings like this (e.g. a walk in the bush) ensure that the children get a lot of speaking practice, and some improvement in the ease with which they express themselves is usually noticeable after quite a short time.

Shops, restaurants, etc.

Depending on the language in question, it may be possible to locate shops, banks, restaurants, etc., where someone knows that language and is prepared to speak it to customers. The children can then see that the language does have certain possibilities outside the home. Even at age 8, for instance, Thomas still finds it an exciting experience to be able to carry out some simple transaction in German, for example buying a book from the German-speaking staff of a Sydney bookshop. The beneficial effect of such an experience is evident from the enthusiasm with which he later tells friends about what he did. Even if a language not known to the children can be heard, for example in a restaurant, this too can be a useful experience for promoting interest and pride in bilingualism. A child can derive a certain amount of satisfaction, when asked, for instance, by a waiter "Can you speak Chinese?", from not having to admit to knowing English only but being able to reply, 'No, but I can speak German."

Ethnic schools and playgroups

In countries of immigration, various groups of interested and concerned immigrants establish "ethnic" schools to give their children instruction in the language and culture of their former homeland. These usually hold classes outside normal school hours, either in the late afternoon or at the weekend. For younger children, playgroups may be organized at other times.

It is estimated, for example, that in Australia today there are approximately 1,000 ethnic schools attended by about 100,000 children each week.[237] Ethnic playgroups and schools can provide parents with valuable support in preserving and fostering a language. The children — and the parents — then realize that there are others in the same position as they are, and that it is feasible to retain a linguistic (and cultural) system different from that of the community at large, whilst still being able to function adequately in that community. Such schools are particularly useful in making children literate in the language of the home, as many parents are unsure about how to teach their children to read and write or are apprehensive about tackling this on their own (see also pp. 210ff. for discussion of biliteracy).

However, such schools do have their problems. Firstly, they usually take place *in addition* to the children's normal school hours. If held in the late afternoon, the children are not only tired after a full day at the normal school but may regard it as an imposition when their monolingual peers are free to play or watch television. This applies probably even more so to classes held at the weekend. Secondly, many parents shift most of the responsibility of language maintenance on to the ethnic school. They rarely, if ever, speak the language to their children at home or encourage the children to speak it to them, and then expect the ethnic school to teach it to them in, say, three hours every Saturday morning. For such children the ethnic school is virtually a foreign language school. Unfortunately, this attitude is even held by some of those running ethnic schools. For example, at a migrant studies seminar held in Melbourne in 1979, the co-ordinator of a number of Saturday schools for a particular language, when asked if the children who attended the classes also used the language at home, remarked, "No, very little — we think it's a bit much to demand that children use the language at home."

Ethnic schools can be successful if considered as an *aid* to, not a substitute for, someone in the home regularly and consistently using the language for communication with the children. Without the support of the home, such schools can, in the limited time available, impart but a smattering of the language.

A solution to the problems caused by the ethnic schools being conducted outside normal school hours would, of course, be for the teaching of the home language, or even for some teaching *in* the home language, to be incorporated into the normal school curriculum. However, this is only possible with the co-operation of the school authorities and normally only if a particular minority language group constitutes a significant proportion of the school population. But when children's bilingualism is acknowledged and provision made for it in the normal school, studies show that the results can be very pleasing. Not only does the minority language receive in this way a certain amount of status — it is now part of the normal school curriculum just as arithmetic is — but the scholastic progress of the children can actually be improved. Lambert,[238] for example, reports on an experiment conducted in the northern regions of Maine (U.S.A.), where French is spoken by 85% of families. Several schools were permitted to teach about one third of their elementary curriculum in French, and the progress of the children in these schools was compared to that of other bilingual children of comparable intelligence and socio-economic background who received instruction only in English. After five years the children who had received part of their instruction in French clearly outperformed those children in the all-English schools in *English* language achievement tests and on academic content such as mathematics, learned partly through French. Moreover they were bi-literate, having learned to read and write both English and French, whilst the children in the all-English schools had become literate only in English.

Similar evidence is emerging in the Australian context. For example, in 1980 McGill[239] reported that at Milingimbi in the Northern Territory, Aboriginal children taught at school in *both* English *and* Gupapuyngu (one of the more than one hundred Aboriginal languages still spoken in Australia) have been found to perform significantly better than children in an English-only programme on such measures as *English* reading, *English* written composition, oral *English* and arithmetic.

In the case of Thomas and Frank, there is no language except English taught at the primary school which they attend. Only Thomas had any experience with an ethnic school. Between the ages of 3;8 and 4;1 he attended the kindergarten section of a German Saturday school in Melbourne for 2½ hours on Saturday mornings. It was beneficial in that it brought him into contact with other German speakers. However, it was not, unfortunately, as successful as it could have been, because many of the children attending spoke little or no German at home, so that the teacher often used English to communicate with them. Trying to cater for children of disparate linguistic competence is a problem faced by many ethnic schools.

Parents may also provide their children with reading and writing instruction in the minority language themselves at home, either instead of or in addition to using an ethnic school. Details of how this has been attempted with Thomas and Frank are given in the section on biliteracy (pp. 210ff.).

Visits to and from the linguistic homeland

An ideal aid in establishing and maintaining bilingualism in the home would be for the family to make regular trips to a country where the language is spoken, or to be visited fairly regularly by relatives and/or friends from that country. Of course, the feasibility of this will depend on geographical, political and financial considerations. For example, someone making a trip from London to Helsinki, Moscow or Ankara has less distance to cover (and consequently less to outlay in fares) than someone travelling from Sydney on one side of Australia to Perth on the other side of the country, not to mention someone departing from Sydney to Europe. Immigrants who are refugees often do not have ready access to their former homeland.

However, if such visits to the homeland can be managed, the benefits are many. Both the children and their parents are for a time totally immersed in the language, the children come into contact with the language of children of their own age (something usually lacking in a foreign environment) and see the language being used as a completely viable means of communication in all spheres of life. It is an opportunity for their language to be revitalized.

Similar, but not so striking, benefits can result from visits by grand-parents, etc., to the new country, as their presence increases the amount and variety of language used in the home, particularly in mixed marriages. Some immigrant families, of course, have this benefit on a permanent basis, in that the grandparents are also immigrants and live with or near the family; their presence means that the home language is heard and *used* much more by their grandchildren. Smolicz & Harris's[227] interviews in 1977 with 70 children of Polish parents in Australia showed, for example, that 94% of them spoke only Polish to their grandparents, whereas only 57% spoke only Polish to their parents.

Correspondence

One way of getting children interested in reading and writing the language is for them to be encouraged to regularly exchange letters in it with friends and/or relatives, particularly with children of similar age and inter-ests in a country where the language is the majority language. Another possibility is to obtain a penfriend who speaks the language by writing to a magazine with a "Penfriends Wanted" section, or by contacting an organiz-ation which puts prospective correspondents in touch with each other.

Language maintenance for parents

In many ways the quality of language acquired by children mainly or only from their parents in a foreign environment will obviously depend very much on the quality of language they hear from their parents. It therefore follows that if parents wish to pass on what they regard as a good standard of the particular language, they should offer their children a good model. This requires some effort and vigilance on the part of the parents to keep their own language active, fresh and up-to-date. Many of the points already mentioned in this section are also useful here: reading of newspapers, magazines and books, writing letters, listening to records, cassettes and radio broadcasts, watching films in the language, etc. All of these can help parents not only to maintain their language but also to extend it by introducing them to new vocabulary and idioms which have come into being in the linguistic homeland and which may not even yet be found in diction-aries, e.g. on the occasion of the first flight by the American space shuttle Columbia, the father in this study learned immediately from a shortwave news broadcast beamed towards Australasia by the DEUTSCHE WELLE (*Voice of Germany*) in Cologne that this new concept was expressed in German as *(Welt)raumfähre* (literally "space ferry"), and he was thus able to use the correct specific term when discussing the event with the children.

Nevertheless, a good quality dictionary is virtually indispensable for checking and finding information. Brand new vocabulary (such as "space shuttle" just mentioned) can be written in for later reference.

Opportunities can also be sought to speak the language as frequently as possible with other speakers of the language; in countries with immigrants, many ethnic groups have formed various clubs and organizations (cultural, social, sporting, religious, etc.) which could be joined or whose functions could be attended.

There is much truth in what Haugen[240] says:

"Once acquired, an extra language is like swimming or dancing or bicycling, in not being easily forgotten in disuse. But for successful and skilful performance, it requires, like these, constant practice and effort."

11 Conclusions

Given the disproportionate amount of exposure Thomas and Frank have had to the two languages, the results obtained in this experiment in creating bilingualism would seem to be very satisfactory. Both children, it is true, are more fluent and accurate in English, but have approximately equal vocabularies in German and English. In the home they function equally well in English and German. Outside, they can be indistinguishable from monolingual English-speaking peers, and can also communicate effectively with German-speakers.

Moreover, their German has been acquired at no expense to their English, the official language of their country. Knowing German has not impeded the children's speech development in English, nor has being able to speak, read and write in German had any deleterious effect on their educational progess in an English-speaking school. In this regard, it is worth recalling that there is much evidence to suggest that bilingualism can enhance children's intellectual capacity in various ways.

Family harmony has not been disturbed by the use of two languages in the home. Indeed, in some ways family relationships may well have benefited from this home bilingualism, for example, the relationship between the father and the children — the father's endeavours to ensure that they are exposed to as much German as possible means that he spends as much time as possible talking to and playing with them.

No formal *teaching* of German has been required (except in reading and writing); instead, the children have been given the opportunity to *acquire* the language (just as monolingual children acquire their native language) by being consistently spoken to in German and by being encouraged to use the language themselves as a natural means of communication. Once using a language like this becomes the established routine in a family, much of the language like this becomes the established routine in a family, much of the battle is already won. Nevertheless, as has been seen, some effort and perseverance have been required to establish and maintain German in the home in a predominantly English-speaking environment. But the effort required is by no means daunting and is more than compensated for by the rewards. The important thing is not to give up at the first hint of difficulties. If parents are patient, determined and persistent, it is very likely that they will succeed in raising their children as bilinguals.

It is hoped that the results obtained in this one Australian family, as well as the evidence from other studies referred to throughout this book, will help remove some of the mystery and doubts about bilingualism in the family, and that as a consequence other parents who speak languages other than the dominant language of their community will be encouraged to pass on their languages to their children. This can only mean enrichment for the community, the parents, and the children.

Notes

These notes list the author and date of publication of works which have been referred to throughout the book. Where appropriate, specific page numbers are also given, so that the relevant section of a work can be easily located. The titles of the works and other publishing details can be found by looking up the author's name in the bibliography.

1. FISHMAN, 1967.
2. DIXON, 1980, p. 32 and p. 69.
3. The statistics given here are based on an analysis of the Census by CLYNE, 1979 and 1980.
4. KLOSS, 1966.
5. CLYNE, 1974, p. 65.
6. HOFMANN, 1957.
7. BRANDT, 1957.
8. VENT, 1957.
9. SMOLICZ, 1979, p. 132.
10. BOOMFIELD, 1933, p. 56.
11. THIÉRY, 1976.
12. ANDREWS, 1980, p. 273.
13. LEOPOLD, 1939–49.
14. LEOPOLD, 1949b, p. 139.
15. SCHLIEMANN, 1881, p. 9.
16. HAUGEN, 1953, p. 7.
17. DIEBOLD, 1961.
18. HAAS, 1953.
19. HAUGEN, 1973, p. 508.
20. PEAL & LAMBERT, 1962, p. 8.
21. DOYLE *el al*, 1978, p. 16.
22. BALKAN, 1970.
23. MACNAMARA, 1967.

24. WEINREICH, 1953, p. 1.
25. CLYNE, 1967.
26. ANASTASI & CORDOVA, 1953, p. 32.
27. CLYNE, 1972, p. 24.
28. HAUGEN, 1956, p. 72.
29. JESPERSEN, 1922, p. 148.
30. WEISGERBER, 1933.
31. WEISGERBER, 1966, p. 85.
32. DE REYNOLD, 1928.
33. SAER, 1923.
34. MORRISON, 1958.
35. HAUGEN, 1956, pp. 80–84.
36. PEAL & LAMBERT, 1962, p. 15.
37. WILKINSON, 1971, p. 100.
38. PEAL & LAMBERT, 1962, p. 20.
39. MACNAMARA, 1966.
40. LAMBERT & ANISFIELD, 1969.
41. ANISFIELD, 1964.
42. SEGALOWITZ, 1977.
43. IANCO-WORRALL, 1972.
44. FELDMAN & SHEN, 1971.
45. CUMMINS, 1978.
46. CUMMINS, 1976, p. 33.
47. BEN-ZEEV, 1972.
48. LEOPOLD, 1949a, p. 188.
49. SCOTT, 1973.
50. LAMBERT, 1977, p. 17.
51. CARRINGER, 1974.
52. GENESEE, TUCKER & LAMBERT, 1975.
53. BEN-ZEEV, 1977b, p. 41.
54. LIEDTKE & NELSON, 1968.
55. PEAL & LAMBERT, 1962.
56. CUMMINS, 1976, p. 23.
57. DOYLE et al, 1978.
58. BEN-ZEEV, 1977a.
59. BERGAN & PARRA, 1979.
60. SEGALOWITZ, 1977, p. 131.
61. MACNAMARA, 1967, 1971.
62. MCLAUGHLIN, 1978, pp. 190–193.
63. KOLERS, 1968, p. 83.
64. PRICE, 1977, p. 345.
65. PAUWELS, 1980, p. 177.
66. RŪĶE-DRAVIŅA, 1967, p. 100.
67. SWAIN, 1972.
68. WODE, 1978.

69. HUERTA, 1977.
70. LEOPOLD, 1957.
71. BAETENS BEARDSMORE, 1982, p. 25.
72. MCLAUGHLIN, 1978, p. 99.
73. RŪĶE-DRAVIŅA, 1967.
74. RŪĶE-DRAVIŅA, 1967, p. 91.
75. Quoted in TOLL, 1977.
76. CLYNE, 1967, p. 116.
77. THOMPSON, 1980, p. 205.
78. RONJAT, 1913.
79. VON RAFFLER-ENGEL, 1970.
80. VOLTERRA & TAESCHNER, 1978.
81. FANTINI, 1976, 1978a, 1978b.
82. ZIERER, 1977.
83. HAUGEN, 1972, p. 10.
84. BUBENIK, 1978.
85. OKSAAR, 1971, 1977.
86. ELWERT, 1959.
87. SAUNDERS, 1979, 1980a, 1980b, 1982a, 1982b.
88. PAST, 1976.
89. DIMITRIJEVIĆ, 1965.
90. STEPHENS, 1952.
91. SWAIN el al, 1981.
92. RONJAT, 1913, p. 106.
93. LEOPOLD, 1957, p. 5.
94. LEOPOLD, 1949b, p. 95.
95. LEOPOLD, 1949b, p. 107.
96. LEOPOLD, 1949b, p. 125.
97. LEOPOLD, 1949b, p. 135.
98. LEOPOLD, 1949b, p. 146.
99. LEOPOLD, 1949b, p. 58–9.
100. LEOPOLD, 1949b, p. 143.
101. LEOPOLD, 1957, p. 6.
102. LEOPOLD, 1949b, p. 102.
103. LEOPOLD, 1949b, p. 159.
104. LEOPOLD, 1949b, p. 160.
105. LEOPOLD, 1949b, p. 164.
106. HARRISON & PIETTE, 1980, p. 220.
107. ELLIOTT, 1977.
108. RONJAT, 1913, p. 109.
109. HUERTA, 1977.
110. PADILLA & LIEBMANN, 1975.
111. BAIN, 1974.
112. BURLING, 1959.
113. RONDAL, 1980.

114. FRIEDLANDER, 1971, 1972.
115. NYGREN-JUNKEN, 1977.
116. IMEDADZE, 1967.
117. OKSAAR, 1976.
118. OKSAAR, 1977, p. 300.
119. VOLTERRA & TAESCHNER, 1978, p. 322.
120. HAUGEN, 1956.
121. SMOLICZ & HARRIS, 1977, p. 96.
122. CLYNE, 1970, p. 35.
123. BETTONI, 1981, p. 50.
124. FANTINI, 1978a, p. 290.
125. OKSAAR, 1973.
126. LEOPOLD, 1949b, p. 127.
127. ELWERT, 1959, p. 330.
128. RONJAT, 1913, p. 10.
129. LEOPOLD, 1949b, p. 62.
130. RŪĶE-DRAVIŅA, 1967, p. 37.
131. FANTINI, 1978a, p. 296.
132. ELWERT, 1959, p. 331.
133. CARL MEMLING, *Little Cottontail*. Sydney: Golden Press, 1974.
134. LEOPOLD, 1949b, p. 101.
135. LAURA LEE HOPE, *The Bobbsey Twins at Snow Lodge*. Manchester: World Distributors Ltd, 1955.
136. GINA RUCK-PAUQUÈT, *Die Tante und der Seehund*. München: Betz Verlag, 1965.
137. STOLT, 1964.
138. CLYNE, 1972, pp. 24–5; 1975, p. 29.
139. CLYNE, 1967, pp. 84–91.
140. CLYNE, 1967, p. 89.
141. HAUGEN, 1953, p. 65.
142. TIMM, 1975, p. 475.
143. KOUZMIN, 1976, p. 108.
144. FANTINI, 1978a, p. 297.
145. HASSELMO, 1970, p. 198.
146. HAUGEN, 1953, p. 53.
147. RONJAT, 1913, p. 94.
148. CLYNE, 1972b, p. 139.
149. HASSELMO, 1970, p. 201.
150. CLYNE, 1972b, p. 140.
151. ROSEMARIE GRIESBACH, *Deutsche Märchen und Sagen*. München: Hueber Verlag, 1977.
152. HAUGEN, 1953, p. 63.
153. HASSELMO, 1970, p. 204.
154. *Monster geht in den Zoo*. Stuttgart: Ernst Klett Verlag, 1976. A translation of the English story by ELLEN BLANCE & ANN COOK.

155. PEGGY PARISH, *Ootahs Glückstag*, trans. URSULA BAHN. Reinbek bei Hamburg: Carlsen Verlag, 1976.
156. HESSE, 1980, p. 55.
157. MÉTRAUX, 1964, p. 650.
158. BERTHOZ-PROUZ, 1976, p. 121.
159. JOHNSON, 1967.
160. JOHNSON, 1967, p. 299 and pp. 543ff.
161. ISAACS, 1977, p. 90.
162. HOFFMEISTER, 1977, p.34
163. SØNDERGAARD, 1981.
164. GROVER, 1982.
165. FANTINI, 1978a, p. 288.
166. ELWERT, 1959, p. 291.
167. CLYNE, 1973, p. 100.
168. FANTINI, 1978b, p. 186.
169. RONJAT, 1913, pp. 83–84.
170. LEOPOLD, 1949b, p. 132.
171. SAUNDERS, 1980a, p. 141.
172. VON RAFFLER-ENGEL, 1965, 1970.
173. RONJAT, 1913, p. 93.
174. CLYNE, 1967, 1972, 1973.
175. CLYNE, 1967, p. 103.
176. FANTINI, 1978a, p. 298.
177. CLYNE, 1967, p. 101.
178. FANTINI, 1978, p. 296.
179. RONJAT, 1913, p. 9.
180. RONJAT, 1913, p. 108.
181. WILIAM, 1971.
182. PEÑA & BERNAL, 1978.
183. NORDBERG, 1976.
184. TAYLOR, DE LACEY & NURCOMBE, 1972.
185. MCLAUGHLIN, 1978, p. 172.
186. HELEN BANNERMAN, *The Story of Little Black Sambo*. London: Chatto & Windus, 1899.
187. LEOPOLD, 1949b, pp. 155ff.
188. CLYNE, 1967, p. 19.
189. DAVID BERGAMINI, *The Land and Wildlife of Australia*. New York: Time Inc., 1964.
190. DAVID BERGAMINI, *Australien. Flora und Fauna*, trans. WOLFGANG VILLWOD. Reinbek bei Hamburg: rororo, 1975.
191. COLIN THIELE, *Die Insel des Flötenvogels*, trans. GERTRUD RUKSCHCIO. Mödling: Verlag St. Gabriel, 1974.
192. CLYNE, 1967, p. 112.
193. BERNHARD GRZIMEK, *Mit Grzimek durch Australien*. Gütersloh: Bertelsmann, 1971, p. 13.

194. GRIMM, 1975.
195. HORGAN, 1978.
196. CARSTENSEN, 1965, p. 237.
197. CLYNE, 1967, p. 56 and 1981, p. 32.
198. A. BRÖGER & G. KALOW, *Das wunderbare Bettmobil*. Stuttgart: Thienemanns Verlag, 1975, p. 13.
199. M. DU BOIS-REYMOND & B. SÖLL, *Neuköllner Schulbuch I*. Frankfurt a. M.: Suhrkamp, 1974, p. 47.
200. ASTRID LINDGREN, *Astrid Lindgren erzählt*. Hamburg: Verlag Friedrich Oetinger, 1971, p. 9.
201. ILSE CHRISTENSEN, *Jakob im Wald*. Reinbek bei Hamburg: Carlsen Verlag, 1976, p. 25.
202. HANCOCK, 1977, p. 164.
203. WEINREICH, 1953, p. 51.
204. CLYNE, 1975, p. 17.
205. HAVILAND, 1979, p. 164.
206. DIXON, 1980, p. 8.
207. CLYNE, 1967, p. 71.
208. CLYNE, 1967, Appendix III.
209. HAUGEN, 1956, p. 55.
210. CARSTENSEN, 1965.
211. *Kinderduden*. Mannheim: Bibliographisches Institut, 1970.
212. CLYNE, 1972, p. 9.
213. PENFIELD & ROBERTS, 1959.
214. LENNEBERG, 1967.
215. SCOVEL, 1969.
216. KRASHEN, 1973.
217. SCHNITZER, 1978.
218. PRIESTLY, 1980.
219. MENYUK, 1971, p. 76.
220. SØNDERGAARD, 1981.
221. BECK, 1979, p. 91.
222. POLITZER, 1978.
223. REITMAJER, 1975.
224. ZEHETNER, 1977, p. 19.
225. EDELMAN, 1969, p. 175.
226. CLYNE, 1977, p. 130.
227. SMOLICZ & HARRIS, 1977, p. 98.
228. SAVILLE & TROIKE, 1971, p. 26.
229. LADO, 1977.
230. CHRISTIAN, 1977.
231. DOMAN, 1975.
232. SHARP, 1973, p. 53.
233. GAARDER, 1967.

234. THOMAS JEIER, *Der letzte Häuptling der Apachen*. München: Heyne Verlag, 1977.

235. LEO POLITI, *Moy Moy*. New York: Charles Scribener's Sons, 1960.

236. JURI KORINETZ, *Dort, weit hinter dem Fluß*, trans. HANS BAUMANN. Weinheim & Basel: Beltz Verlag, 1971.

237. KRINGAS & LEWINS, 1981, p. 1.

238. LAMBERT, 1978.

239. McGILL, 1980, p. 202.

240. HAUGEN, 1953, p. 6.

241. CLYNE, 1977a.

242. HEARST, 1981.

243. LEOPOLD, 1949b, p. 70.

244. ROSIER & FARELLA, 1976.

245. HEARST, 1981.

246. MEIJERS, 1969.

247. CLYNE, 1968.

248. SMOLICZ & HARRIS, 1976.

249. The 1b generation means those children who immigrated before their speech habits had become fixed, i.e. before about age 12 (see p. 201).

References

ANASTASI, A. & CORDOVA, F. 1953, Some effects of bilingualism upon the intelligence test performance of Puerto Rican children in New York. *Journal of Educational Psychology*, 44, 1–19.

ANDREWS, I. 1980, Look at bilinguals. *International Review of Applied Linguistics*, XVIII/4, 273–88.

ANISFIELD, E. 1964, *A comparison of the cognitive functioning of monolinguals and bilinguals*. Ph.D. thesis, McGill University.

BAETENS BEARDSMORE, H. 1982, *Bilingualism: Basic Principles*. Clevedon: Tieto Ltd.

BAIN, B. 1974, Verbal regulation of cognitive processes: A replication of Luria's procedures with bilingual and unilingual infants. *Child Development*, 47, 543–46.

BALKAN, L. 1970, *Les effets du bilinguisme français-anglais sur les aptitudes intellectuelles*. Bruxelles: Aimav.

BECK, M.S. 1979, *Baby Talk. How your Child Learns to Talk*. New York: New American Library.

BEN-ZEEV, S. 1977a, The influence of bilingualism on cognitive strategy and cognitive development. *Child Development*, 48, 1009–18.

— 1977b, Mechanisms by which childhood bilingualism affects understanding of language and cognitive structures. In P. HORNBY, (ed.), *Bilingualism. Psychological, Social and Educational Implications*. New York: Academic Press, 29–55.

BERGAN, J. & PARRA, E. 1979, Variations in IQ testing and instruction and the letter learning and achievement of Anglo and bilingual Mexican-American children. *Journal of Educational Psychology*, 71(6), 819–26.

BERTHOZ-PROUX, M. 1976, L'enfant de travailleur migrant à l'école française. *Langue française*, 29, 116–26.

BETTONI, C. 1981, *Italian in North Queensland*. Townsville: James Cook University.

BLOOMFIELD, L. 1933, *Language*. New York: Holt.

BUBENIK, V. 1978, The acquisition of Czech in the English environment. In M. PARADIS, (ed.), *Aspects of Bilingualism*, pp. 3–12, Columbia: Hornbeam Press.

BURLING, R. 1959, Language development of a Garo and English speaking child. *Word*, 15, 45–68.

CARRINGER, D. 1974, Creative thinking abilities of a Mexican youth. The relationship of bilingualism. *Journal of Cross-Cultural Psychology*, 5(4), 492–504.

CARSTENSEN, B. 1965, *Englische Einflüsse auf die deutsche Sprache seit 1945*. Heidelberg: Carl Winter Universitätsverlag.

CHRISTIAN, C. 1977, Minority language skills before age three. In W. MACKEY & T. ANDERSSON (eds), *Bilingualism in Early Childhood*, pp. 94–108. Rowley: Newbury House.

CLYNE, M. 1967, *Transference and Triggering. Observations on the Language Assimilation of Postwar German-Speaking Migrants in Australia*. The Hague: Nijhoff.

— 1968, The maintenance of bilingualism. *The Australian Journal of Education*, 12, 125–30.

— 1970, Some aspects of the bilingualism and language maintenance of Australian-born children of German-speaking parents. *ITL*, 9, 35–47.

— 1972a, *Perspectives on Language Contact*. Melbourne: The Hawthorn Press.

— 1972b, Some (German-English) language contact phenomena at the discourse level. In E. FIRCHOW *et al.* (eds), *Studies for Einar Haugen*, pp. 132–44. The Hague: Mouton.

— 1973, Thirty years later: Some observations on "Refugee German" in Melbourne. In H. SCHOLLER & J. REIDY, (eds), *Lexicography and Dialect Geography, Festgabe für Hans Kurath*, pp. 96–106. Wiesbaden: Franz Steiner Verlag.

— 1974, Language contact and language ecology in Australia. In M. RADO, (ed.), *Bilingual Education. Papers Presented at the Third Language Teaching Conference held at La Trobe University*, pp. 51–76. Bundoora: La Trobe University.

— 1975, *Forschungsbericht Sprachkontakt*. Kronberg: Scriptor Verlag.

— 1977a, Bilingualism of the elderly. *Talanya*, 4, 45–56.

— 1977b, Language contact and inter-cultural communication breakdown and conflict. In C. MOLONY, H. ZOBL & W. STÖLTING, (eds), *Deutsch im Kontakt mit anderen Sprachen/German in Contact with other Languages*, pp. 129–146. Kronberg/Ts.: Scriptor Verlag.

— 1979, Community languages in Australia — what the 1976 Census will (and will not) tell us. Paper presented at the A.G.M. of the Society for Linguistics and Education, Melbourne.

— 1980, Community languages and language policy: A demographic perspective. Paper presented at Applied Linguistics Association of Australia Conference, Melbourne. (Also published in M. GARNER, 1981, 13–36.)

— 1981, *Deutsch als Muttersprache in Australien: Zur Ökologie einer Einwanderersprache*. Wiesbaden: Franz Steiner Verlag.

CUMMINS, J. 1976, The influence of bilingualism on cognitive growth: A synthesis of research findings and explanatory hypotheses. *Working Papers on Bilingualism*, 9, 1–43.

— 1978, Bilingualism and the development of metalinguistic awareness. *Journal of Cross-Cultural Psychology*, 9(2), 131–149.

DIEBOLD, A. 1961, Incipient bilingualism. *Language*, 37, 97–112.

DIMITRIJEVIĆ, N. 1965, A bilingual child. *English Language Teaching*, 20, 23–28.

DIXON, R.M.W. 1980, *The Languages of Australia*. Cambridge: Cambridge University Press.

DOMAN, G. 1975, *Teach your baby to read*. London: Pan Books Ltd.

DOYLE, A., CHAMPAGNE, M. & SEGALOWITZ, N. 1978, Some issues on the assessment of linguistic consequences of early bilingualism. In M. PARADIS, (ed.), *Aspects of Bilingualism*, pp. 13–20. Columbia: Hornbeam Press.

EDELMAN, M. 1969, The contextualization of schoolchildren's bilingualism. *Modern Language Journal*, 53, 179–82.

ELLIOTT, L. 1977, The French Correction. *Reader's Digest*, 9, 53–56.

ELWERT, W.T. 1959, *Das zweisprachige Individuum: Ein Selbstzeugnis*. Mainz: Verlag der Akademie der Wissenschaften und Literatur.

FANTINI, A. 1976, *Language Acquisition of a Bilingual Child: A Sociolinguistic Perspective*. Vermont: The Experiment Press.

— 1978a, Bilingual behavior and social cues: case studies of two bilingual children. In M. PARADIS, (ed.), *Aspects of Bilingualism*, pp. 283–301. Columbia: Hornbeam Press.

— 1978b, Emerging styles in child speech: Case study of a bilingual child. *The Bilingual Review*, No. 3, 169–89.

FELDMAN, C. & SHEN, M. 1971, Some language-related cognitive advantages of bilingual five-year olds. *The Journal of Genetic Psychology*, 118, 235–244.

FISHMAN, J. 1965, Bilingualism, intelligence and language learning. *The Modern Language Journal*, 44, 227–36.

FRIEDLANDER, B. 1971, Listening, language and the auditory environment. In J. HELLMUTH, (ed.), *Exceptional Infant (Vol. 2)*. New York: Bruner/Mazel.

— , JACOBS, B., DAVIS, B. & WETSTONE, H. 1972, Time-sampling analysis of infants' natural language environments in the home. *Child Development*, 43, 730–40.

GAARDER, A. 1967, *Bilingual Education*. A prepared statement presented to the Special Subcommittee on Bilingual Education of the Committee on Labor and Public Welfare, United States Senate. Washington, D.C.: United States Government Printing Office. (Quoted in G. LLOYD, *Studies of Infant School Children 3 – Deprivation and the Bilingual Child*. Oxford: Blackwell, 1977, p. 106.)

GARNER, M. (ed.), 1981, *Community languages. Their role in education*. Melbourne: River Seine Publications.

GENESEE, F., TUCKER, G. & LAMBERT, W. 1975, Communication skills of bilingual children. *Child Development*, 46, 1010–14.

GRIMM, H. 1975, On the child's acquisition of semantic structure underlying the worldfield of prepositions. *Language and Speech*, 18, 97–119.

GROVER, M. & M. 1982, Readers' Response. *Journal of Multilingual and Multicultural Development*, 3, 61–62.

HAAS, M. 1953, Results of the conference of anthropologists and linguists. *International Journal of American Linguistics*, 19, 42–3.

HANCOCK, I. 1977, Lexical expansion within a closed system. In B. BLOUNT & M. SANCHES, *Sociocultural Dimensions of Language Change*, pp. 161–71. New York: Academic Press.

HARRISON, G.J. & PIETTE, A. 1980, Young bilingual children's language selection. *Journal of Multilingual and Multicultural Development*, 1(3), 217–230.

HASSELMO, N. 1970, Code-switching and modes of speaking. In G. GILBERT, (ed.), *Texas Studies in Bilingualism*, pp. 179–209. Berlin: de Gruyter.

— 1972, Code-switching as ordered selection. In E. FIRCHOW *el al.*, (eds), *Studies for Einar Haugen*, pp. 261–280. The Hague: Mouton.

HAUGEN, E. 1953, *The Norwegian Language in America: A Study in Bilingual Behavior*. 2nd printing, revised 1969. Bloomington: Indiana University Press.

— 1956, *Bilingualism in the Americas*. Alabama: University of Alabama Press.

— 1972, Bilingualism as a social and personal problem. In R. FILOPOVIĆ, (ed.), *Active Methods and Modern Aids in the Teaching of Foreign Languages*, pp. 1–14. London: OUP.

— 1973, Bilingualism, language contact, and immigrant languages in the United States: A research report 1956–1970. *Current Trends in Linguistics*, 10, 505–592.

HAVILAND, J. 1979, How to talk to your brother-in-law in Guugu Yimidhirr. In T. SHOPEN, (ed.), *Languages and their Speakers*, pp. 161–239. Cambridge, Mass.: Winthrop.

HEARST, S. 1981, *Ethnic Communities and their Aged*. Richmond: Clearing House on Migration Issues.

HESSE, S. 1980, Reflections on an Australian bilingual. *Journal of Intercultural Studies*, 1(3), 53–5.

HOFFMEISTER, W. 1977, *Sprachwechsel in Ost-Lothringen*. Wiesbaden: Franz Steiner Verlag.

HOFMANN, M. 1957, Can the mother tongue be retained for children of German immigrants? *The American-German Review*, Aug.–Sep., 15–17.

HORGAN, D. 1978, The development of the full passive. *Journal of Child Language*, 5, 65–80.

HUERTA, A. 1977, The acquisition of bilingualism: A code-switching approach. *Sociolinguistic Working Paper No. 39*, 1–33.

IANCO-WORRALL, A. 1972, Bilingualism and cognitive development. *Child Development*, 43, 1390–1400.

IMEDADZE, N.V. 1967, On the psychological nature of child speech formation under conditions of exposure to two languages. *International Journal of Psychology*, 2, 129–32.

ISAACS, E. 1976, *Greek Children in Sydney*. Canberra: A.N.U. Press.

JESPERSEN, O. 1922, *Language. Its Nature, Development and Origin*. London: George Allen & Unwin Ltd.

JOHNSON, W. 1967a, Stuttering. In W. JOHNSON *et al.*, *Speech Handicapped School Children*, pp. 229–329. New York, Evanston and London: Harper & Row.

— 1967b, An open letter to the mother of a "stuttering" child. In W. JOHNSON *et al.*, *Speech Handicapped School Children*, pp. 543–54. New York, Evanston and London: Harper & Row.

KOLERS, P. 1968, Bilingualism and information processing. *Scientific American*, 218(3), 78–86.

KOUZMIN, L. 1976, Some patterns and conditions of code-switching from Russian to English. *Talanya*, 3, 107–16.

KRASHEN, S. 1973, Lateralization, language learning, and the critical period: Some new evidence. *Language Learning*, 23, 63–74.

LADO, R. 1977, Acquisition and learning in early reading. *Hispania*, 60, 533–5.

LAMBERT, W. & ANISFIELD, E. 1969, A note on the relationship of bilingualism and intelligence. *Canadian Journal of Behavioral Science*, 1, 123–8.

LAMBERT, W. 1975, Culture and language as factors in learning and education. In A. WOLFGANG, (ed.), *Education of Immigrant Students*. Toronto: Ontario Institute for Studies in Education.

— 1977, The effects of bilingualism on the individual: cognitive and sociocultural consequences. In P. HORNBY, (ed.), *Bilingualism. Psychological, Social and Educational Implications*, pp. 15–28. New York: Academic Press.

— 1978, Some cognitive and sociocultural consequences of being bilingual. In J. ALATIS, (ed.), *Georgetown University Round Table on Languages and Linguistics 1978*, pp. 214–29. Washington: Georgetown University Press.

LENNEBERG, E. 1967, *Biological Foundations of Language*. New York: John Wiley and Sons.

LEOPOLD, W. 1939, *Speech Development of a Bilingual Child: A Linguists Record.* (Vol. I): *Vocabulary growth in the first two years*. Evanston: Northwestern University Press.

— 1947, *Speech Development of a Bilingual Child: A Linguists Record.* (Vol. II): *Sound learning in the first two years*. Evanston: Northwestern University Press.

— 1949a, *Speech Development of a Bilingual Child: A Linguists Record.* (Vol. III): *Grammar and general problems in the first two years*. Evanston: Northwestern University Press.

— 1949b, *Speech Development of a Bilingual Child: A Linguists Record.* (Vol. IV): *Diary from age two*. Evanston: Northwestern University Press.

— 1957–8, American children can learn their German mother tongue. *The American-German Review*, 24, 4–6.

LIEDTKE, W. & NELSON, L. 1968, Concept formation and bilingualism. *Alberta Journal of Educational Research*, 14(4), 225–32.

MACNAMARA, J. 1966, *Bilingualism and Primary Education*. Edinburgh: Edinburgh University Press.

— 1967, The bilingual's linguistic performance – a psychological overview. *Journal of Social Issues*, 23, 58–77.

— 1971, Linguistic independence of bilinguals. *Journal of Verbal Learning and Verbal Behavior*, 10, 480–7.

MCGILL, G. 1980, Bilingual Education in the Northern Territory. In T. LÊ & M. MCCAUSLAND, (eds), *Proceedings of the Conference Child Language Development: Theory into Practice, September 1980*, pp. 195–205. Launceston: Launceston Teachers Centre.

MCLAUGHLIN, B. 1978, *Second-Language Acquisition in Childhood*. Hillsdale, N.J.: Lawrence Erlbaum Associates.

MEIJERS, J.A. 1969, *De taal van het kind*. Utrecht/Antwerpen: Uitgeverij Het Spectrum.

MENYUK, P. 1971, *The Acquisition and Development of Language*. Englewood Cliffs, N.J.: Prentice-Hall.

MORRISON, J. 1958, Bilingualism: Some psychological aspects. *The Advancement of Science*, 56, 287–90.

NORDBERG, B. 1976, Sociolinguistic research in Sweden and Finland. *International Journal of the Sociology of Language*, 10, 5–16.

NYGREN-JUNKIN, L. 1977, *The interaction between French and English in the speech of four bilingual children*. Master's thesis, Ontario Institute for Studies in Education, Toronto.

OKSAAR, E. 1971, Zum Spracherwerb des Kindes in zweisprachiger Umgebung. *Folia Linguistica*, 4, 330–58.

— 1973, Implications of language contact for bilingual language acquisition. Paper presented to the IXth International Congress of Anthropological and Ethnological Sciences in Chicago, Aug. 28 – Sept. 8, 1973.

— 1976, Code switching as an interactional strategy for developing bilingual competence. *Word*, 27.

— 1977, On becoming trilingual. A case study. In C. MALONEY, (ed.), *Deutsch im Kontakt mit anderen Sprachen*, pp. 296–306. Kronberg: Scriptor Verlag.

PADILLA, A. & LIEBMAN, E. 1975, Language acquisition in the bilingual child. *The Bilingual Review*, 2, 34–5.

PAST, A. 1976, *Preschool Reading in Two Languages as a Factor in Bilingualism*. Ph.D. thesis, University of Texas at Austin.

PAULSTON, C. 1975, Ethnic relations and bilingual education: accounting for contradictory data. *Working Papers on Bilingualism*, 6.

PAUWELS, A. 1980, *The Effects of Mixed Marriages on Language Shift in the Dutch Community in Australia*. M.A. thesis, Monash University, Melbourne.

PEAL, E. & LAMBERT, W. 1962, Relation of bilingualism to intelligence. *Psychological Monographs*, 76, 1–23.

PEÑA, A. & BERNAL, E. 1978, Malpractices in language assessment for Hispanic children. In *Occasional Papers on Linguistics No. 3*, pp. 102–16. Southern Illinois University at Carbondale.

PENFIELD, W. & ROBERTS, L. 1959, *Speech and Brain Mechanisms*. Princeton: Princeton University Press.

POLITZER, R. 1978, Errors of English speakers of German as perceived and evaluated by German natives. *The Modern Language Journal*, LXII, 253–61.

PRICE, C. & PYNE, P. 1977, The immigrants. In A. DAVIES *et al.*, (eds), *Australian Society. A Sociological Introduction*, pp. 331–55. Melbourne: Longman Cheshire.

PRIESTLY, T. 1980, Homonymy in child phonology. *Journal of Child Language*, 7, 413–427.

REITMAJER, V. 1975, Schlechte Chancen ohne Hochdeutsch. *Muttersprache*, 310–24.

REYNOLD, DE. 1928, In *Bieler Jahrbuch – Annales Biennoises II*, 105.

RONDAL, J. 1980, Fathers' and mothers' speech in early language development. *Journal of Child Language*, 7, 353–69.

RONJAT, J. 1913, *Le développement du langage observé chez un enfant bilingue*. Paris: Librairie Ancienne H. Champion.

ROSIER, P. & FARELLA, M. 1976, Bilingual education at Rock Point – Some early results. *TESOL Quarterly*, 10(4), 379–88.

RŪĶE-DRAVIŅA, V. 1967, *Mehrsprachigkeit im Vorschulalter*. Lund: Gleerup.

SAER, D. 1923, The effect of bilingualism on intelligence. *British Journal of Psychology*, 14, 25–38.

SAUNDERS, G. 1979, Creating bilingualism. Paper presented at the Fourth Annual Congress of the Applied Linguistics Association of Australia, Sydney University. (Published in 1980 in *Australian Review of Applied Linguistics*, 3(2), 122–30.)

— 1980a, Adding a second native language in the home. *Journal of Multilingual and Multicultural Development*, 1(2), 113–44.

— 1980b, Some factors affecting the fostering and maintenance of bilingualism in the family. Paper presented at the Twelfth Annual Conference of the Australian Linguistic Society, Monash University.

— 1982a, Der Erwerb einer zweiten "Muttersprache" in der Familie. In J. SWIFT, (ed.), *Bilinguale und multikulturelle Erziehung*. Würzburg: Königshausen und Neumann.

— 1982b, Infant bilingualism: A look at some doubts and objections. *Journal of Multilingual and Multicultural Development*, 3(4).

SAVILLE, M. & TROIKE, R. 1971, *A Handbook of Bilingual Education*. Washington: TESOL.

SCHLIEMANN, H. 1881, Autobiography of the author. In *Ilias, the City and Country of the Trojans*. Reprinted New York: Benjamin Bloom, 1968.

SCHNITZER, M. 1978, Cerebral lateralization and plasticity: their relevance to language acquisition. In M. PARADIS, (ed.), *Aspects of Bilingualism*, pp. 149–155. Columbia: Hornbeam Press.

SCOTT, S. 1973, The relation of divergent thinking to bilingualism: cause or effect? Unpublished research report. McGill University.

SCOVEL, T. 1969, Foreign accents, language acquisition, and cerebral dominance. *Language Learning*, IX, 245–53.

SEGALOWITZ, N. 1977, Psychological perspectives on bilingual education. In B. SPOLSKY & R. COOPER, (eds), *Frontiers of Bilingual Education*, pp. 119–58. Massachusetts: Newbury House.

SHARP, D. 1973, *Language in Bilingual Communities*. London: Edwin Arnold.

SMOLICZ, J. 1979, *Culture and Education in a Plural Society*. Canberra: Curriculum Development Centre.

— , & HARRIS, R. 1976, Ethnic languages and immigrant youth. In M. CLYNE, (ed.), *Australia Talks*, pp. 131–73. Canberra: A.N.U.

— , and HARRIS, R. 1977, Ethnic languages in Australia. *International Journal of the Sociology of Language*, 14, 89–108.

SØNDERGAARD, B. 1981, Decline and fall of an individual bilingualism. *Journal of Multilingual and Multicultural Development*, 2(4), 297–302.

STEPHENS, K. 1952, Reader's letter. *The Linguist*, Nov., 307.

STOLT, B. 1964, *Die Sprachmischung in Luthers Tischreden: Studien zum Problem der Zweisprachigkeit*. Stockholm: Stockholmer Germanistische Forschungen.

SWAIN, M. 1972, *Bilingualism as a First Language*. Ph.D. thesis, University of California at Irvine.

—, LAPKIN, S. & ANDREW, C. 1981, Early French immersion later on. *Journal of Multilingual and Multicultural Development*, 2, 1–24.

TAESCHNER-FRANCESE, T. 1978, Zwei Sprachen als Muttersprache. *Umschau in Wissenschaft und Technik*, 23, 738.

TAYLOR, L.J., DE LACEY, P. & NURCOMBE, B. 1972, An assessment of the reliability of the Peabody Picture Vocabulary Test. *Australian Psychologist*, 7(3), 167–9.

THIÉRY, C. 1976, Le bilinguisme vrai. *Études de linguistique appliquée*, 24, 52–63.

THOMPSON, S. 1980, *Australia Through Italian Eyes*. Melbourne: OUP.

TIMM, L. 1975, Spanish-English code-switching: El Porqué y How-Not-To. *Romance Philosophy*, XXVIII/4, 473–82.

TOLL, C. 1977, Frühe Zweisprachigkeit im Unterricht und die deutschen Auslandsschulen. *Zielsprache Deutsch*, 2, 15–24.

VENT, H. 1958, Letter to the editor. *The American-German Review*, Jan., 39–40.

VOLTERRA, V. & TAESCHNER, T. 1978, The acquisition and development of language by bilingual children. *Journal of Child Language*, 5, 311–326.

VON RAFFLER-ENGEL, W. 1965, Del bilinguismo infantile. *Archivio Glottologica Italiano*, 50, 175–80.

— 1970, The concept of sets in a bilingual child. In *Actes du Xe Congrès International des Linguistes*. Vol. III. Bucharest: Romanian Academy Press.

WEINREICH, U. 1953, *Languages in Contact*. New York. (8th printing, The Hague: Mouton, 1974.)

WEISGERBER, L. 1953, Zweisprachigkeit. *Schaffen und Schauen*, 9.

— 1966, Vorteile und Gefahren der Zweisprachigkeit. *Wirkendes Wort*, 16(2), 73–89.

WILIAM, U. 1971, The construction of standardized tests for Welsh-speaking children. *Educational Research*, 14(1), 29–34.

WILKINSON, A. 1971, *The Foundations of Language*. London: OUP.

WODE, H. 1974, Natürliche Zweitsprachigkeit: Probleme, Aufgaben, Perspektiven. *Linguistische Berichte*, 32, 15–36.

— 1978, Developmental sequences in naturalistic L2 acquisition. In E. HATCH, (ed.), *Second Language Acquisition. A Book of Readings*, pp. 101–17. Massachusetts: Newbury House.

ZEHETNER, L. 1977, *Bairisch. (Dialekt/Hochsprache − kontrastiv 2)*. Düsseldorf: Pädagogischer Verlag Schwann.

ZIERER, E. 1977, Experiences in the bilingual education of a child of preschool age. *International Review of Applied Linguistics*, XV/2, 143–9.

Index

Accents 150, 225
Accuracy 172
Active vocabulary 43
Ambilingual 7
Animals 71
Arbitrariness of language 17
Australian Aboriginal languages 1, 193, 194, 241
Australian fauna 184, 194
Australian life 198

Bilingual education 5, 240
Bilingualism
– adolescent 13
– and the brain 21, 230
– and intelligence 14, 164, 241
– attitudes to 14, 113, 219
– balanced 9
– child 13, 30
– consecutive 30
– definitions of 7
– degree of 207
– infant 13, 29
– in world 1
– receiving 9, 37, 140
– "true" 7
Biliteracy 33, 210, 224, 240
Blocked switching 97
Books 89, 107, 190, 232

Calque 180
Case 175
Cassettes 150, 233
Census 2, 27, 28
Circumlocution 196

Code switching 11, 39, 48, 52, 58, 65, 92, 98, 106, 129, 135
Cognate 180
Cognitive development 21, 40
Communicative competence 204
Concept formation 20
Correspondence 135, 214, 242
Creative thinking 19
Creative writing 214
Culture 22, 152, 160, 204, 236

Dialect 98, 206, 225
Dictionaries 147, 243
Divergent thinking 19
Domain 12, 207
Dominance 10, 29, 207
Dreams 71

Equilingual 7
Errors 165, 174, 223
Ethnic schools 239

Fluency 165
Formality 204, 232
Free speech 171

Games 238
Gender 175
Grandparents 31, 126

Homophone 180
Homophonous diamorph 92

Immersion programmes 34
Incoining 193
Integration 194
Intelligence 14, 159, 164

Kindergarten 134, 241

Languages 227
Language maintenance 2, 232, 242
Language shift 2, 27
Linguistic relativity 230
Loan meaning 181
Loan rendition 194
Loan translation 180
Loanword 93, 194, 199

Medical personnel 114
Memory 21
Mimic gestures 197
Mixed marriages 27
Monolinguals 9, 113, 118

Outings 238
Overall code 44

Peabody Picture Vocabulary Test 10, 159
Peer Group 127
Playgroups 239
Playmates 121
Poetic language 233
Preformulated sequence 109
Private speech 65
Proficiency 159
Pronunciation 88, 147, 186, 201, 230

Quotational switching 98, 106

Radio 24, 151, 234
Reading 210, 222
Receptive vocabulary 43, 159
Records 233
Role play 59, 84

Sandwich words 95
School 5, 117, 134, 223, 239
Semantic extension 181
Separation of sound and meaning 18
Social sensitivity 19
Storage 21, 231
Storytelling 89, 106, 165, 232
Stuttering 115
Style switching 98
Switching 11, 39, 48, 50, 58, 65, 92, 98, 106,
    128, 129, 135

Teachers 30, 117
Teasing 60, 78, 126
Television 225, 234
Threshold level 20
Toys 73
Transference
 – lexical 11, 61, 75, 92, 194
 – phonological 11, 201
 – semantic 11, 147, 180
 – syntactic 11, 47, 175
Translation 102, 118, 126, 202, 236
Triggering 13, 92
 – anticipational 94
 – consequential 94
 – contextual 60, 96

Vocabulary 17, 20, 146, 232, 237
Vocabulary gaps 102, 143, 183, 195

Word order 177
Writing 210